The Beings:
A Story of Extraterrestrial Visitations

By Virginia Leonard

Copyright 2013 by Virginia Leonard
All rights reserved.

Preface

The following story relates my experiences as they happened with intelligent life forms either from outer space or another dimension, and at times I have thought it was both. I found that although there are many agencies and groups whose focus is on UFOs and aliens, there have been none that were supportive but then, I have to ask the question, what could they really do for me? It has been my finding that unless there are multiple witnesses watching a person being floated up to the UFO, claims are not taken seriously. I was fortunate in being led to a supportive buddy whom I have never met other than through email. Over the years she has kept both of my feet on the ground through trying times of fear, confusion, frustration, and anger.

There seems to be a set of rules and variation from them makes the experiencer suspect, in other words, people like me whose experiences do not fit into the accepted pattern are rebuffed. It has been impossible to convince anyone that these beings are in my home almost daily leaving my claims suspect. They are still here or, at least, a form of them is.

Some people publically claim to have been abducted while others hesitate to talk about their experiences for fear of ridicule, possibly jeopardizing their jobs and in some instances, their position in life; others want the experience so badly they fabricate stories. There are those who are unable to accept the idea of living beings from a more advanced civilization, be it a planet or dimension, and there are the hecklers who have a narrow attitude towards anything they are unable to see in their mirror.

In the beginning and after I had somewhat conquered my terror, I felt privileged to be exposed to living intelligent life from not of this earth but this sense of privilege, over time, developed into the realization that we humans are considered inferior to them and technologically, I would not disagree. They are well advanced in mind control; they are able to subdue us mentally; they are able to delve into our inner most thoughts using them for their studies; they are able to do all of this without our prior knowledge and consent. They think differently than we do so they cannot be measured and held accountable by human standards, yet I believe that they have a moral code. They are not angels sent from The Creator to save our world, as some people want to believe, but are living beings that will die the same as you and me. They are no better than humans and while some of them respond to this statement in a tolerant, humoring manner, as if I am a young child, others become insulted and hostile.

The beings have insisted from the beginning that they are scientists here to study our species. They view us as subjects and not as individuals in the way that we view ourselves and each other as individuals. They will do whatever it takes to complete their agenda of study if that is their actual agenda. As you read you will see that I seem to be committed to something of which I have no idea what it is but am reassured that I can remember if I want to, and that I will know what it is when the time comes.

I have awakened in the morning with multiple bruises, needle marks, a black eye, blood on my pillow, a small incision in my umbilicus, and aches and pains that were not present when I went to bed. I have found my nightclothes on backwards, the doors unlocked and the alarm system turned off many a morning. I have found my animals locked outside on the back porch and on one occasion shut in the closet. It has been my experience that the aliens have been both physically and mentally invasive to me in my home as well as aboard their ships.

The majority of activity and dreams begin in my bedroom and include the adjoining bathroom. The bathroom has water and water is a conduit, so do they use water as a facilitator? No, they do not. They have told me that it can be used, however, in my situation I believe the bathroom plays a key role because it has a commode. In nearly every dream or "trip" at some point the need to use the bathroom is involved. The "interfered with" dreams were tailored around my past and present daily life camouflaging the dreams to make them acceptable to me, almost always beginning in a setting in which I was comfortable then easing into their agenda. The people I see are those they want me to see, usually family members, to watch my interaction in conditions the beings have devised. I found it necessary to record in a journal the dream or event as soon as possible otherwise it would be forgotten, indeed, I had forgotten many of the incidences in this book until I reread the journal.

I have had an MRI of the brain for ringing in my left ear and was diagnosed with TMJ and a recent CAT scan for dizziness. No mention of finding an implant was made nor did I tell them to look for one. The CAT scan was negative for a brain tumor and CVA. The ophthalmologist has found nothing wrong with my vision except for cataracts that were removed and now I only require over-the-counter reading glasses. The dentist did find a small hard smooth white object the shape and size of a fat sesame seed caught between the bridge and the gum throwing it away, saying it was an unusual looking piece of bone.

Through the years I have searched for answers by reading books that normally would not hold my interest hoping to find something of use revealed, by searching the Internet, and by utilizing other sources, I learned of several Native American beliefs and customs that I have incorporated into my life.

I learned more about the paranormal. I learned that we have power within ourselves but do not always recognize it; I learned that some of us are intuitive; I learned some of us have the ability to see things others cannot and are frightened left feeling vulnerable; I learned some of us are able to sense an unseen presence while others are able to talk to the dead. There are psychics who are able to see the beyond providing insight to those seeking answers to unresolved questions. There are those who do not recognize that they have any of the above or that it even exists. By learning of my own power I found a means, a weapon so to speak, to make the beings visits as unpleasant and difficult as possible by using the intangible against the intangible and the tangible against the intangible. I want them to leave.

The entire UFO situation is a conundrum to everyone and until it is proven beyond a shadow of a doubt it will remain so. I understand why our government will not forthrightly admit the beings exist because the government recognizes it is unable to have a controlling force over them. We are not equals in ability or technology giving the beings the upper hand, and if they wanted to destroy or take over our planet, it is my opinion they could do so with little effort on their part.

Over the years I have wondered how many other people have had experiences similar to mine but because we lack a UFO suspended above us and witnesses, we don't fit into the accepted criteria; our experiences are considered extraneous. This book is written for those who carry the heavy burden of which cannot be spoken. They do not carry this burden alone, I carry it too.

My story is centered on the beings and their effect on me. Regarding them, everything else in my life seemed inconsequential at times. This story is laden with their and my interaction excluding my normal human life for the most part. It will lead you from the discovery of the beings and the terror experienced as each new thing is revealed while I strive to convince myself that I have not become insane. You will follow me as I remember past events that seemed to have no meaning at the time but are slowly fitted into a pattern of significance. I will share with you on a daily basis my thoughts and reasoning as written in my journal while I work through the acceptance of their presence, their effect on my life, the struggle to gain respect as another life form, and the strong desire to get rid of them.

Chapter 1

Who am I?

Seventy-one years ago a young couple birthed their first child, a baby girl, me, in a small town in America's corn and grain belt of the Midwest. It's hard to believe that I was ever a baby but I have a lovely picture taken of a plump baby dressed in pink, laughing at the camera as proof. I have heard people say they remember little of their childhood but I have a lot of memories.

I remember the mailman knocking on our front door assuring me the large package he held in his hands had my name on it; placing in my arms a long large box sent by my dad's foster brother who was in the Army stationed in Germany. It was a beautiful doll with a Bisk head, little white teeth, eyes that opened and closed and brown human hair dressed in a Nazi uniform. I remember the breathless trembling excitement of surprise and wonder that I had received a package in the mail; a package so large that mother had to help me carry it into the living room to open. Seventy-one years later, I still have that doll although most of the uniform has been lost and the arms are missing. This was the only surviving doll from my childhood; the only one cared for becoming the first of my doll collection. I had no interest in playing with dolls; I would rather play with humans.

I remember standing in our small unfenced backyard looking at the tops of the trees in the wildly over-grown gully where a small stream ran through the middle; the edge of the gully only a few feet away, so tempting to explore but I was tied to the clothesline because I was a curious child that was there one minute and gone the next. I ran up and down the line playing within a safety zone until unexpected lightning struck nearby. I love adventure, to see what lies around the corner.

I remember sitting on the couch with Dad watching him draw stick figure cartoons and telling me stories. He always had time for me and was interested in my thoughts. It was well into adulthood that I realized that he was my only source of unconditional love. He simply loved me for me.

I remember Mom and me lying on the bed while she read *Ozma of Oz* to me eating the whole box of raisins herself while I ate one because I had swallowed a penny. I didn't like raisins but didn't tell her because raisins were better than a laxative. The one raisin was effective.

I remember our small wooden ice box and the iceman delivering ice in an open top wood sided truck with a tarp to cover the ice, the huge tongs used to carry the blocks of ice into the house, and on hot summer days being given ice chips to savor by the iceman. Unexpected gifts can come in unusual ways and should be recognized and appreciated.

There is memory of being sent to the small neighborhood grocery store three doors down and around the corner to get a loaf of bread, and on this particularly hot day a loaf of bread, and a cold bottle of strawberry pop, to be put on the tab. I remember the mischievous glint in the grocer's eye, and his smile because he knew that I was doing this without my mother's permission, and I knew that he knew. He told me to tell her when I gave her the loaf of bread. I knew that

I would have to tell her because he would make sure that I had. I could be sneaky, always "testing" but in the end learning to choose wisely because every action has a consequence. I learned to ask permission.

I remember my first spanking when I had crossed a busy street to play with a friend and being found by my dad on the other side ready to come home. He flew across the street, I don't think his feet touched the ground, grabbed my left arm and whaled the daylights out of me all the way home. I remember the embarrassment and confusion then anger because I had done what he had taught me to do when crossing a street, and now I was getting spanked in front of the entire neighborhood for doing it. Sometimes it's not the punishment but the embarrassment that is the path to the intended result. I was one of those children who thought they were older than they were. I was a handful.

When both of my parents worked days the neighbor ladies babysat me. I called the elderly twins my nannies, Nanny Mable and Nanny Maude; I loved them dearly. I loved the smell of their large old house, their personal smell of Ivory soap and the rocking chairs scattered about the sitting room. This lovely way of life ended when on one summer afternoon the Nannies found me at the end of the long walkway leading from the street to their front porch. I was sitting on the top step yelling insults at an older heavy-set boy riding his bike down the street in my direction. I watched him stop, get off of his bike and begin to walk in my direction wondering what was going to happen. Both Nannies came running, grabbed my arms and escorted me back to the house after telling the boy to be on his way. I received a lecture from them and an unending one from my mother. Mother's lecturing was to be a lifelong trait of hers; she never hit my sister or me instead using her tongue as a weapon that in the end was worse than getting spanked because it seemed to never end and the story could be told to everyone.

It wasn't long after my challenge to the bicycle boy that I had a new and much younger babysitter called "Red". Red had a grade school aged son whom I called "Babydoll," and who I loved to tease because he was bashful. Over the years I have developed a subtle teasing humor and those not listening miss it.

Meanwhile during these years of early childhood my grandmother, my father's mother, would visit us, and we would visit her and grandpa at their house as we all lived in the same town. Little did I know this part of my life would soon end as a result of my grandmother's declining health.

Sometime between my age of two and half and three years old we moved in with my grandparent's so the adults could care for grandma. Mom being a registered nurse cared for her during the day, grandpa during the night after working all day, and dad helped grandpa during the night as needed as he too worked. There were occasions when all three were helping at the same time as grandma's condition declined and me, at my age, watched, listened, and tried to make them all happy, especially my grandmother.

It really wasn't a bad time for me as I had a new neighborhood with so many new people to learn about, homes to explore if invited in, and more kids my age. I was still the same feisty kid ready for battle remembering only one incident when an older and much bigger neighborhood girl made a long forgotten comment about my family or me in connection with my family. I remember as if it were yesterday. The German-Irish blood coursing hot through my veins when as quick as a flash, I shimmied up her much taller body as I would have a tree, and wrapping my legs around her waist I began pummeling her in the head with my little fists. Someone uncoiled me from her body, probably daddy who always had at least one eye on me posted nearby. I watched the big baby cry with satisfaction while I cried with anger at what she had said. I had a temper and still do but better controlled as I grew older.

One day in August, 1946, my grandmother was taken to the hospital for a blood transfusion and while there she died. I remember the phone ringing and both my father and grandfather hurrying out of the house to get into the car only to return quiet and subdued. Grandpa went into the room that he and grandma had shared closing the door, and dad sat down on the couch. He sat leaning forward with his elbows on his knees, his face buried and hidden within the open palms of his hands. His whole body shook as he sobbed as hard as I had ever done in my short life. I had never seen my daddy cry, and in my innocence, I had not connected my grandmother being in the hospital to the phone call received, and the rushing out of the house. I tried to comfort him standing next to him with my little arm on his shoulder but his loss was too fresh, too intense, and too final for him to be aware of anything beyond his own grief; an immense grief that years later, at the death of my daughter, I learned to understand. My mother ushered me into the bedroom, and to bed where I lay in fear of what unknown thing had happened that could cause my daddy to cry, and not knowing or understanding the few words said, I cried myself to sleep. I was four years old.

I remember Grandma's viewing and daddy holding me so I could kiss her on the cheek for the last time, to tell her goodbye, and that I loved her. Several years later we moved into another house not far from the cemetery where she was buried. Over the years I would ride my bike to her peaceful burial site, to sit on her headstone, to think about her and what she had meant to me, and to think about the mystery of life and death. Death does not frighten me, it is inevitable; it is the manner of death which is concerning.

The fronts of the houses in this neighborhood faced the street but behind the houses ran an alleyway down to the side streets. The fronts of the houses on each side of the alleyway faced a different street. Trash and garbage were placed at the back of each house and the garbage and trash trucks would drive down the alleyways picking up refuse rather than in front of homes as is done today.

On this particular day I had no one to play with, and to occupy my time, which we had to do in those days being there was no TV, computers, or hand games; I meandered down the alleyway behind the houses across the street. I picked colorful hollyhocks fitting them together forming hollyhock dolls, and as I proceeded to mid-block, I could hear a man yelling and a dog yelping, whining and crying. I hurried to where the sounds were, stopped and peered through the wire fence between the leaves of a bush to see a man beating a dog. I silently sat and watched horrified by the cruelty of what I was seeing sympathizing with the dog.

When the man went into the house the dog hid behind the bushes by the back fence, and with a little gentle coaxing on my part, he came to stand before me, a medium sized white dog with big black and brown spots on his back and a black head. He leaned against the fence, and I leaned against the fence, able to get my small arms through the wire fence holes to hold him, mumbling sympathy and love into his black ear, crying while he whined telling me about his life and the mean man he lived with. That night at dinner I told my family what I had seen.

Not long after that encounter that white dog with the brown and black spots on his back, and a black head was sitting at my back door. My family agreed that he was now my dearly beloved dog, and I named him "Spot". He was my guardian, and no one dare to appear to harm me or they got bit much to my grandfather's dismay, when he suddenly reached out to playfully grab me. Spot bit him on the hand before grandpa even touched me, and Spot did not let go growling and shaking grandpa's hand. Grandpa had just arrived home from work; dad was already home, and both he and mom were in the kitchen when they heard the commotion, and ran to the back door to see what was going on. One look sat everyone into motion. Dad ran to start up the green Pontiac; Mom ran to get clean dish towels to apply pressure to stop the bleeding and wrap the hand; Grandpa stood holding his wrist, and I kneeled wide eyed on the ground next to Spot with my arms protectively around him.

After a trip to the hospital, Grandpa was brought home with stitches covered by a large white bandage on his hand. Grandpa was a barber so cutting hair was going to be difficult for him until his hand healed.

Dinner was eaten in silence as each of us independently thought about what should be the outcome of this situation. After dinner, the family gathered in the living room to hold a meeting. When Spot first arrived, he had been taken to the vets and had received his rabies shot and grandpa was given a Tetanus shot at the hospital. It was decided that based on how Spot had been treated by his former owner, and how he and I had met culminating in his resulting escape and appearance at our house, Spot's reaction could be expected. Spot was my guard dog and fully carried out his self-appointed job when he bit grandpa after making a sudden movement in my direction. Grandpa thought about this and agreed never touching me again when Spot was around, however, I could run and jump on Grandpa for hugs and kisses, and this did not upset Spot. After that incident each kept their distance from the other.

My parents were pleasantly assured that there was no way in hell that I would ever be harmed by anybody when Spot was around; they could relax a little.

I started first grade at the age of six walking the five blocks alone to school in the morning, home for lunch and back to school then home again after school and like the mailman, this was done in sunshine, rain and snow. School was never closed for inclement weather. No one was bussed; it was a neighborhood school. I knew to watch out for strangers having been taught the same safety measures that I taught my children and the children of today are still taught. Nothing has changed.

In February, 1948, I was sent for a visit with my cousins in a neighboring state. I thought this was strange because if I went to visit my mother's sister, my aunt, uncle, and cousins, it was always in the summer but I welcomed seeing them all again. My little bags were packed, my homework was in order, and Dad drove me the 70 mile one way trip. The next weekend Dad picked me up, and we drove home. Dad said that they had a surprise for me but wouldn't tell me what it was; it was a surprise!

I was a loud boisterous child who embraced life with exuberance but that was to change the moment I entered the house, and was told that I had to be quiet. Quiet? Quiet is for church. They led me into our bedroom, and there and behold was a baby crib with a baby, my sister, my unannounced unprepared for sister, my surprise. You have to understand that I had been a well loved only child for six years, and had been happy being that only child, and now I had to tip-toe and whisper while the baby did not care if any of us slept through the night without interruption. The worse of it was this baby demanded everyone's attention, now not later, and I had to wait. That baby couldn't play because she was too little unable to do anything but lay there, and I wasn't allowed to touch her unless someone was with me. Finding the whole situation unsatisfactory, I wanted the baby sent back. I was jealous and angry; the seeds of selfishness were sown.

I began to look outside of my home rather than inside my home for comfort and satisfaction at the early age of six. My parents were too busy with my sister and I wanted nothing to do with her. That's pretty much how I felt most of my growing up years. I came home to use the bathroom, eat and sleep otherwise I was out of the house.

I began to suspect that I was adopted, why else would I be treated as a cast off? One Saturday morning, dad drove me to the bank where we entered an imposing vault, and after producing the proper key he withdrew from a locked box my birth certificate as proof that I was their natural child. I was not impressed and although this certificate had an official seal I knew by then, having listened to people talk about adoption, that adopted children received a new birth certificate with the adopted parent's names. My father, deflated, and I left the bank and drove home. I eventually out grew this phase of being adopted. Today I can look in the mirror and see my mother, my aunt, and my father's aunt but mostly my mother looking back at me; genes do not lie.

My sister and I are now close but when we speak of our growing up years, we speak of two different sets of parents, and yet they were the same parents only more experienced with their second child who had a different personality and needs than their first.

We were raised with Midwest values, God, family and country. Family members had been called into WW II followed by the Korean War and fortunately everyone returned. As school children, we filled Red Cross boxes with toothpaste, toothbrushes, Hershey bars, soap and washcloths for the children of war torn Europe. Children can have intenseness for other children who are caught up in a war knowing they are helpless and as dependent as they themselves are. Then came the "cold war", and should the Communists drop "the bomb" on our little town, we had practice drills taking cover under our desks. Then we were moved to the basement under the daunting double wide metal staircase leading to the first floor with each of us realizing that if that staircase should fall we would be smashed. We had heard the bomb could be dropped on us but none of us thought much about it except that we got out of class for a good 20 minutes.

At the age of nine we moved into a larger home located in a new neighborhood, a neighborhood nearer to where Grandma was buried.

In 1952, the polio epidemic hit our small town, and mother returned to nursing. The crisis was such that we were not permitted to play with others nor go anywhere where there was a crowd. We learned about the dying children first hand from mom as she sat weeping talking to dad, and that was pretty much all we needed to hear to keep away from others. It was a sad time for many people but fortunately not our neighborhood as it had escaped the wrath of the disease.

I was a child who required explanations as to why I should or shouldn't do something, and to this day I still want an explanation. The simple statement of "you can't do that" was not enough because whatever it was not to be done, found its way to the top of my list to do. I wanted to know why, why can't I do this or that; what will happen? My father was the one who invariably patiently provided explanations that satisfied my yearning to understand.

An example of not knowing why occurred on a well remembered short trip taken with a friend whose mother wanted to visit her friend in another town. The beautiful old home was on an estate surrounded by a brick wall and steel gated entrance located within the town. The owner took my friend and me around showing us the areas where we could play; she then led us to a shed where we stood at the door, and as she pointed to it, she said, "You must not open this door. Do you understand? Do not open this door." With that final statement she left us to walk to the veranda to be with the mother of my friend.

Having never been a submissive obedient child, and a curious one at that, the shed with the door not to be opened held my fascination as we played. Why can't we open the door? What could be behind it? Having played everywhere else we eventually ended up in front of the door. Placing our ears against it, we could hear no sounds within; there was nothing alive in there! Perhaps it was furniture to be refinished with dangerous chemicals sitting around, maybe an old car or garden tools we were not to touch. With some persuasion, I convinced my friend that we had to open the door and we did. There was nothing there, and then we saw it, an enormous white goose standing in the shadows off to the side. We stood eyeing each other, me with wonder, as I had never seen a living goose, a Mother Goose just like in the stories without a hat!

The women were sitting on the shaded veranda drinking coffee when we came charging up chased by this honking monster with flapping wings thrusting its head forward nipping at our heels. I could run like the wind but my friend was slower than I, and I held my breath as I stood on the veranda watching as the goose closed in on her. Eyes wide with terror she threw herself up the two steps onto the veranda, and lay on her back gasping for air. Both women were now standing having witnessed the commotion. The goose stopped at the bottom of the veranda steps settling down to peck at whatever geese peck at within the grass. The visit was over, and I was never again invited to go on a trip with them.

I have laughed at this over the years, and have wondered if the woman had told us there was a vicious goose behind that door, would I have still encouraged my friend to open it just to see what a vicious goose looked like? I might have, I am curious.

My world revolved around my friends, mostly boys in the neighborhood because they were more fun than the girls who played pretend house, pretend dolls, cutout paper dolls and dress-up using old adult cloths. I was a tomboy climbing apple and cherry trees to get the best ripened fruit, jumping from garage roofs into sand boxes, playing baseball and basketball. I preferred adventure always pushing towards the limit and was an explorer who knew every nook and cranny in our neighborhood. I liked to work with my dad in the basement where he taught me to use his drill press, electric drill, band saw, metal lath and other tools. I have my own toolbox and can fix about anything I set my mind to except anything electrical and some plumbing. Before I graduated from high school my aptitude test results were, number one, an airplane pilot and number two, a mechanic, neither likely in 1960.

It was after moving into this new house that I began having experiences with the paranormal. When I was a child, grade school was first through eighth grades and high school was ninth through twelfth grades; there was no such thing as middle school. I was probably in the fourth or fifth grade when I suddenly woke up to see a transparent figure with long white flowing sleeves standing by my sister's bed facing my sleeping sister. Our twin beds were approximately three feet apart allowing me a good view of the figure. I squeezed my eyelids tightly closed because I didn't believe what I was seeing, and when I opened them again the image was gone. I was absolutely convinced that it was my grandmother who had died before my sister was born. Who else but angels wear long white flowing sleeves, and stand by your bed at night. There was no question in my mind I knew that my grandma was an angel.

The second experience was suddenly waking up aware of feet running up and down the hallway outside our bedroom door, and whatever it was had short legs because the running sounded like it was taking little running steps. The running steps again passed the door heading into the living room, and sounded like it had circled around the dining room table running back past our door to the end of the hall and stopped. Again it ran past our door. By this time I am grossly awake sitting up in the bed, holding the sheets tightly in my fists, eyes as wide open as I could get them, trembling, intently concentrating on those running feet, and where they were going. All animals slept in the basement at night, so it wasn't one of them. Only adults with long legs live in this house except for my sister and me, and I can see her asleep in her bed next to mine. The running stopped in the dining room, and I heard a teaspoon fall onto a piece of china mother had setting below the spoon rack. The running began again, faster now, and I am holding my breath as it pauses by our bedroom door then runs to the end of the hall and stops again. Surely I cannot be hearing what I am hearing! Why isn't anyone else hearing these running steps as it runs by three bedroom doors multiple times? And then it runs to our bedroom door, stops, and I can hear the distinct sound of the door knob turning! I let out a blood curdling scream but there is no sound except for a loud wheeze! I draw another deep breath, and let out a scream to wake the dead.

I wasn't finished with the scream when I heard my father's feet hit the floor in the bedroom next to ours the bedroom door flew open and bounced off of the closet door behind it. I have never felt safer in my life then to see my dad standing there with his gun in hand ready to save me from those running feet. My grandfather is now up as well as my mother; my sister still lies asleep in her bed three feet from mine. I blubber out my story of the running steps, the teaspoon, and the doorknob. Gun in hand, dad and I walk to where the teaspoon would have fallen onto the china but there is no fallen teaspoon. All spoons are hanging where they should be hanging. The entire house is searched, nothing is overlooked, and nothing out of the ordinary is found.

The next day dad explained that he thought it was probably a poltergeist, a prankster entity that tend to bother children whose bodies are developing into adult bodies, and I was of that age. He told me not to be frightened of it but to be aware that this or something like this could happen again but it never did.

Upon entering high school, I became less impulsive, less adventuresome and followed the rules becoming one of the flock, so to speak. I did not want to get into trouble bringing shame and embarrassment to my family or myself becoming the talk of the small town. There were big kids in high school, and I was a "greenie", a freshman. I wanted a good reputation and to liked.

In high school my world expanded and I made new friends. I continued to enjoy learning about people, and how they lived, where they lived, how their family interacted, what they thought and why, how their homes were furnished, what their routines were, and how they were different or the same as my family.

People were fascinating to me, and I was to learn that we are all pretty much the same regardless of who we are, rich or poor, and that we go about the struggle of life in different ways. No one is right, no one is wrong, everyone is different and that is okay. Some were role models whom were better to emulate than others. It was during these years I found myself being a confident to several adults, parents of friends as well as strangers; people needing to find an ear that would listen and not judge, and I was good at listening because I learned from them. It was also during these years the family thought I was sleep walking, as many a morning mom, the first to rise each morning, would find me sleeping on the couch or in a chair with or without my pillow.

In my senior year, mother decided that I should become a nurse thinking I would be good in that profession; nursing was very low on my aptitude test list with my councilor saying I wasn't "hardboiled enough", too compassionate. I became a registered nurse, no discussion. After graduation I married a divorcee whose employer transferred him to the East Coast where our children were born and raised in a country setting. In the early 1970's new people moving into this area were considered foreigners. Both of us coming from city life found this to be a unique experience.

Our married life lasted for forty years when we divorced amicably. We moved on in our lives, him remarrying for the third time while I enjoy my independence. Despite our differences the one thing well done was raising the children who were first and foremost in our life together. We enjoyed every minute of their successful individual thrust into the world of adulthood.

After our divorce, I bought a home in a southern state where I resided with my feline family of four, the babes, Cleo, Lolly, Jezebel and Buster. I am retired but work part time in a position that involves children whose untainted essence brings me great pleasure. They are a constant reminder of how frightening and fragile childhood can be, and how one simple act given freely can have a positive influence in the life of a child and in mine.

My mother at the age of eighty-six moved in with me until her dementia made her presence dangerous for both of us having inadvertently set fire to the kitchen twice when unsupervised while I was asleep. I was able to place her in a personal care home, then an assisted living facility where she happily resided until she fell asleep in her chair sliding out and fracturing her hip. She was admitted into a nursing home following her hospitalization, rallied around then fell and broke her other hip, the precursor of her death at the age of ninety.

The story I am about to relate begins on the 17th of September 2005. While rereading my journal I realized this story probably began long before this date, and I was able to make some sense of unexplained events that had happened in the past especially in the country house. As I read I was surprised how I waffle back and forth between acceptance and loathing of the beings. One day I want to serve them a meal, the next I want to dash their ships against the rocks as I work my way through their unabated assaults. You will see that certain characters appear and reappear throughout, as well as certain subjects are brought forth multiple times as if searching for a fine distinction. Initially, before and after many of the events, I suffered unprecedented fear affecting my daily life leading me into the realization that I was experiencing post traumatic stress syndrome; but when I am in their element, I recall having no or little emotion, and usually act without feeling. I have a single purpose and act accordingly.

I started recording events, dreams and my thoughts in a haphazard manner, careless with dates and time, in the effort of seeking relief from confusion and fear. I had this notion that when it was written it would look different from what I had experienced but it didn't. For seven months I floundered, as if a drowning victim grasping for something solid to cling to, until I realized I needed to be specific about dates and times as much as possible leading me to the day-by-day descriptive record. In April, 2006, Chapter 8, you will see an abrupt change from paragraph form to a daily journal entry. The daily entry presented clear reference to time and events and I hoped, would allow patterns to be identified, and the emergence of facts about the beings. The events and dreams were usually recorded soon after I experienced them. There is no physical evidence to present as proof any of it actually occurred. While I have a pretty good imagination the story I am about to tell is well beyond my wildest abilities to create.

There isn't a dream I will reveal that has not been influenced by my daily life. It was created using my daily life, family and friends, then "interfered with" resulting in a dream not solely of my sub-consciousness, and it is the interfered with portion that captivates my interest. I want to know what that portion reveals about the beings, and what they are seeking; is it the understanding of the human mind or of an individual mind? Do they categorize us as we humans do by putting people into prejudged slots? Are they looking for consistency? What is their purpose?

This writing covers eight years of the journal. Every night starts out about the same, I go to bed, I read, I turn out the light and there are white balls and flashing lights.

Chapter 2

In the dark night hours of Sunday, 17 September 2005, I awoke to use the bathroom. While I walked from the bed to the bathroom, I looked to my left and saw, standing just outside my bedroom doorway, a huge black figure. "It's a ghost," I mumbled to myself deciding it was unlike any ghost I had ever seen or heard described. Once glimpsed ghosts vanish, and an empty doorway is what I expected to see on my return to bed. I looked to the right as I exited the bathroom, and still standing in the doorway was the huge black figure I had seen moments earlier. A light behind the figure drew my attention to the computer desk where standing in front of the desk was a smaller image of it. A light was illuminating from the top of the desk behind the smaller figure. Not in any way alarmed, I snuggled back into my warm bed and fell asleep.

The next morning when I tried to sit up to get out of bed, my right wrist was sore as if I had flexed it and then lain on it. Flexing it back and forth until it was no longer painful to move, I could put my weight on it to sit up. I put my feet on the floor to stand up and found that I could not place the left foot flat on the floor due to tightness in the Achilles tendon. I moved the foot up and down to loosen the tightness, and then I was able to get out of bed. I limped to the kitchen to start my morning routine tuning in CNN on the way to see how our planet was fairing.

I sat on the couch sipping the hot nectar of the gods, coffee, and smoking one of many cigarettes for the day, facing the TV with my bedroom door to the right of it. I didn't hear a spoken word. My attention was riveted on the bedroom door and the strange event of the night before. There was no question in my mind of what I had seen. I had seen a space suit standing at my bedroom door; I had seen a little space suit standing in front of the computer desk; I had seen a cold white light shining behind it, and my right wrist and left ankle had, in some way, been injured while I slept. Why the hell did I go to bed when there were strangers in my house; why had I done that! I took a long contemplative drag off of my cigarette followed by a sip of hot coffee and was puzzled. I got up, and stood just outside the bedroom door looking into my bedroom, seeing what it must have seen with the exception that I had been in the now empty bed.

I wiped my face with a cold wet washcloth and studied it in the bathroom mirror. I looked the same, yes; it was my face, the face I have known all my life. I am still me; I look the same as always. What the hell happened last night? What was it I saw? I began trembling and felt chilly digging into a drawer for a sweater then becoming hot and sweaty throwing it on the floor. My body became a vehicle in motion, aimlessly wondering around the house touching this and that, as if to reassure myself that all was real, while my mind flitted unable to land in a spot that was familiar, solid and safe.

"Just stop this nonsense!" I said out loud to myself, "Stop and think!" In a flash I remembered that several weeks before I had seen a huge black shape standing in the bedroom door but I hadn't gotten out of bed. I had rolled over in the bed huddling under the magic blankets of childhood, and praying until I fell asleep. Did I imagine that? Did I imagine last night? No, this morning my right wrist and left ankle were painful to move, and I did not imagine that. Did I see a ghost both times? No, last night they were not ghosts. The first time had been a black image in the dark. Last night there were two black images, a tall one and a short one, both of them in some sort of outfit, and there was a light! Humans require light to see in the dark, and that light was unlike any light I have ever seen. It was white, cold, and intense, illuminating not the entire room but only a small area at the computer desk, just enough, so that I could see both of them.

Why wasn't I afraid? I see what looks like two space suits standing in my house, and I go to bed and sleep! If they hadn't frightened me then why didn't I go over to the one in the doorway and ask what it was doing there? Why did I think only of going back to bed? "Okay, okay, take a breath and think; something's not right here," I said to the babes who lay about watching me roam throughout the house muttering to myself. Then it occurred to me that they had probably seen it too! If only they could talk! I sat down on the couch, my left hand automatically reaching to stroke Buster who lay patiently waiting by my side.

Both forms were dressed in outfits that resembled space suits with helmets. Except for the helmets the outfits also resembled attack dog training outfits. Up again, I searched the Internet finding the attack dog training suits that most resembled the ones I had seen with the exception that the sleeves and pant legs were shorter exposing the hands and shoes. The suits I had seen last night looked padded with a clear cut off at the hands and feet but I hadn't seen hands or feet. The sleeves were longer than normal human sleeves but they would be if the hands were covered by them. The pants legs went down to the floor showing no feet or footwear.

Both beings had looked solid. I did not see through the tall one at the bedroom door nor did I see the computer desk and light through the little one. I could clearly see above and to each side of both of them from head to floor. They each had on an elliptical shaped helmet similar to what our astronauts wear. No light reflected off of either one as if their outfits absorbed light. If they had stood next to me in a dark room I would not have seen them.

Maybe this will make sense if I put it into a context that I can understand. I grabbed the tape measure out of my toolbox and began measuring distances. My bed was nine feet from the commode. Measuring from the bathroom doorway to the bedroom doorway was twelve feet. From the bathroom door to the computer desk, where the little one stood, was twenty-two feet and four inches. The bedroom doorframe is eight feet high leading me to estimate the height of the tall one to be about six feet. The little one was about four feet tall based on measuring the height of the computer desk, and where the top of the helmet appeared against the monitor seen behind it. Their bodies had to be shorter to fit into the helmets so the tall one was taller than me; I am five feet six inches.

How on earth did they get in? I hadn't heard any noise that would indicate someone breaking into the house. I checked the deadbolt and doorknob locks on the steel front door, and the lock on the steel and glass storm door finding both locked. I checked the sliding glass door at the back of the house, and found the wooden dowel preventing the door sliding open in place. The door on the back porch was locked. All of the windows were locked. I even checked the attic to see if there was some way someone could gain entry; there was none. My house was totally locked, as it is every night, and yet, the space suits were standing at my bedroom door and in the living room. How the hell did they get in?

The suits appeared to be thick and padded like the ones used for training attack dogs. Astronaut suits also appear thick and padded plus astronauts wear helmets and these two had on helmets! If the outfits were attack dog outfits, I would have been able to see hands, feet and the heads, unless it had a face mask and then it would be hidden but none were seen. If they were astronauts, which is beyond my comprehension at this point, did they need the suits to survive or were they worn as camouflage? It seemed obvious that they wanted me to be aware of their presence; I woke up at the time they were present; I saw both of them at the same time; I was unafraid. Was this entire incident a message to tell me there are entities that do come to earth from another planet? If this is true then why did they come to my house? And if the huge black image standing in the door the first time that had frightened me so badly, is the same as the one seen last night, do they need the suits as protection from me?

I thought about this for awhile when it hit me, "Oh my God! Maybe it's the devil!" I wailed, as visions of art the masters have painted of tortured souls captured in hell drifted through my mind backed by sermons of preachers heard throughout childhood of the relentless hunt of the devil for sinners. A different kind of fear, a hopeless fear, shot through me, as an endless stack of my sins, real or imagined, began to pile one upon the other without end. "Dear God in Heaven help me!" I pleaded, "I'm doomed. It was the devil in a space suit trying to fool me!" I began to pray for forgiveness; wallowing in self-pity I groveled in front of the Lord, when, as if a message from Him, the thought struck me that I had not sensed evil from the presence of the space suits, in fact, I had sensed nothing at all. I knew when evil is about; its presence is felt. I murmured a sincere, "Thank you, God for this message. I love you," and prayed for guidance.

I am constantly thinking about the space suits, and the possibility of alien entities; for weeks there has been no relief from thinking about what I had seen, and what it might mean. They must have been standing there watching and waiting. Will they do it again? The fear of the unexpected, for they surely were the unexpected, mounted day by day. The darkness of night was no longer part of the twenty-four hour day to which I looked forward. It was no longer a time of rest and recuperation for the next day. I worried about why they were here, if they still were here, and what was happening, if anything, when I thought I was sleeping. As the late afternoons advanced into night a sense of dread poked its ugly head into my normal reality.

I would lie in bed watching the bedroom door and jerk out of a light sleep to look at the door. I tried sleeping with the bedside light on using a sleep mask, ripping it off periodically to look at the bedroom door. I changed to reading most of the night then lying half awake watching the door for the rest. I was consumed with the need to be aware and prepared for their next visit should they come back, if they came back. I had a lot of unanswered questions, and I was angry with them for invading my privacy and home. I was sleep deprived, on edge, and snapping at everyone.

Then one night I suddenly awoke to see a grayish square object hovering in the air several feet from the head of the bed. I kept blinking, willing it to go away, wishing that I had a gun as I wanted to shoot the hell out of it. I was livid that they had invaded my home again, and not having the gun, I did the first thing that came into my mind; I propped myself up on my right elbow and using my left hand, I began violently shaking and waving my bed linens, yelling with the stern authority of an agitated mother and grandmother, "Get! Get!" It didn't move continuing to hang midair as if in defiance. In one swift motion I leapt out of the bed while simultaneously groping for the bedside lamp-pull nearly yanking the lamp off of the bedside table.

The grayish square object was now white and looking proper sitting on the lamp. It was the lampshade! In my restless sleep I had slightly changed my angle in the bed, and when I opened my eyes I was looking towards the bathroom door rather than the bedroom door. Moonlight shining through the bathroom window had caused the white lampshade next to the bed to appear free floating, the base hidden in shadow.

I had shot out of that bed ready to fight, ready to let them know just how much I resented their uninvited intrusion. The adrenalin was pumped and the body ready for action to fight a lampshade! I collapsed onto the bed laughing. I needed to seriously re-evaluate what I was doing to myself. I closed the bathroom door, and turned to look fondly at the four babes stretched across the bed, blinking, looking at me with sleepy eyes as if to say, "What's going on, Mom?" I continued to laugh at myself, this time with relief.

Weeks of restless nights continued with sleep arriving as a result of exhaustion. And finally, the realization hit home that when I turned off the bedside light, and searched the shadows here and there in the bedroom, the adjoining bathroom, and the living room, it didn't matter what I did because if they wanted in they would get in. They could be standing in a shadow in the room at that very moment, and I wouldn't be able to see them. They were the color of night. I slept.

Chapter 3

During the day, every moment not requiring my attention was fixated on the visitors. Had this been a random visit but there had been two visits! How many times have they been here, and how long have they been coming? Have they been coming all of my life, and I'm just now finding out? Why now?

Thoughts led to my father who raised my sister and I to have an open-mind; to be aware that what is considered fantasy today may be reality tomorrow. I remembered summer nights we had sat outside in the backyard gazing at the star filled sky sharing our thoughts. He was a science fiction buff who believed in the possibility of intelligent life on other planets, and so my sister and I do too. Dad also believed there was a Roswell cover-up although he never explicitly said this but one could deduce his opinion. How dad would have loved this experience or would he have? He slept with a gun and had the philosophy of shoot first and ask questions later. Would he have shot the huge one in the doorway or would he have gone back to bed and slept like I had done? I have heard that generations of humans have been followed by alien beings; could this be true? Had dad's family been one of the chosen ones or was it mother's? But mother ran from anything paranormal while dad stood his ground looking for explanations. I remember dad telling me the witnessing of a child being taken while drawing water from the family well at night. Was this a story he had heard or was this a story handed down in his family? I'll never know the answer because dad died in 1978.

My thoughts turned to The Creator of everything, a creator

who has no limits; to believe that humans are the only intelligent life form in the vast universe is a huge limit, one set by man.

I am watching any program I can find on UFOs, looking for anything that is similar to my experience. I am not aware of being transported to their laboratory for painful probing and tests, or having unborn babies yanked from my body as some people report. Should I experience just one big needle thrust up my nose or anywhere else into my body, I would most likely have cardiac arrest and die on the spot. I have seen an occasional light in the sky but nothing like what is shown on the UFO programs. I have watched interviews about alien abduction, unidentified flying objects, and witnesses seeing strange life forms running around on our planet. And if these things are true then I am selfishly relieved that it happened to someone else and not to me. I've only seen two space suits and that is enough for me, I require nothing more.

Then I remembered that several months prior to seeing the space suits, my neighbor had casually asked me if I had noticed a bright light shining through the top of my blinds late one night. She said the light was only at the top of the blinds spooking her so much she got out of bed and watched TV for over an hour until it finally went away. She was my chosen target of release, and I told her about the space suits standing at my bedroom door. She said the light has not come back nor has she has seen strange visitors in her home leading me to wonder if they have been back, and she is unaware. Years later she was to tell me that she has found herself sitting on the side of her bed yelling, "NO, NO, NO," but does not know why and remembers nothing.

I came to the conclusion that they had not come to hurt me but that didn't relieve the unease as the sun began to set. The only time that I felt I might be safe from them was when I was with other people. I learned later that was a fallacy, a wished for belief.

I have seen and experienced phenomena such as ghosts, orbs and things that go bump in the night since I was a little girl and, yes, I was terrified until I eventually learned to keep calm using the "I'm alive and they are dead" thought giving me control. I have never sought out these things; they come to me no matter where I live. Mother had told me that these entities gain strength, and therefore power from your fear, and to avoid discussing events where they dwell preventing acknowledgement of their presence. I never really know what is there. I just have a feeling of good, bad, even indifference, sometimes anger, and some can start out one way evolving into another. The ones I have seen vanish when you blink or look away and then back but the space suits hadn't remaining in place like statues. I hadn't felt anything from them; they were a blank.

Chapter 4

Having somewhat calmed down and resuming my normal sleep pattern, I found that I couldn't see anything when I turned off the bedside light one night. My peripheral vision was sharp but I couldn't see a thing straight ahead. When I moved my head around I could peripherally see the different shades of night light and shadows in my room. I slept little that night fearing that I was going blind yet I had no problem with my vision the next day. The next night the same thing occurred but this time I got up and watched TV for hours. This went on nightly for weeks.

Then one night I suddenly awakened to a pitch black room smelling what I thought was something similar to an antiseptic. The smell was strong and seemed to be emanating from my right side towards the foot of the bed. It smelled of a combination of Clorox and something else I couldn't identify. Once I had identified what I could, I wasn't the least bit concerned, rolling over and falling back to sleep remembering nothing the next day.

On the morning of 4 October 2005, I woke up with my belly hurting. My first thought was that I had eaten something that had upset my stomach; mentally listing everything eaten the day before nothing was found. Resting my hand on my abdomen, I found that it was too tender to bear the weight of my hand. Touching the belly button caused intense pain. Most women will admit that they don't remember the actual pain of childbirth, just that it was painful but with the next baby, and the first labor pain she remembers it all too well. I identified the pain as the same as when I required laparoscopic surgery forty-one years ago;

the pain was the same and I couldn't imagine why I would be having it now. What had happened to me while I was sleeping? I wondered about the night I had smelled the antiseptic. Was that last night? No, it was several weeks ago.

I got up, dressed and went to work and found the discomfort diminished as the day wore on. Days later, when the area was less tender, I found a small red line in the twelve o'clock position of the umbilicus. The little red line was about a quarter inch long and has now healed without scarring. I was at a loss as to how this might have happened and knew that it was "them"; who else could it be? They had done this to me but why? I thought about it for days and realized that I had been seizing a roll of fat, fat I had never had in my life until I took a sit-down job, fat unflatteringly spread across my belly; seizing it with both hands saying to it go away, go away. I wanted that roll of fat to go away. If that is what happened, either they don't understand English or they misunderstood thinking that I was having pain and investigated to find the cause. Had I known they were going to surgically investigate I would have opted for the removal of the entire roll of fat and willingly submitted. But what was the real reason for the laparoscopy? To this day, I do not know because I remember nothing.

It amazes me how I am becoming complacent and accepting about what is happening but then what can I do? Should I have called the police to report having had a surgical procedure during the night that I had not authorized, and performed by someone, whom I do not know? I can only imagine how that scenario would unfold. Of course, I experience waves of anxiety, who wouldn't? But following the anxiety is the feeling of helplessness, that there is nothing I can do, anything is possible, and I won't know what that possibility is until I wake up in the morning. I've never been a laid-back individual; when anything untoward happened I was there investigating, trying to figure out what, why, and how, so it could be prevented from reoccurring. The anger and resentment began to mount up, anger for violating my privacy and extreme anger for violating my body, and resentment that it was all done without my permission or knowledge beforehand.

On the morning of Monday, 11 October 2005, I awoke extremely fatigued. I had had an unusual dream the night before that had been arduous.

I am in an observation room where I look through the large window into a testing room while someone unseen on my left is talking to me. The testing room is white and has a large projection screen on the facing wall. On the wall adjacent and to the right of the screen is an exit door near the corner. On the adjacent wall to the left are cabinets and a door to a storage room. A table is in the middle of the room with piles of large cards laying on it. I know what is expected of me as I have done it before. Suddenly I am standing in the testing room next to the table holding one of the piles of cards in my hands looking at them.

The cards are approximately eight by four inches, thicker than playing cards, and have colors on one side, and black and white on the other. I don't pay attention to what the designs are because they are familiar. I've seen them before. I am to throw the cards in proper placement, forming a cube that will not lose its shape or collapse; if either happens then I haven't completed the task properly.

The test is timed beginning when I throw the first card. If I remember the proper sequence I will throw each card into the correct area, and they will latch onto one another eventually forming the cube. It is not a test that can be done slowly because the cards will not remain latched falling to the floor. It is not only physically tiring because the cards must be thrown accurately with a certain force to create the latching but mentally as well, because I have to remember how each cube is constructed. I am finishing up the third cube having had to throw the last card three times before it successfully locks together and glides off to the end of the room with the other two. From the table, I pick up the next group of cards to start the fourth cube while mentally measuring how far I have to throw them, and decide that I am too tired to continue. I lay the cards on the table, turn around and walk from the room through the door to the right of the projection screen. When I walked from the room, I found myself awake and in the process of getting out of bed, or maybe I was getting into bed, I don't know.

The weirdness of the dream bothered me running through my mind like a greyhound on a racetrack. How strange to build a solid cube with locking cards, and it hadn't been a new experience for me, I had done it before but when? Everything was familiar, the room, the cards, and the test. I knew that in the past I had made more than three cubes. I regretted not paying more attention to the design on the cards because if there were earthly scenes and pictures of humans, then it would be just a frustration dream inspired by my work for a national greeting card company. Later I learned that this was most likely a dream "interfered with".

An obstacle that I have encountered since finding the space suits in my house is the inability to state date and time when strange events occur. My mind becomes blank, was it last week, this week, sometime this month, or sometime last month? It is so abstract that I have learned to jot down what I can remember, and if lucky, then I will remember another piece, and another, until most of it comes back; or I just simply don't remember until something occurs jolting my memory. Most often it just doesn't seem that important and yet it really is, to me. My practice now is to go from dream or experience to the computer recording every detail I can remember if I am allowed to remember anything at all.

During the month of October 2005, I experienced two unusual events.

The first event occurred after I had turned the light out and lay in bed willing sleep. I no longer fall asleep easily, and can toss and turn that is annoying to me as well as the babes. I can't ever remember falling asleep on my back but will lie on my back for a while if I can't get comfortable on either side. This particular night I lay on my back searching the shadows and yawned. When I closed my mouth the roof of it was stinging and there was a bitter taste. That's the last thing I remember. I remember nothing. Lesson learned, I no longer yawn in the dark without covering my mouth.

The second event caused me to know that they, whoever or whatever "they" are, were back. I suddenly became aware of a small beam of very bright white light penetrating through the blind and curtain at the upper right side of the bedroom window while the rest of the window and room remained dark. The light hit me in the face but didn't hurt my eyes when I looked at it. The light was steady, not moving or wavering, and whatever was holding the shining light in the window had to be a minimum of seven feet tall. I immediately thought of my neighbor and the bright light shining through the top of her bedroom window late one night. I stealthily got out of bed and hurried into the dark living room intending to go out back to see what was causing the light to shine in my window. I looked in the area of the computer desk first then towards the sliding glass door opening onto the back porch. On the closed vertical blinds of the sliding glass door were three solid red circles, the size of baseballs, forming an upside-down triangle. They didn't seem to be pulsating or if they were, it was so rapid that I was unable to detect it. I was held spellbound by feet having turned to lead.

I stood about eight feet from the triangle alert watching the red circles to see what they would do. I figured it was "them", and I was curious to see what would happen next hoping that one of them would materialize in front of me. Questions were running rampantly through my mind. Were they being transported within the three red dots, is that how they get in? Once the process of transportation begins can it be stopped? Would one or both of them materialize in front of me? Whatever, I wanted to see it happen, and I was going to stand there and wait until something did. It was years later that I decided that each red ball was probably an individual transport device.

It was a stand-off. After three or four minutes, an eternity, had passed and nothing happened, I thought about putting my hand in the triangle then decided that might not be a good idea; I need both of my hands. I then considered throwing an object into the center of it then wondered if there might be an explosion destroying them, me, the babes, the entire building, maybe the whole block. I was becoming impatient and decided that throwing something into the middle of the triangle and run like hell would work just fine. Never taking my eyes off of the red circles, I took a step towards the desk with my right arm outstretched to grab whatever loose object lay on top when I abruptly decided that I was tired and should go to bed. And that's what I did. I turned around, the mystery of the triangles forgotten, and marched off to bed and slept.

All my plans were scattered in the wind. I was going to approach the beings if they came back. I wanted to know who they are, where they are from, and what they expected to accomplish in their visits to me. I wanted to know how long they have been coming and where else they have been on earth. I wanted to know about them as living beings. But I was thwarted, sent to bed, making me more angry and resentful of their treatment towards me, and yet, at the same time, I was more curious than ever about them.

Apparently they can read my mind; on the other hand, perhaps they understood my action when I reached towards the desk. One thing is definite, based on two past examples they can make me do what they want. If the red dots had vanished or melted through the vertical blinds when I walked into the room I would have thought it was my imagination, instead, they hung there like a De Vinci painting on a museum wall captivating my interest. Perhaps my presence was unexpected, and they didn't know what to do until I became a potential threat, then again, maybe it was planned.

Chapter 5

When I get up in the morning events and dreams are fresh in my mind, if I remember anything at all but always become fragmented and seemingly unimportant. If a memory of something pops up, I write it down which has worked in the past but now I develop headaches when I try to remember. If I let my mind wander or become focused on some mundane daily thing the headache vanishes returning when I begin to refocus on the previous night's events.

I confided in my sister about what was going on, and she suggested I read *Communion* by Whitley Strieber. I found the book at the library, and had difficulty absorbing anything as I became anxious just opening it. I had to lay the book down for several days then force myself to pick it up and read and reread every line until I began to absorb the written word. At several points in the book, I was struck by some similarities of our respective experiences that I found comforting and somewhat reassuring.

I also do not believe that they have come to our world to do us harm, not at this time anyway at least with me so far. They must be curious about our world in general otherwise why would they be here? From accounts they have visited many people, and their ships have been seen throughout the world. This indicates to me that by now they probably recognize the differences between races and nationalities as well as the sameness that we share. They seem to be careful about the interactions between them and us, and I feel that they respect the unpredictable behavior of humans. But for me the bottom line is the beings are always in control, and I end up doing what they instruct me to do, and I suspect it may be the same for everyone else. Strieber writes about the greys. At this time, I have only seen two space suits, a short one and a tall one, a beam of light, and three round red balls. I have no idea what the beings look like.

As for locking doors and windows, it is an ineffectual endeavor as they seem to be able to ease through glass as if it does not exist, and that thought juggled my memory of my oldest son about the age of nine. We lived in the country house at the time. Every night before he went to bed he checked every door in the house to see if it was locked. When asked why he did this, he replied that he was just making sure they were locked. The phase passed but I still thought it was unusual.

The children were privileged to grow up in a country setting learning not only strong family values but strong community values as well. Their friends were the children of many folk who were descendents of generations who had settled in the area. Country children, especially adventurous boys, could roam acres without meeting another individual and our youngest and his friends were roamers. I believe it was in the early 1980's that he and one of his friends began telling me about strange looking people wearing long brown coats they would see in the fields. He said they never saw their faces.

Sometimes, the boys said, they were chased by them, and I recall several occasions when they came flying in through the door looking terrified. I knew there was something to their stories because they wouldn't go back outside on those days. At other times they talked about seeing UFOs flying over while in the fields, and sometimes they just made up stories to tease me. Whatever their stories, there was no way to check them out because by the time I would get to the area whatever had been there would be gone. I began taking long walks down deserted roads among the fields but didn't see anything strange.

Around that time my mom and dad were living with us in an unattached apartment. Dad said that he had seen what looked to him like a lion outside his bedroom window. He verified this by saying that his cat sitting in the open window went ballistic. I had heard strange noises like grunting at night outside our bedroom window but never a noise that I would think a large cat would make, unless it were sick and had difficulty breathing. I did find a strange paw print but it was destroyed before it could be identified. Eventually the talk of UFOs, strange looking people and the grunting creature all stopped and life settled down to normal.

Then one day when my youngest son was around eleven years old he complained about a sore area on his back that bothered him. Examining his back in the area he said was sore; I noted the skin was intact and that there was redness below the right scapula. I told him that as often as he hurt himself playing in the woods and fields he most likely may have a small foreign object embedded under the skin and his body would work it out advising it be left alone for right now. It was nearly a week later while I was working in the yard that he pulled up beside me when riding his dirt bike. He again complained of the area on his back. I took another look at it, and this time it was a raised red area. "Pinch it!" he demanded, "Get it out! It hurts!" And that's what I did, I pinched it. I was able to place both thumbs under the red area squeezing and lifting up at the same time when a small object appeared. Impatient now, my son insists to keep pinching, to get it out. One more effort exposed a tiny clear plastic looking triangular shaped object slightly larger than a quarter inch from tip to tip to tip lying on the skin surface. It was unlike anything nature made. With the thumb of my right hand I attempted to brush the object into the palm of my left hand to get a better look at it when it seemed to jump from my hand falling into the grass at our feet. Instantly he said his back didn't hurt anymore and thanked me for getting it out, meanwhile I'm on my hands and knees looking for it but it was not to be found. There was little blood from the open area, and it healed quickly with antibiotic ointment and a band-aid leaving a small scar. Not having heard of implants neither of us thought much more about the event now, however, now we both wonder.

Another event happened which also looks very different to me today than it did at the time.

My parents were no longer living with us having moved to be with my sister and her family. The unattached apartment where they had lived was attached to the main house. It was quite late, the lights in the house were turned off, and I was the only one up standing in the dark looking out through the screen door for fox listening to their calls as they hunted. I was concerned and searching for our calico cat, Ruth, who liked to lie on the hood of the car parked near the door. A definite "click" sounded, and a very bright white light shown down on the roof of the house where I stood spilling over onto the parked car in front. I could see Ruth was not on the car hood. I craned my neck to look at the spotlights attached to that side of the house but they were not turned on. I had not heard anything fly over the house, and there was no noise after the light turned on but I felt there was something hovering above it. There was a sense of heaviness all around me making me feel pressed or dense. The light was on for approximately fifteen or twenty seconds, certainly no more than a minute, and then disappeared. I did not hear a click when the light went off and I heard nothing fly away but I could feel the heaviness lift off around me. I wasn't about to go outside to investigate. A US Air Force Base was near, and I thought someone was probably trying out a new type of aircraft in the darkness of the woods, and wondered if perhaps the boys had experienced something from the base as well.

Today I would venture that it may well have been one of the beings smaller ships taking one or both of my boys who lay sleeping in their beds above me. Can you possibly have any idea how this makes me feel as their mother? I was worried about our cat when I should have been running up the stairs to where my boys lay in their beds but I didn't know about the beings then or what they could do.

I had another strange experience while living in that country house, supernatural or real, that terrified me. I couldn't talk about anything else for days. I didn't know what it was, and I still don't but now I have my suspicions.

It was in October 1980 or 1981, the anniversary of my father's death. My husband got up to go to work at the usual time of four in the morning, and I rolled over for a few more hours of welcomed sleep then decided to go into the bathroom before sinking back into oblivion. From the bathroom I could look across the hallway through a kitty hole in the bottom of the basement door allowing the cat's access to their pans in the basement. I saw a bluish glow coming from the hole and thought the dryer door had popped open leaving the dryer light on; it had happened before with heavy jean loads. Had I not been half awake I would have remembered that this was a new dryer that did not have a light in it. My intention was to go downstairs, shut the dryer door, punch the button turning it back on and go back to bed. I had on a pair of slippers.

I opened the basement door and saw that the light was actually a strange bluish glow covering the basement wall as far as I could see on each side of the basement steps. I thought this was strange as the light from the dryer would be concentrated in the dryer area on the side of the steps, and wondered what could be the source of this bluish light. The thought had barely passed through my mind when in a nanosecond, the bluish glow collected into a faceless shape, flew up the steps, hovering above them slightly lower than the level of my face.

I was looking at something that had no head, no arms, and no legs but I knew where the head was although I could see no features. It looked as if a short sheet had been draped over it and I thought of *Casper the Friendly Ghost*.

We faced each other in the dark, it radiating a soft bluish tint, and me pale with only my feet covered. My hair didn't stand on end; I wasn't cold or hot; I wasn't even frightened; my heart rate probably picked up a little because I was astounded. But those sorts of things I didn't think about when I was facing this unknown entity; I was too busy summing up what was before me.

My body was frozen in position with my right hand still clutching the edge of the door I had just opened. Immediately I sensed that whatever it was had intelligence, and it was just as curious about me as I was of it. Suddenly I became embarrassed that I was naked because it knew that I was! Two hands are not enough to cover three targeted areas of a woman's naked body especially when one of those hands still remains firmly clutched to the basement door. It was then that alarm sprang through me like a herd of buffalo followed by a roaring prairie fire, and thoughts spewed forth, "it knows I'm naked, what will it do to me if anything, and oh-my God-what-will-it-do-to-the-children if it knows where they are!" My last thought before flight was it has to follow me. I slammed the basement door with the strength of biblical Samson hoping to scare it away and if not then to lead the blue tinted Casper to follow me down the hall by fleetingly stomping my way to our bedroom. Again with biblical strength, I slammed the bedroom door so it would know where I was. I jumped into bed, scrunched up into a ball, and lay shuddering with fear under the protective magic blankets. I prayed every prayer I had ever learned and created many new ones. Sometime during my feverish praying I fell asleep.

Now in retrospect there is no doubt that I attempted to lead a clear path away from my children but at the same time I didn't consider that if anything might awaken the children it would be two massive explosions one after the other. Bleary eyed with nerve ends still sizzling throughout my entire body, I asked the children the next morning if they had heard any loud bangs during the night with all three indicating they had not. Thank you, God.

I saw "Casper" once more, about a week later in the middle of the night when it came up out of the ground at the side of the house, paused, then glided at tremendous speed towardthe neighbor's house. I was grateful that it didn't look towards the bedroom window where I stood. I never made an effort to look for it again; I really didn't want to know if it came back. From that day forward I wear nightclothes when I go to bed, after all, you never know who or what you will meet in the dark in the middle of the night.

As I read and search for answers the sense of strange happenings throughout my life seem to be taking on a significance that never existed prior to 17 September 2005. Life does go on, and when my oldest son calls and says, "Yo! What's happening?" I reply with "Nothing much." You can't tell anyone or even act a bit strange, as someone might ask something, and with the need so great to talk about what's been happening to you, it could pop out and you would regret it. So life goes on as if, for the benefit of other people, nothing unusual or of interest has happened to you since you were born, a mundane life of "nothing much" that is, in actuality, anything but.

Chapter 6

Things continue to happen and you want to be prepared so as not to miss anything. Your senses are sharpened and you are waiting not knowing when or where the next event will take place. You don't even know if you will be aware of it, if it does, but you want to be ready.

Perhaps the beings have been doing this for years, as some people believe, maybe eons, and had never been seen unless they had wanted to be. I have seen their presence twice now; I think they want me to know. I will begin to look for patterns maybe I can learn something about them.

The nights I went to bed and the babes left as soon as I turned off the light were the nights I suspected the beings were coming or already there, and I slept little. If the babes remained on the bed, at least until I fell asleep and didn't know they had left, I slept better.

I tend to lie on my left side initially, and that is the side facing the window. One night a flash came in through the window as I lay there looking at it. Ah ha, they were checking to see if I am asleep! I was out of the bed standing in the dark living room facing the vertical blinds in the blink of an eye. Nothing happened but I couldn't go back to sleep. My theory was destroyed all of the babes had been on the bed when the flash occurred.

Another night the babes were asleep on the bed when a flash inside the bedroom went off. My eyes were closed but I was awake waiting to fall asleep. Jezebel took off like a torpedo leaving a rip in the quilt from her back claw. I turned on the light, and read a book until the words blurred together finally falling asleep.

Since November 2005, periodically I see small bright white balls flying through the air. They are about the size of a marble, and can occur with the lights on or off. These are not the same as the larger "orbs" that also occasionally float around. When the lights are turned off I can see small red dots or a larger undefined blob of red that vanishes when I look at it. Usually I catch the blob out of the corner of my eye.

For days in January 2006, I was doing computer work that required concentration. In the afternoon of the third day, I was glued to the computer screen when a hand lay very gently on my right upper arm. It didn't just touch my arm it laid there and then disappeared.

The position of the hand indicated that the body it was attached to was standing behind my chair. I was struck with the compassion that I had felt from this gesture.

On another day while working at the computer I looked up at the ceiling, and found above me a large white rectangle with clear edged borders. Standing at the edge of one of the side borders was a grey looking down at me. I could see only the arms, shoulders, neck and head as the arms seemed to be resting on something, perhaps a banister, as he leaned slightly forward looking down at me. Shortly two more joined him on the side of the rectangle looking down at me as I looked up at them. The eerie feeling of being watched squirmed its way into the reality of having the beings know where I live. How do they do this? Where are

they as they watch me through the ceiling?
One day when I walked from the kitchen to the bathroom accessed through my bedroom, I could smell human body odor in two places. One was in a narrow area from the kitchen to the living room and the other was in the bedroom by my bed leading to the bathroom. After the third time, I said, "You need to take a bath" and the odor disappeared. I smelled it again yesterday evening, 18 March 18 2006, this time it came from the chair next to the couch where I was sitting. I didn't say anything, and kept glancing in that direction to see if something would materialize but the odor went away. I've also smelled foot odor coming from that same chair on several occasions. Are they with me all the time, day and night and have the ability to be invisible because I sure can't see them? I can't be certain that the odors are coming from them or where they are originating. If I am the only human in the house it lends me to think the odors are coming from someone or something else but human odors? Days later, I smelled vomit. Do aliens vomit?

One night I awoke extremely distressed following a dream.

I am shouting at someone regarding a staphylococcus infection, and how it needed prompt attention. I pop out of my body and see someone sitting next to me attempting to calm me down by patting my right shoulder leaning forward into my face trying to get my attention. I pop back into my body, and continue yelling that antibiotics are needed immediately, searching my memory trying to remember which one they should use. I am sobbing, and explaining that we have terrible bacteria on this planet, that he had probably gotten it when he had touched my arm, that if "you care about this person you must do it now, and you can save him". I continue sobbing and yell "do it now and you can save him," over and over becoming more upset each time when I awoke in my bed hot and drenched in sweat.

I sat up remembering as if it were this morning that our daughter had died as a result of MRSA. He had touched my arm and now he was dying having no immunity to earth germs. I felt badly that he should die this way, and wondered if they had antibiotics for earth germs hoping they had listened to me. But why did I assume it was a being that had touched my arm?

Was it a dream or was I physically with them in another setting? How can I be sure anymore what's real and what's a dream? If it wasn't a dream then who or what was in my face trying to calm me down? Why did I pop out and back into my body witnessing what was happening? I was later to learn that when in their presence popping out and into my body would be a common occurrence.

The next strange dream was 19 March 2006.
I am looking at snapshots of people in a book while the pages turns and point to each picture when I decide that I need a bathroom break and stop.

The snapshots were like those placed in school yearbooks, and I had been looking at one snapshot after another saying "yes" or "no" indicating whether I knew them or not when I woke up. I lay in the bed thinking that I hadn't recognized any of those people, and why the heck was I looking at them anyway. I mulled over the other dream I had had about staph and now this one showing pictures of people, and wondered if they were probing my mind while I slept or were they just simply dreams.

If there are no physical visitors, and I am imagining all of this, then I need some serious help but I can still function, talk, walk, carry out commitments and function in daily life. I don't see strange things everywhere I look or get messages from the TV or microwave. Strange, it's so strange.

I was awakened by another dream.
I throw a cigarette into my bed and crawl in with it, and continue repeating this dream until I decide that I need to wake up.

I sniff the air expecting to smell smoke but there is none, and the fire alarm has not been triggered. I lay there thinking how strange this dream has been and what it might mean; yes, there was no doubt that I needed to quit smoking, and that must be what the dream was about. Then the odor of hot metal wafted through the closed bedroom door. I went into the kitchen to find that my elderly mother had put the teakettle on high and had forgotten about it. The water had boiled dry and the copper-bottomed kettle was melting onto the burner. Did they have anything to do with the dream or was it my own intuition?

I began to remember other strange dreams that I have had one dream in particular, three different times over a several year period before the space suit stood in my doorway.

I am always walking behind the leader; there are others behind me as we walk in single file across a room, always taking the same path that passes what looks like a rectangular box shaped metal frame on our left. I am able to see many of these frames that extend off into the distance because the room is enormous. The first time we walk by it, I ask the leader in front of me what it is; I am told it is a bed. The second time we walk by there is a man sleeping in it. I am surprised and curious about him, and wondered what he does here, who he is, and how he can sleep in this big open room with the lights on, people walking by, and not be disturbed. He has on what looks like a solid blue frontal closure one-piece outfit with long sleeves, lying on his back with his arms at his sides, floating within the frame. There are no blankets, pillows or mattress, and I think, "Cool". The third time we walk by it is empty, and I ask the leader in front of me if I could lie in the bed, and am given permission. I expect to fall to the floor as soon as I set to lie down, or have the need to flick a switch before I sit down instead I float in the air. I do not hear the humming of a motor or the sounds of a compressor; there is no sound whatsoever. I look at the top of the frame wondering how it functions, considering how it would prevent the formation of pressure sores on people who are unable to reposition themselves because I feel no pressure anywhere. I am floating in air. When I asked permission to lie on the bed, I held the same expectation and excitement as if riding on a new carnival ride, and now I am somewhat disappointed. I feel exposed because there is nothing under or over me, and I have no pillow to lay my head on. The bed is not uncomfortable just very different from what I am use to. I wonder if one can turn onto their side but I am hesitant to try not knowing how I could get leverage to do so while floating, so I get up. I have never had the dream again.

Since September, I crave coffee. My habit for many years has been two cups when I first get up, and one cup in the afternoon around three o'clock. I have probably doubled the daily amount with even more on some days. I can drink it anytime finding that it soothes me making me drowsy, and can hardly keep awake at times. Along with this craving for coffee is the desire for more salt, lots of salt; salt it and if you can't taste it, salt it some more.

Sometimes I talk to them and explain about earth and how we live, or at least I live. I keep telling them that with all of their powers, they should help me win the lottery and stop smoking but neither has happened. There are times when I'm pretty sure they are here with me all of the time, especially after seeing them on the ceiling, but as evening draws closer, I still become anxious.

There have been many doubts regarding their purpose in my home, and my imagination has run rampant searching for reasons and answers. If you are old enough to remember the captivating series "The Twilight Zone", you will remember an episode where the friendly aliens came to Earth to transport thousands of humans back to their world with the promise of a better life. People were pushing and shoving to get onto their ship when one human eventually deciphers their written words, and realizes that it is a menu on how to prepare and serve the new food source being shipped.

That sheds an unthinkable light on the possible intentions of aliens. On the Internet, some say the reptoids eat humans, others say they have seen large vats with human body parts floating around and little grays swimming in it. I don't want to let myself think about the possibility that humans are a food source. It's totally unnerving when they are visiting you, and personally, I don't think that is the purpose of their visits.

Then I think of another episode of "The Twilight Zone" where an old woman is terrorized by a space ship that lands on her front porch eventually making its way into her home. She struggles with this thing finally destroying it with her broom; she smashes it all to hell, and you are cheering her on with every whap of the broom. Then the camera pans onto the insignia on the side of the tiny crumpled ship as it sends out its last desperate communication, "The United States of America". I feel like that old woman with the broom. I want them gone and yet, I am curious about them.

A government plot has certainly wondered through my growing suspicious mind while searching for answers. These beings wear space suits similar to what is used by earthlings for space travel; on occasion I have smelled body odor, stinky feet, and one time vomit that I wouldn't think is a by-product of aliens but of humans. Is one of our government agencies so technologically advanced in using invisibility and in transporting that they can now come into my home or any other home?

If the visits are genuinely from alien beings, it is apparent their mission is a one-way street of not giving knowledge but to gain knowledge; they are takers not givers at least so far with me. I feel that everything that I have learned about them has been unplanned and accidental, but then why do I always feel they are in control, as if I am being led?

My father taught me to appreciate the order of the universe, and gazing at the night sky helps to put my life in perspective when I consider that I am an infinitesimal speck living on a speck of the entirety. The thought that perhaps other life forms are gazing at their view of a star filled sky and thinking what I'm thinking is comforting because that makes us somewhat alike. Gazing at the stars is peaceful, relaxing, and comforting to me. It reassures that there is organization somewhere, if not in my life, and as I look at the stars I wonder about the beings and their lives.

Chapter 7

I have ruled out that the visitors are ghosts because they didn't look or behave like ghosts, and the events that have happened are not ghost-like; the visitors are living entities. I heard someone on TV state that you do whatever a ghost tells you to do, and I disagree, however, with the beings, I am finding that you do what they tell you to do, and you remember what they want you to remember. We are alive and have free agency, and are able to overrule ghosts by forcing them to leave while the beings do what they want regardless of what you want. I believe there are both ghosts and the beings in my home. I will try to explain.

I moved into a newly constructed home in March of 2000. Along with my personal belongings I brought the babes, a Siamese named Lollie, and three shorthaired domestics named Cleo, Buster and Jezebel. They had all been homeless taken in by our daughter who had also adopted a homeless dog. Upon her sudden death, the dog was found lying next to her, and the cats were lined up on the edge of the bed above her, watching and waiting until her body was discovered later in the day. These faithful friends of hers were not to be abandoned; her father took the dog and I took the cats.

Buster is a lap cat who thrives on attention and no one is a stranger to him. If someone will pet him he will welcome it crawling up into their lap to be reached more easily. Jezebel, however, is skittish and if anyone wants to see her let alone touch her, they will have to find her first, and be prepared for a battle when they try to drag her out of her hiding place. Lollie will let anyone touch her if they are eating and willing to share their food; she is very smart noticing and investigating any change or addition made in the house. Cleo watches all of us and has a restrictive rule, "look but don't touch", yet there are times she will sit next to me to be gently stroked and have her ears and chin scratched. Cleo is the dominant animal; the others always have at least one eye on her, knowing where she is and what she is doing. Since the arrival of the beings, poor little Cleo and Lollie have passed on. Lollie's death was unrelated to their presence, but when I found Cleo, I had the impression that she had been frightened to death; it was the way she was laying, almost hidden, as if she had been running and simply collapsed. The age of all of the cats was around 14 years, so a natural death for Cleo cannot be ruled out.

After work in the evenings, I would do genealogy searches on the computer, watch TV, or read a book. The babes were great companions for me; they were close, grooming each other, snuggling up together to take naps, and playful with each other or alone as they amused themselves with their basket of toys.

There were times during the evenings the cats would go crazy, running around as if they were chasing or playing with something other than with each other, ganging up on whatever it was; a feline pride in action. Sometimes they would be facing the same direction with their heads following something moving quickly around the living room. Their heads would move in unison, up and down in the same direction at the same time, as if watching the same thing. I thought perhaps there was a flying bug in the room, and once in a while I would see one of them pounce on something, and that would be that, a bug. However, more often than not, the behavior would simply stop, and they would resume being their normal selves. During January 2002, I purchased an hp 318 digital camera, and began taking random flash pictures when the babes acted strangely but I didn't see anything unusual in the pictures.

My habit before going to sleep was and remains reading in bed to clear my mind of the days stress losing myself in a good mystery novel. The babes would snuggle up to me until I turned out the lights then I noticed that each of them would take a position at each corner of the bed. Buster always lay to the right of my head and Cleo to the left. Lollie would lay to the left of my feet and Jezebel to the right. All of them would be facing away from my body. I found this amusing and thought of them as Earth, Wind, Fire and Water, my little protectors. I also found this rather odd. In the morning I would find two or more of them curled up next to me and the others elsewhere in the house.

When dusk approached, those minutes before artificial lighting is required, I would see glimpses of "orbs" some larger than others flying around in the living room. They would shoot off sideways and disappear. And later, when I lay in bed reading, having propped the book on a pillow that lay on my chest, and to the right of the edge of the opened book, I could see different heights of human shaped shadows passing in front of the mirror that hung over the living room couch, moving towards the sliding glass door one after the other. Sometimes there were only a few while at other times there was a continuous stream. They did not disappear when I blinked or when I squeezed my eyelids tightly together; the procession continued seemingly unaware of my presence. I began to wonder if there was a portal in my living room, and if so, I thought I knew where it was. I wondered if the shadows were of the dead passing through or were they the living from another dimension entering into our world. I had no way of knowing or proving a portal even existed. I had heard of portals but knew nothing about them. The shadows were not bothering me seemingly intent in moving to the sliding glass door, and not knowing what to do about this situation, I ignored them. I considered the possibility that in some way, the beings played a role in this affair. If they were testing me then they must have been disappointed to not have gotten a reaction. Eventually the shadows moving across the living room mirror stopped appearing.

Then something new arrived, something that moved very fast. Perhaps you have seen comic books where a figure would move and lines or a cloud of dust would be drawn behind it to indicate that it was moving fast, this was sort of like that. It must have disturbed the atmosphere as it moved, and that disturbance was enough that I could see it.

I first noticed it one evening when I was in the bathroom seeing something black flash across the bathroom doorway, and as it came to rest against the wall by the doorjamb, I could see it clearly. It was trying to hide behind a four inch doorjamb with its head peeking around at me. It seemed to be aware that I had seen it because it looked at my face, and then shot back the way it had come. It was about a foot and a half tall, black with white eyes, and on its head was a tiara of elongated triangles across it from ear to ear reminding me of the headpiece on the Statue of Liberty. It was slender but not skinny, well formed, and moved agilely like a small child but much faster.

Many an evening after work, Jezebel would lie next to me where I sat on the couch watching TV or reading, and Buster would be at the sliding glass door looking out. He was spending a lot of time looking out onto the back porch at night, which he has always done but he was been doing it more often, and for longer periods for the past several months. In the past when the babes started acting strange I took random pictures, and this evening, because of his behavior, I begin taking pictures of the vertical blinds and back porch.

After downloading the pictures into the computer and letting them set sometimes orbs appear as well as faces. The pictures then stream across the computer as a screen saver, and there are times that I enjoy watching the random shots that include family and friends. I noticed one picture of the vertical blinds seemed to have brown on it that resembled a shoulder that I hadn't noticed before, and was one of the first I had taken in 2002.

I printed the image on plain white paper and looked for the shoulder instead finding a set of blue eyes. They were below and to the right of the sliding glass door handle and set in an intelligent looking black smiling face unlike any face I had ever seen. Only the head, shoulders and arms were visible, and it seemed to be wearing a brownish outfit with a cowl neck. I studied the creature and was relieved because it proved to me that I hadn't lost my mind.

In another picture the creature looked like a short barrel

chested male running into the room, and although the features were not human they were humanoid, eyes, ears, nose and mouth all in the right places. The head had wide set eyes the color of sapphire blue, oversized human shaped ears, and was wearing a big gummy smile obviously pleased with what it was seeing. It was the same being further into the room. I was thinking that this was truly amazing. Here he had been in my living room years ago, my living room of all places.

My hands began trembling, and I felt lightheaded and nauseous. This picture frightened me more than finding the space suits in the doorway because those I had seen, while this creature, also in my house, had been invisible. I warily looked about the room wondering if he was here now, and if so, where? I wondered what else might be in the room that I am unable to see. It is now the end of December 2005 and this was taken in the winter of 2002 almost three years ago. My mind whirled, everything else in my life was insignificant compared to this, and I needed to know more. I needed some reassurance! I needed help to understand what was happening to me.

The next morning I reexamined the picture. I stared at the black face with the wide gummy smile looking for more details then noticed that there were two other faces in the picture I hadn't seen the day before. The one face at the top looked like a cartoon face of a clown. To the right of the clown face and slightly lower was a light brown, almost tan, human shaped figure stepping into the room through the glass door and vertical blinds, the side of the sliding glass door that doesn't open,. I couldn't fathom why they were here. What were they? Were they part of the space suit group? They had not hurt me and heaven knew they had plenty of opportunity. I put the picture aside, and tried to forget what I had just seen, immersing myself in mundane normal chores around our little home, desperately trying to get in touch with reality, normal earth human reality.

That night I studied the picture again using a high intensity light, reading glasses and a magnifying glass, and found that holding the picture with the top angled slightly backward, I could see more detail. The suit of the little man-like creature was brownish color and appeared quilted; I could see that under the right circumstances it could probably blend into the dark and look black. It was now further into the room by the oriental screen with a portion of its left sleeve on this side of the screen. Cleo was behind the creature looking in its direction, and Lollie was in front of it with her ears laid back looking alert. Above and behind the creature at the top of the vertical blinds was the huge clown-like white face laughing with rubbery lips spread into a wide smile extending well beyond the width of its narrow head. Sitting on the bodiless head were teddy bear-like ears. To the right of the clown face and slightly lower was an unfriendly looking being whose visible body appeared light brown with small plates similar to alligator skin. There were also more faces in the picture that seemed to obscure and make locating the original three more difficult; the picture seemed to be changing. I suspected they had the capacity to simply vanish from the picture, as if they had never existed except only in my mind.

The fear I had experienced the night before returned with such impact that I could hardly breathe, hyperventilating, unable any longer to think rationally. I felt isolated and helpless; things were in my home that I could not see! Were they there that minute, watching me examine these pictures and my reaction to them? I was frantically trying to act like this picture was no different from any other, as fear is not a good thing to let unknown things know you are experiencing, especially beings who have abilities greater than your own. They had changed the picture each time I looked at it. Had there even been anything unseen by me in my home when the pictures were taken? I would have to answer yes, based on the actions of my animals that had prompted me to take the pictures in the first place.

I got on the Internet and started looking for someone to contact who would take me seriously, and not exploit the situation. There were lots of addresses but which ones were legitimate? I was watching all of the UFO programs on TV, and taking notes with names and titles. I looked up Stanton T. Friedman from MUFON as I had seen him on a number of UFO programs, and emailed MUFON hoping for a reply.

Giving myself some time to gain control over my fear, my curiosity led me to look at more of the pictures. I pulled up the next image.

This picture showed the little man-like creature at the bottom of the vertical blinds in the same area looking at the Chinese screen. His wide toothless mouth is slightly curved downward, and his expression looks as if he is concentrating. Can he read Chinese? The brownish suit is the same, the eyes are not blue in this picture, and the face is ape-like. The clown face at the top of the picture has changed and is large and tipped slightly backward so that the eyes, nose and mouth can be seen clearly, and the skin looks either wrinkled or alligator-like and wears a stern expression. The third one to the right is still standing but is not as clear as in the first shot. There are many other faces in this picture as well.

Having seen these pictures and completely undone, I searched the Internet again. I had to talk to somebody who would listen and not laugh in my face; this was a serious matter to me. I ended up with MUFON again, and completed the form provided stating I had pictures, and hoped that would get someone's attention, and it did. I received an email from Mark Ausmus of Georgia State MUFON on 20 March 2006 asking for copies of the pictures; he didn't have to ask twice, I sent them. He replied asking me to point out exactly where, and what I had seen in the pictures leading me to believe that he hadn't seen anything or couldn't find what I was seeing.

On March 22nd I resent some of the pictures with detailed directions on where to see the beings. I did not want to give him too much detail about the creatures, as that would be leading him. He either saw what I did or did not, and I'm waiting for a reply, today is March 27th. I am hoping that he has more computer savvy then I, and can isolate the beings making them clearer. I have had the thought that perhaps I am the only one who can see them as I've asked them so many times to let me see them. I keep telling myself that none of us can help what we look like but that wouldn't be very sustaining had one actually presented them self in the flesh unless, of course, they do their keep-calm magic. I had mailed the same picture to my sister prompting her to call me asking what it was she was suppose to see in it. So disappointing, and even more isolating when you see things others do not. Oh, dear Lord, I am losing my mind!

I have reviewed the pictures many times over the years looking for what I had originally seen but since those first views the pictures have changed; the beings and faces are no longer there.

One night, I woke myself up snoring, cheeks blowing in and out, lips vibrating together, every sagging facial muscle quavering to the rhythm of my steady breathing. I was laying on my right side with my head half off of the pillow and my face hanging downward towards the mattress. It's everybody's fate to grow old, if they live long enough, and watch your body turn into something foreign and unfamiliar, and now it's my turn. With humiliation and gratitude that no one else could hear this except the babes who had vacated the bed and wouldn't tell a soul, I rolled over and slept on. The next night I became aware of someone snoring, and realized that it was me in the exact same position with the same results. I could hear laughter, and was instantly awake. It had to be them amusing themselves at my expense. I sat up and yelled, "Don't do that again!" I pounded the pillow into shape and chuckled as I fell back to sleep. It couldn't have been a pretty sight, and had to be funny to watch. They have a sense of humor and that is reassuring.

I had found and sent two other pictures taken of the back porch to Mark Ausmus of MUFON, as there was a square on three of the pictures that looked as if there was writing in it. Whatever was in the box was so small that I could not determine what it was. He replied saying it was a reflection of the exterior siding off of the glass door, and that I should be able to replicate it under the same conditions. Relieved, I happily replicated the little box under the same conditions on another day.

My house seems to make a lot of noise at night, bumping, thumping, pings, squeaks and creaking, so many noises that I hadn't noticed before. Some of them are probably due to the icemaker, some to the settling of the structure, and some to noise from neighbors. When there were four cats I could always blame one of them for any noise. Now when I hear a noise I lay there wondering what it is, and am torn between I want to know, and I don't want to know. When the babes are on the bed with me then I know it is not them making the noise, and the times I have checked there has been nothing there I could see.

Last August, many nights I could hear what sounded like objects being moved around in the attic, always at a time when I was in bed for the night. Nothing ever looked out of place when I investigated the next day, and I wondered, if it was them, why are they doing this?

If they could make noise in the attic then it stood to reason they could be making the noises on the ground floor. If they are, then I wanted to sit up a situation where they would make an unexpected noise as a result. I was bent on trapping them; I wanted to be in control for once. I chose plastic grocery bags because of their distinctive sound when brushed. I loosely attached the bags in different areas throughout the house placing many more of the bags in my bedroom, closet and bathroom. If a being glided by the bag, the air movement would create a sound from the plastic bag movement.

I heard nothing. But one night when I had gotten up without a specific reason, I found sitting in the middle of the living room floor a plastic bag, as if it had been filled with air, and sat with the open end on the floor. I stepped back and flicked on the overhead light thinking that one of the bags had become loose, and found there was nothing on the floor, nothing. Were they letting me know that they were aware of my trap? I'm guessing they were.
I have started taking pictures at night of the sliding glass door and porch in the effort to capture the image of a being, or maybe even replicate what I had found several years ago.

One picture appeared to have a large quantity of floating dust lit by the flash of the camera; another had many faces, faces of different races and some that didn't seem to be of this earth. Are they gathering on the porch to move back into the house, to walk in front of the mirror to re-enter the portal? I shivered at the thought. I have not seen the shadows in front of the mirror for quite awhile, now I find these faces on the porch. Then I wondered, if there was a portal, is it open only at certain times, and were they gathering waiting for it to open? If there is a portal to where does it lead? Further pictures taken showed nothing but the porch and furniture, however, those taken of the vertical blinds would occasionally have an orb present.

I found two other pictures taken in February 2006 that had been glanced over thinking that the light rectangular object seen was a reflection from a mirror or glass on a picture. I sent them to Mark, and with nerves stretched like banjo strings, I admitted that I was scared to death. Both of these pictures were taken while I was setting on the couch in the living room and are of my unlit bedroom. Facing me as I sat on the couch, sitting cattycornered on the corner of the foot of the bed is a rectangular box shape with four compartments, three across the top and one in the middle on the bottom. Through the middle of the two centered pictures is the shadow of the corner bedpost.

Originally, although distorted now, the first compartment on the top left had four human faces with unclear features looking in my direction. The top center compartment has the shadow of the bedpost in the middle, and is also distorted from the original which showed two large colored hieroglyphics that I took to be their writing. The top right compartment also somewhat distorted but still showing the grey standing in front of a flat panel with, in the original, had several buttons and knobs. His left hand is resting on a knob while he is looking in my direction as I take the picture. On his forehead was something thin and red that I took to be an antenna. In the bottom compartment the shadow of the bedpost can be seen dividing the compartment. Two burly figures are seated one behind the other with their hands resting on their thighs, and in the original they were the color of tanish brown.

In the second picture all of the compartments are distorted. The bottom compartment originally had a standing burly brown figure but over time this is also becoming distorted.

Every time I come upon something new the chill of fear hits me like a speeding cement truck. These two pictures were so unexpected, creating a fear so strong and overwhelming, that I was unable to think, wanting to run away! At first I thought the first compartment of the first picture had alien observers but when I looked at it closer I could see they were human heads looking in my direction as if I was an animal in the zoo.

What would humans be doing with the greys observing me, or was I seeing what they wanted me to see? I realized that the picture of the little lit rectangular box could probably be created by a clever person, and had I been computer savvy perhaps I could have but I don't have the skill, the imagination or the interest to do something like this. Mark replied asking if I remembered what was written in the second compartment of the first picture that I did not, and although I looked at them I was concentrating on the grey in the third box. I believed he had seen what I had, and although he never said this, his question was enough.

On the evening of 22 March 2006, I had a fleeting glimpse of a large brownish being coming out of the hallway towards the kitchen. He stopped and disappeared in the area where I suspected there might be a portal.

I realized the rectangle sitting on my bed could go anywhere in the house sitting on any flat surface, so I began moving things around creating fewer free surfaces. Then I realized this was fruitless as there were the ceiling fan-blades, the top of the cabinets, the seats of the chairs, the floor itself and who knows, the damn thing can probably float in the air if need be or cling to a wall. Everything in the compartments had been miniaturized, and I felt like it was everywhere; that it could go everywhere, and become any size that it needed to be. Every motion I made, everything I did was being monitored and observed by any number of beings. I felt violated and frantic.

Every time I stripped to take a shower, I felt like I had an audience, and would look around the room to see if I could spot them. I was embarrassed. I had seen balls flashing in the shower, so they were even in there. Everything I did, every movement I made no matter how insignificant, was being observed not by one but possibly by many. I came out of the bathroom one night, crawled into bed, and turned off the light; when I turned around to lean forward to pull the covers over my shoulders, evenly spaced covering the entire bedspread were lit balls the size of marbles that simultaneously went dark as if they wanted me to know they were there. I was at the drive-in and I'm the movie. I shook the covers to get them off of the bed. I want them gone.

There are people who believe that they have been coming for hundreds if not thousands of years to study earth, keeping tabs on man's progress, and maybe even give us a boost in knowledge periodically. I don't know, I do not have the answers, but it would seem to me, if they have known man for thousands of years then they have no need to study us. From what I have observed in my own home, we cannot duplicate their technology and knowledge at this time. I think we share things in common, for instance a sense of humor. I think that there are times when they might get bored and tease us to see how we will react, and what we will do, or maybe, just to amuse themselves.

This picture was taken 8 March 2006 at 10:38 PM in the living room.

Chapter 8

Tuesday, 28 March 2006, I awoke with incredible left shoulder pain shooting down the arm and up into the neck. The entire shoulder, shoulder blade and ribs hurt when I moved the arm but if I held still there was no pain. What had been done to me during the night? I verbally accused them of hurting me.

That night I had to place supporting pillows around the shoulder and arm to gain a comfortable position in which to sleep, and again, I accused them of hurting me wondering what on earth they had done to me. The next morning I couldn't lift the bed linens up to get out of bed. I could feel Buster between the sheet and the cover but his weight has never prevented me from moving the linens. Jezebel was lying on my left at chest level on the top of the covers. I was perplexed why I couldn't lift the linens on the right side of the bed, yanking on them several times, when abruptly something black jumped up and off of the foot of the bed disappearing as it ran into the living room. They sleep as we do!

Thursday, 30 March 2006, I couldn't sleep last night so I watched TV until about 3AM. The left shoulder, back and chest were painful, and I couldn't find a comfortable position accusing them again of hurting me.

The high-pitched sound in my ears which has been there for weeks is gone today. It was so quiet when I lay down. I was just getting comfortable in the bed when I could hear a high pitch sound by the closet door. It grew louder until now I have it all of the time again. They can turn the volume up or down, and had it up so high one day when I was preparing supper that I couldn't think. I yelled, "Turn it down!" and the volume decreased immediately.

Friday, 31 March 2006, I slept like the dead last night. This morning I was paying bills and reading the mail, placing some in a pile to be shredded, and some in another pile to sort through. Annoyed at seeing my money going out faster then it comes in, I grabbed an envelope yanking out the letter as I pulled it towards me, and heard what sounded like little mechanical musical noises. I looked in the envelope to see if there was one of those thin musical playing discs in it but there wasn't. I must have caught them off guard and "tipped" their world for an instant.

I had to run errands this morning and the past several times that I have had to go somewhere I have had this feeling of impending doom, but once I get about three blocks from the house the feeling subsides. Either they can't go with me, or they are afraid of our transportation, and the doom feeling is their own. Perhaps it is the driver.

Monday, 3 April 2006, I have printed out a hard copy of everything written so far and started a journal. I also copied the pictures onto a CD-R to send to Mark per his request. I am determined to have somebody else see what I am seeing. I later realized that I had not kept a record of what I had sent to him.

Tuesday, 4 April 2006, the time changed to daylight savings on Sunday, and an hour of sleep has been lost but I am still on the old time and finding it difficult to go to sleep at a decent hour. I puttered around, read, watched TV and played my hand game until I finally dropped off around 12:30 AM.

Sometimes there is a part of me that is very aware of my dreams and I go along with them to see where they will take me knowing that my subconscious is at work. I am dreaming.

I am holding a conversation with someone that I cannot see as well as my oldest son when I hear a mechanical musical sound play three notes and somehow I know that it is A-E-E. My son says, "What's happening?" and I respond, "I don't know".

My brain surfaced to reality; I rolled over onto my back and lay looking at the ceiling while mulling over the notes and my son's question. Why would I think that the notes were A-E-E? It had been far too many years since I had played the violin to be sure of the names of the notes, so I really couldn't say what they were. I connected the notes to the mechanical sound I had heard when I picked up the envelope, were they the same notes? It didn't matter; I knew they were toying with my mind. I studied the shadows but couldn't see anything in the room with me. Buster was laying to my left cuddled next to me giving himself a bath and Jezebel was not on the bed. I started to become anxious because I had no way of knowing where the beings were, and what they were up to.

I lay looking at the ceiling watching a large dark shadowed square above the bed, the size of the mattress, surrounded by a lighter area except for the portion that was at the head of the bed. The edges were definitive and the dark dense shadow was colored evenly. I wondered if it was some sort of a container with them in it hanging above the bed, and after seeing the tiny little beings in the box on the bed I felt it could be possible. There was nothing but a dim night light in the room which lit only the bottom drawer area of the file cabinet in the corner and the bottom corner of the curtain, and would be incapable of providing enough light to surround the square above the bed. It dawned on me that the source of the light was coming from under the bed escaping around the sides causing the bed itself to form the shadow.

If I got out of bed they could grab my ankles and pull me under which has been a childhood fear, something unknown under the bed grabbing my ankles. I would not even sleep with an arm hanging over the bed for fear of the monster grabbing it. Hell, I tried never to sleep with my mouth open for fear of something being poured into it while I slept. Until I went to nursing school, I slept with the magic blankets over my head and wrapped around my body like a cocoon.

Taking a deep breath and mustering all of my will power, I leapt out of bed and turned the bedside light on looking about the room seeing nothing. I fell to the floor and saw nothing under the bed. There is a dark blue bed skirt, so the light had to be bright to illuminate through it. I ran to the living room, and checked the vertical blinds, then to the sliding glass door flicking on the porch light seeing nothing there. I ran through the house turning on all of the lights, checking every nook and cranny, nothing. I suddenly became tired and while repeatedly yawning, I started turning off the lights to head back to bed, but instead I resisted because I knew that was what they wanted me to do. I filled a glass with water from the tap, sat on the couch with Jezebel, and watched programs recorded earlier. Becoming restless I then began searching for aliens on the Internet finding a source naming the different types and providing people's experiences.

The type of aliens that I have seen in the pictures taken in my home is a grey, what looked like heads of humans, and possibly a reptilian. I did not see a tail, ridges on his head, wings, nor could I see the hands and feet, but he did have brownish skin with small plates like an alligator. Apparently the "greys" and reptilians have been known to work together. I can't imagine where all of this information has been gathered but suspect from eyewitness accounts given by people who have been abducted. It was 4:27AM when I turned off the lights except for the back porch and slept.

Wednesday, 5 April 2006, last night I had gone to bed about 8:30PM waking at 11:23 PM, hot and sweaty. I could feel Buster beside me. Jezebel was not on the bed. I searched the shadows in the dark room then looked over towards the bathroom door seeing the white lampshade and lamp on the bedside table then started to look at the bedroom door. As my head began turning to look at the bedroom door, a small lit rectangle, approximately 4 x 1 1/2 inches appeared on the lampshade. I stared at it waiting for the compartments that I had seen in the rectangle on the foot of the bed to become visible but they did not appear, the whole thing disappearing instead. I knew it could still be there watching and waiting to see what I was going to do. Slightly unnerved yet curious to see what else they would do, I got out of bed and went into the living room, booted up the computer to make this note in the journal.

The next thing I remember I am in bed very uneasy, looking at the large dark, dense, heavy shadow above the bed. I glance at the clock; it is 1:23 AM. I feel as if I could put my hand into it, as if it has substance. The edges of this shadow are not distinct, there is no light surrounding it, and is much larger than the night before. I waste no time getting out of bed again, turning on the TV, and brewing a cup of tea. It is times like this that I am frightened of the unknown, and my powerlessness to control what is happening to me. My mother is in the other bedroom but her presence has not prevented their visits since I became aware last September. I have not told her about the beings, I don't want to frighten her. There are times that I wonder if she knows about them.

Mark from MUFON has not responded, however I don't know that they could do anything anyway. I told him I was terrified, and I'm sure they don't want to be involved with a hysterical woman. They want clear pictures, and otherworld items to support their theories of extraterrestrials; it's like Big Foot without a body, it does not exist even though many suspect it really does. Beings from another world are living with me, and are not being terribly subtle knowing there is nothing I can do about their presence. I can't prove their existence beyond the pictures suspecting that only I can see what they want me to see in them. For me, it's the idea that I wouldn't be "alone" if someone else knew what I'm going through. I would like to tell my family which I will do, but I am not able to take any ridicule right now. The beings understand our situation, and use it to their advantage giving them more power over the humans they involve themselves with. It's the simple strategy of divide and conquer. These guys are not evil or destructive but that doesn't mean they are "good" either.

Those who have endured contact, and continuing contact, need some place where they can record their experiences and read about other's experiences without ridicule. Until the abduction situation is accepted and examined, and many have tried, people like me live with a secret. Acknowledging this does happen does not mean it will stop the beings, but it would expose more detail that will enable us to learn more about them. The denial by our government of alien existence could very well signify that they do know they exist but lack the knowledge of how to protect themselves, militarily or otherwise, from the aliens. If you deny there is a sun then you don't have to explain why it is shinning.

I would like to get a good night's sleep and live the docile life of my choice, either that or be told what my mission is so that I can get on with my life. It's 3:20 AM, and the ringing in my ear continues seemingly to become more annoying when I write about them, and yet, I don't think they really care.

Friday, 7 April 2006, at 6 PM a black shadow man walked by my kitchen window.

Saturday, 8 April 2006, I watched *Cosmos* today by Carl Sagan. The probe sent into space with information about Earth and humans was the Voyager II which had a "Golden Record" attached to the side of the craft. Whoever hadn't known about earth will only need to use the map as a guide to find us; welcome to earth. I viewed the golden record on the Internet and wondered how primitive it would look to an advanced civilization. I hope it disintegrates.

Sunday, 9 April 2006, since I am not one to let go of things I don't understand, I reviewed the pictures I remembered sending to Mark. I used HP Photo Image and found I could adjust the display setting to 640x480 screen resolution. Behold! What had looked like shoulders covered with material were the arms of the wicker chair and the lattice covering the porch screen! I humbly apologized to him and feel really stupid, but the box on the bed remains a mystery.

Chapter 9

Tuesday, 12 April 2006, I didn't wake up exhausted this morning. I had turned off the light about 12:30 AM and could feel them there, in the dark, waiting for me to fall asleep. It was an uncomfortable feeling, as if they could hardly wait. I turned on the light, and don't know what time I turned it off, as I didn't look at the clock.

I suspect they are draining me of my life forces or so it has felt, not knowing if that is even possible. I have wondered what they are doing to me, and suspect that whatever it is, it is not a good thing. I've been rather dizzy and disoriented the past couple of days, and have had to force myself to follow my normal daily routine because at night I want to sleep. If I nap during the day then I won't sleep well at night. Right this minute, I would say that these are not "good" guys, and I need to keep calm. It is surreal that I am writing about this. I have always believed that it was possible for life to exist on other planets but I never said that I was a believer to the point that I wanted a one-on-one house visit.

I am headed to Mississippi this Friday morning, and I will be glad to get away from here for a few days.

Thursday, 13 April 2006, the neighbors tell me that mom knocks on their doors asking if they will take her places when I am at work. The woman across the street has agreed to help me with mom while I am at work since she now requires 24/7 supervision. They go out to lunch, shop, stay here and visit, or sometimes they take long rides; mom is resentful about having a "babysitter". Other than the hours

I work at a part-time job, mom and I are constant companions. Her behavior has become unpredictable, and I have learned to sleep with one ear open listening for her movements in the house, and one eye open watching for the beings. She accidently set the second kitchen fire the other day, and it was fortunate that I smelled it in its early stage but unfortunately it has forced me into making a decision I have been delaying. I made arrangements for her to live in a personal care home.

I picked her up today to take her to out to lunch; she loves a double cheeseburger, fries and a small coke. I was relieved when she told me she liked her new home. She talked about what she does to keep busy, and introduced me to her new friends then took me on a tour of the moderate sized house. She said that she is attending church with one of the other residents, and talked about the church, the people, and the pastor. I was happy for her, and at the same time, saddened that it was necessary to place her in the care of someone else, someone who didn't know her or love her.

As I drove home reviewing our visit, what she had said about the pastor kept running through my mind but I couldn't put my finger on why it should. I am spiritual but not religious, having no need to be force fed someone else's belief in God, nor do I need to be threatened with eternal damnation when I see the forces of evil right here on this beautiful earth right now while I live. I have not been to church in years. Why should I be dwelling on the pastor, a pastor I have never met? Then while showering later that evening, I remembered the dream I had last night.

I am naked setting on a bench next to a naked man I do not know nor have ever met. Neither of us is embarrassed by our situation, it simply isn't an issue. He tells me that he is a pastor that I should not lose my faith, and he will pray for me. I said thank you and thought that it was very kind of him to be saying this to me but it didn't mean much since he was in the same position I was, naked, two strangers sitting on a bench in a strange place.

As I dressed for bed a vision flew through my mind that only I was naked, and he was dressed in a black suit. Why would I put clothes on him and not me? I would certainly cloth myself before I would him! Where the heck were we and what really happened? If mom had not talked about the church pastor, would I have remembered this? What else has happened that I do not remember?

Mark from MUFON looked at the pictures that I had sent to him and has asked me to repeat taking several of them thinking that I should get the same results. I couldn't replicate them but I did get orbs. I don't know what to think. I sent all of them to him and stated what I saw in each one; he didn't mention the box on the bed. I'm sure that he thinks they are reflections or contrived in some manner, but they are not.

Tuesday, 18 April 2006. Before I left to go to Mississippi I decided that I didn't want any knowledge of what's going on in my home. Ignoring everything it took a couple of days to calm down and relax. Why I think that they don't go on the road is ridiculous but there it is; I don't want to believe they can find me when I travel. I was with my ex-husband and told him a little bit of what's been going on. I have to admit

he was pretty good about not laughing in my face but he had no interest in this, and not asking one question or making one comment, the subject was dropped.
We stopped at the small Mississippi Crane Wildlife Center and looked at the exhibits. As we walked around in the peaceful setting, I found tears running down my cheeks at the thought that these beautiful birds are endangered with only thirty remaining, thirty birds, only thirty of them. I was surprised how emotional I became, as if it were a personal loss but when you look at the whole picture, it is.

I love Gulf Port, Mississippi, the Gulf of Mexico, and the beautiful homes across the street from it on US 90. It is a barren spot now since Hurricane Katrina swept them away, so sad, but nothing in this world is permanent, everything is in constant change, even people. I slept well the entire trip but I am always glad to be home.

I had contacted and received a reply email from Deborah Lindemann. She stated that "from years of study in this area, (she has) to say that it is most unusual to have these experiences every night. By the fact that (I) say there is an odor involved, it sounds more like poltergeist type entities or astral "beings" then extraterrestrial."

Is this a confirmation that I have ghosts or poltergeists in my home? I think there are multiple things going on here. Yes, there are the odors, and there is something the cats follow in the evenings. Can poltergeists take the form of space suits and shadow people? Is there a portal in my living room with all kinds of things coming through it, and staying to visit? But what about those two space suits, the three red circles forming an upside down triangle on the vertical blinds, the beam of light shining through my blinds, the sore belly with the slit in the naval ,and the box on the bed? These do not seem to me to be astral or poltergeist entities but the result of living, flesh and form, entities. I remain convinced that the activity here is a mixture of things but is this mixture created by the beings or is each independent of the other? I don't know. It was sure heartening to get a response.

Friday, 21 April 2006, I have taken a lot of pictures since I've been home from Mississippi, and was finally able to reproduce the little boxes found on the back porch door. The afternoon lighting was perfect showing the boxes to be the reflection of the rolled up bamboo blind reflecting off of the sliding glass door. I attached a copy of the replicated picture to an email sent to Mark at MUFON. I still have to figure out the box on the bed. Sometimes I wonder if I haven't imagined everything, that none of this has happened, that I am living in two worlds, the real one and an imagined one.

I've been doing a lot of reading on the Internet about alien abduction and found that keeping a journal is recommended. The weather should be included because abductions seem not to occur during thunder and lightning. Also recommended is keeping track of bruises and blemishes.

It stormed last night, and no new blemishes or bruises noted this morning. I've slept well the past several nights waking up feeling good, and have had a lot more energy.

Sunday, 23 April 2006, it rained hard yesterday morning

then cleared up to become a beautiful cool day. I slept fairly well last night getting up at 8:30 AM to a pleasant cool and sunny morning. Maybe I can leave the windows open again today. I have no new bruises or blemishes.

Jezebel was running around like a crazy person, leaping on my bed and stopping at the edge peering over as if she was looking at something, then she settled down and began cleaning herself. I heard her growling several times, and went in to see why because Buster was in the living room with me, so it couldn't have been him annoying her. When I turned on the light she jumped up, did a double take of my face, looked surprised, then jumped off of the bed, and ran out of the room. What had I looked like to her at that moment? What had she seen? Later she sat next to me on the couch.

From what I have read on the Internet, the appearances of ghosts are part of the alien's deception, in other words, they mask themselves as ghosts, and even religious experiences. When people have been regressed under hypnosis, they reveal that the people they think they are seeing are actually the "greys". What a cruel thing to do but this demonstrates their ability to "play" with our minds. When compared to these beings we are not as sophisticated as we would like to think we are.

When I close my eyes at night pictures of faces appear each one is different, different ages, different expressions, different races but none are all human nor all "greys", and some faces look mean with cold hard eyes. Are they throwing in a few extras to confuse me? I've always been an "eye" person, and may miss other details because it is a person's eyes I am looking into and searching. I never knew what I was searching for perhaps it was something deep within them. My sister says that when she closes her eyes at night she sees eyes not faces.

I received a list of abductees from Debra Lindemann, who have volunteered to communicate with other abductees, and have decided to correspond with one of them. I will start at the top of the list working my way down until I find someone who feels right. The first person was a male and did not respond. I sent an email to the second person and she responded that same night. I don't feel so alone now.

I filled out the form on Dr. David Jacob's site, International Center for Abduction Research (ICAR), at Temple University, **www.ufoabduction.com**. This thing has consumed my life. It seems like I spend every waking moment seeking answers to questions I don't understand, and doubt that I ever will, but I sure as hell am going to try.

The following picture was taken on 26 April 2006 at 9:06 PM in my bedroom. There was an orb above the bed and a small object on the second square of the quilt at the foot of the bed. When enlarged it looks like a little bird.

It is Monday, 24 April 2006, 12:29 AM. The babes have been nervous today. Jezebel has been jumpier than usual, and Buster can't get enough attention but then he never can, he is a lap-cat. When I went outside to talk with the neighbors, he was inside yowling then stopped abruptly when I walked in through the door; he never yowls like this unless he is in the car.

Wednesday, 26 April 2006, I fell asleep reading last night after I heard what sounded like loud flatulence in the living room. I had not heard that noise before and there was no way that I was going to investigate it. No rain that I heard last night and no new bruises or blemishes this morning.

Chapter 10

Thursday, 27 April 2006, I feel great, and have no new blemishes or bruises. There was no rain that I heard last night.

Late afternoon I went into the guest bathroom, and found dirt in the bottom of the bathtub, dirt that had covered the bottoms of flat shoes. Mom had been here earlier today, and had not shut the door when she went into the bathroom. I would have heard her moving the clothes hangers that hung on the shower rod with clothes to air dry. They didn't look like they had been moved, and why would she, an eighty-eight year old woman, crawl into the bathtub just to stand? Even if she had, we had not walked through dirt that would cling to our shoes such as was in the tub. Even with that possibility the dirt would have fallen off in the driveway, the porch, and in other places of the house long before she went into the bathroom. The dirt was not in the tub yesterday afternoon when I hung the clothes on the shower rod, so how did the dirt get into the bathtub? From where did the dirt come?

Later in the evening when I was sitting on the couch watching TV, the little black creature with the crown on his head ran across the living room in front of me towards and through what had been Mom's bedroom door. It came out of her room headed down the short hall then out into the living room disappearing. What is this little creature? Is it looking for mom? Where is it from? She had told my sister and me that when she was a little girl, a small black hand with an extended finger had poked her on the nose one night when she was in bed. Is this that creature?

Yesterday, I had a job interview and sure hope they hire me because I need to get out of here, I am consumed with this conundrum.

Friday, 28 April 2006, I slept well; the nights have been cool and the morning's cold. I have no new bruises or blemishes. I've been corresponding with a woman who I will refer to as "my buddy", and I can truthfully say that it is a relief to tell someone what has been going on.

The dirt is still in the bottom of the bathtub and looks the same as yesterday. I saw a white orb zoom sideways in the living room and a black one fall towards the floor. I think bugs, but why a white bug then a black one following the other? I am looking for meanings in things I would ordinarily ignore. Today my mind feels dizzy and confused, and I am looking for something to hang onto that supports that I am not a crazy person. There is always that doubt in my mind that I've made it all up; I know I haven't but it is there anyway. I'm tired of it all, the deception, the games, and the unknown.

Today the little black creature with the crown on his head ran the same path as yesterday. I am convinced it is looking for mom.

Sunday, 30 April 2006
Around five o'clock this morning I was awakened by someone talking to me. It was a male voice that sounded a little nervous and hesitant. I asked him where he was from, and he gave me two names. I was thinking that I need to write this down before I forget when he said that I could not write them down because the reptoid can read. The reptoid

can read! What is he talking about? Is he telling me that everything I've been writing the reptoid is reading? Let him read it, I could care less.

I asked him what his name was and he told me, repeated it a number of times, and I don't remember it either. I told him this nonsense has gone on too long, and I want to see him now. I rolled onto my back, opened my eyes, looked around and saw a black shadowy thick elongated triangular shape on the ceiling. The next time I look at the clock it is 7:30 AM. This is the first time I am aware of an actual loss of time yet it doesn't seem like a loss of time as I thought that I had fallen asleep but isn't that what I always do when something happens; I fall asleep? What happened during those 2 1/2 hours? Did I sleep?

My sister called today to tell me that she had spoken with her friend who is a psychic, and was told that "they" are afraid of us humans because they have been captured and abused by humans who force them to use their powers against other humans. This psychic must be talking about another group of beings, certainly not mine. I don't believe these guys are being forced.

My buddy advises me to not let them know that I am afraid but I don't think that there would be anyway that I can prevent it. I turn out the lights, and it is dark, my imagination takes over, and that's it, the lights are turned back on. It doesn't elude me to know they could control the lights if that is part of their plan but turning them off would probably send me into hysterics, and a total freak out.

I fell asleep reading a book tonight when a lit white ball flew between the book and my face, zip and it was gone. I woke up at 11:30 then turned out the light and could see the black shadowy thick elongated triangular shape on the ceiling like the one early this morning. They originally used a rectangle above the bed now it has changed to a triangle, and why is that? I would think that it would be the same every night. Are these different groups or are they checking to see if I know my shapes?

There is a fine rain outside, no thunder or lightning. I was on edge in the dark room searching it feeling as if they were everywhere. I looked over at the clock to check the time and it was as if something crossed in front of it and that was it; I was out of the bed in a flash. I am very brave when it's daylight, and convince myself that I am not afraid than at night when I turn off the lights, I am.

There are times that I am grateful that I don't know what is going on, and then there are times that I wish I knew. Because they have blocked it out frightens me, yet there is always the nagging feeling, because it's all so bizarre, that none of it is real yet I know that it is.

Humans are fixed on the idea of "tangibles", prove it, show it to me, while the beings exhibit the "intangible" such as out of body experiences, invisibility, floating in air, riding in crafts that can change shape, size and speed in a heartbeat. We don't understand how any of this is done therefore it doesn't exist because it hasn't been proven mathematically even though we watch it happen.

I think the majority of my fear is the result of not understanding what is happening; I lack the knowledge to understand. If I had the knowledge then I would have the understanding that everything happening to me is explainable, and can be trusted as fact. When I have no knowledge therefore no understanding, and therefore no trust, I have no control; ignorance versus illumination. I think the remaining fear is a result of unexpected suspense of not knowing what will happen next.

Control is an important issue to me. I want control of myself, my actions, where I go, my body functions, how I look, what I say, what I wear, who I am with and so forth, in every circumstance I'm involved in but my desire in this issue is not important to them nor one, I think, they even consider. The beings target a human, swoop in overwhelming them resulting in unexpected sheer terror for the target.

Apparently they realize that we do have some intelligence giving lessons and warnings on how to prevent the destruction of earth to some abductees, and if that is their goal why bother with the rest of us? Leave the rest of us alone. Their method in abducting humans speaks broadly of the lack of understanding us as creatures with intense feelings. We're plucked from the safety of our beds into a foreign world without any preparation, blocking most if not all of the memory allowing only bits and pieces to be revealed creating confusion. They may understand more then I think they do but I don't think they really care.

On Wednesday, 3 May 2006 at 5:48 PM, I saw a short dark shadow man walk past my open front door and apparently through the wall into the bedroom on the other side. He disappeared at the wall so where did he go? I've seen several shadow people walk that same path since I've moved into this house.

Today is Saturday, 6 May 2006. It's been a rather quiet week, and I have gone to bed unafraid of the dark, slept, and have gotten up early, a normal life.

In my mind I heard a male voice talking to me. He had said, "I am from Creed," (I have no idea how to spell it) "which is in another galaxy." I asked him, "What is going on?" and he replied, "You must trust me." I asked him, "When am I going to see all of you, and find out the truth about what has been going on?" and he replied, "When you are ready. You must trust me." I asked him, "What about the ringing in my ears, mostly the left?" and he responded, "That is so you will know that we are always with you." Of course! Why didn't I think of that? He told me, "There are seven of us that come here" (into my home) "but not all at once, usually no more than three at any one time." He then said, "We are not all the same, but are all different." I shut him out; I don't want to hear this. I want them to leave me alone.

My interview was a success! I was hired and will start this new job next Tuesday, and hope that I can shove all of this into a secret recess of my brain and forget about it. It has consumed too much of my life for the past eight months.

During the evening of Friday, May 12th, while I sat on the couch facing the bedroom door, I caught a glimpse of something whitish about four feet high and skinny run around the corner of the foot of my bed. The room was not dark as the sun had not completely set. I was surprised but didn't care.

Saturday, 13 May 2006, this afternoon while in the bathroom, I saw the little black skinny being run to the corner of the doorjamb to the bathroom, and then into the bathroom towards me and disappear. What the heck! Sunday, 14 May 2006, I woke up with my short hair standing on end this morning that indicates to me that I slept in my bed all night, or it should indicate that. I hadn't given a thought about last Saturday morning, May 6th, when I got up with my hair in place, so I am pretty sure that I did not spend the entire night in my bed. I remember being restless that night, and tired when I got up.

This morning I saw the little black skinny being run through the living room onto the back porch where the babes were and disappear. Is this one of the three the voice said would always be here? I think it is the one usually looking for my mother. I don't like not knowing when they come, what they do, why they do it, and who they are. I have so many unanswered questions.

I picked up mom this afternoon, and we went out for dinner then aimlessly drove around as she likes to take rides looking at everything. When she said she was tired I took her home. When I got home I turned on the computer to see if there was new email then watched TV. The atmosphere here was electric, filled with expectation even I was excited looking forward to something but had no idea what. The white and black balls flying around were not as obvious as they have been.

I can communicate at anytime with whatever is in my head,

it is always there. Last night when I turned off the light the voice began talking, and I was not happy to hear it. After we talked I recorded as much as I could remember. I said, "Go away." and he replied, "I will not, I am always with you." "I want nothing to do with you," I said and he replied, "That it is not your choice," and continued saying, "You are needed and have a job to do." I replied, "I will do nothing for you without meeting certain conditions such as, I want to meet all of you personally, and I want to know exactly what the job is, and why I'm supposed to do it." I am on a roll and have had enough of this ridiculous situation and say, "You have the ability to make me think I see one thing, and another is actually there; that is deceitful. You want me to "trust" but you have forgotten that along with trust is honesty, and you have not been honest with me so how can I trust you? I will never be able to believe anything you say when you come in the middle of the night, zap me so that I don't remember a thing, and do things to my body, and allow others to do things to my body which should never be done." No response. Did I win this verbal battle? I felt better even if I didn't.

Monday, 15 May 2006 I woke up this morning with a feeling of calmness that I have not had in weeks, and it feels good, as I have at times thought I would jump out of my skin. There are no new bruises or blemishes.

Today is Tuesday 16 May 2006. When I went to bed last night I read then turned out the light and lay looking at the shadow on the ceiling. A skinny little thing jumped out of it onto a ceiling fan blade and disappeared. I don't become a spastic bundle of nerves like I did in the past, now I wonder what is going to happen.

Sometime before 10:00 PM the phone rang, it was one of my sons. We talked about UFOs and people being taken. He told me of his experience while living in his deceased sister's house. He said a bright light shown through the bedroom window then two beings appeared, one taller than the other, wearing dark cloaks, and a covering over their heads that hid their faces. He was paralyzed, unable to move, as he watched them appear beside his bed. The next thing he remembers is floating several feet above the bed then being dropped onto it, and watching the beings hurriedly disappear out through the window. He said his jaw was so thoroughly clamped shut that he was surprised that he had not broken teeth from the pressure. Our conversation ended and I went back to bed, and fell soundly asleep. I had a sense of relief talking with him about the beings.

I woke up at 2:07 AM looking at the clock just seconds before something started humming a tune in my right ear. I didn't move, and could almost feel their breath on my ear it was so close. It wasn't a human sounding hum, and I thought of something small, childlike and mechanical that could make that particular sound. The tune was not unfamiliar but I couldn't place it. Jezebel lay on her side by my left leg, and Buster was up near my head lying on his four legs as he had been when I went to sleep. I got up walked through the living room checking things out then went back to bed and slept.

The voice in my mind is far away now and isn't with me like it has been the past two weeks although it responds when asked a question. They think that they have nullified my feeling of mistrust and desire to fight them. I still do not believe that these entities have anything to do with good or evil, some are good and some are bad just as we are. They are technically and psychically more advanced then we are but they are merely flesh and blood, so to speak, as we are. What is it they want?

Today is Sunday, 21 May 2006, for the past two nights, I have woken at 5 AM hot and wet with sweat soaking the linens.

I haven't heard from my buddy for two days. She says my experiences are not like what other people have, and I wonder if she believes what I have told her. Unfortunately people who have experienced this kind of phenomenon are a loosely formed group. If it is true what the grey told my buddy, that the gathering has begun, information needs to be collected on every person who has claimed contact. Each one needs to be tracked down, and an update on their abduction activities recorded. There may well be patterns that can be identified. Whatever is going on, we humans need to know.

I worked my first eight-hour day since 2004 and every muscle and joint ached as well as my tired brain. A neighbor dropped in to visit then I heated up a TV dinner, and went to bed about 10:30 but couldn't sleep. Lying in bed I could see tiny white balls flying around, and when one was reflected in the mirror, I knew they were not something I was imagining. I was so restless that I got up. I was too tired to have them mess with me preventing sleep I badly needed. I fixed popcorn and watched some programs that I had recorded.

While sitting on the couch munching on popcorn, a black

ball zoomed across the living room from the couch towards the TV rather than across the front of the TV which is what it usually does. I saw it for approximately four feet then it disappeared. A few minutes later I got a glimpse of it out of the corner of my left eye as it zoomed towards me, and hearing a low pitch humming noise, I wondered if it had flown into my ear. I swatted around my ear and head then looked around the room to make sure that it was not a flying insect finding none. At 1:50 AM, I went to bed, and had hardly gotten settled when Devlin, the new voice in my head, says, "Here I am!" and faces of mean looking aliens began their parade across my closed eyelids, all of them different, many scary looking, and every one of them had cold mean-dead eyes. If eyes are the pathway to the soul, they have no souls.

After the faces had passed, I lay thinking about implants and that I may have one in my left ear. In the late 1980s, during the time I was repeatedly dreaming of falling, I woke up with an earache and a small amount of blood on my pillow and in my ear. I had never had an earache before or since. A nurse practitioner examined my ear several weeks later, and told me the eardrum had been ruptured.

I remember the falling dreams well, as they were terrifying with views from high in the sky onto lit cities and dark vastness far below. There was one instance when I thought I was falling too fast, and the thought came into my mind that if I moved my legs like I was pedaling a bike, I would slow down, and have more control. I remember pumping my legs like a crazy person then popping out of my body watching myself drift off with my arms out in front of me as if holding onto handle bars. I had heard that if you die in your dreams then you die in real life; I didn't know if it was true or not, but what I did know was that I was tired of the falling dreams, and if I was going to die then I would die. The next time I dreamt of falling, I let myself fall, and landed in the bed awake and aware of what I had done. The falling dreams stopped, and I have given them little thought until now, where they may have a whole new meaning.

I said, "Hey Devlin, do I have any implants?" He replied, "Implants are placed by different alien groups. The one in your ear was placed in 1986, and the one in your nose was inserted in 1994." Nose! I don't believe him; I don't want to believe him.

Wednesday, 24 May 2009, today I was involved in a fender bender that messed up the hood of the car, so I am driving a rental until the hood is replaced, fortunately no one was injured. Three things have happened, and I hope that this is the end of events, my accident, mom's positive breast biopsy, and my sister in the hospital for a few days, the cycle is complete.

Friday, 26 May 2006, when I got up this morning I felt like something happened last night almost remembering then it was gone.

Saturday, 27 May 2006, I cleaned the pictures hanging on the bedroom wall earlier today, and when I pulled the picture of dad off the wall a strange mechanical sound abruptly started and stopped. The sound wasn't the same as when I pulled the envelope off of the desk but similar.

Sunday, 28 May 2006, I went to bed early last night and

slept like a log. Since starting work I get up and go to bed earlier sleeping better. I have three days off together, and have worked nonstop getting my home in order so that tomorrow I can do nothing but read and relax.

I have had no new bruises or blemishes since my last writing, and there have been white and black balls, not as many as usual, flitting around the past couple of days.

Devlin hasn't been quite as strong the past few days, but I haven't initiated talking with him either. I feel like something is going to happen and soon. Perhaps they are allowing me to remember some of my visits because I get this strong thought that the battle will be between this world and invaders who want it. There will be us humans with aliens fighting other aliens. We'll see.

Chapter 11

Monday Morning at 4:06 AM, 29 May 2006, I have had a dream unlike any other.

Suddenly I become aware that something is in my bedroom, and by the time I open my eyes I am floating from my bed towards the bedroom door. I can see a "grey" at my feet, and know there is one at my right shoulder even though I cannot see him; the three of us are moving at a fast clip. I grab the rounded back of a chair by the bedroom door. I think we are headed for the front door because I can see the entrance hallway and front door. I am still grasping the chair and won't let go of it, so they are unable to get me through the door that is like a glass storm door rather than the steel front door. I pop out of my body standing behind us and see one of them holding a young girl with long dark hair in an upright position off of the floor at the front door. She is screaming a soundless," Daddy! Daddy!" and has her arms flung out above the grey in helpless supplication; I pop back into my body.

We are at the sliding glass door, and the grey at my feet is struggling to get the chair out of my hand. I hear the grey at my head urgently tell him to "hurry up and get going," and the grey finally succeeds in getting me to let go of the chair. I pop out of my body and watch myself pound him on the head with my freed fist while screaming a soundless "Daddy! Daddy!" and can hear the little grey cry "Oh!" each time I hit him. I am back in my body. I feel myself being pulled upward, and see a large entrance to an empty metal room where I am unceremoniously thrown onto the floor. I pop out of my body and float on the outside of the doorway to watch myself lying on the metal floor then scramble on all fours towards the back of the room away from the open door. I am awake.

I look at the clock; it is 3:27 AM. My heart is beating faster than I would think it possible to beat and still remain alive. I am lying on my right side in my bed, and see something whitish move into the shadows making no effort to see it closer. If I was just abducted why am I in bed? Was I abducted or did I witness someone else being abducted? I felt that the person abducted was a teenager but who was it? And I wondered why I was yelling for Daddy when he has been dead for years? The house was neither the house I live in now nor the house where I spent my teenage years; it was a combination of both. I have chairs exactly like the one I grabbed but there were none like them in my parent's home. None of the chairs are out of place, I've checked.

I lay in the bed with my eyes closed watching alien faces march across my eyelids. These faces are different from the ones I've seen before. I see a female insect, her head is triangular shaped and flat faced with huge black eyes. Her nose is very thin with two nares seen, and her expression is soft, pitying, non-threatening. She looks like a mantis. There is a man with eyes that glow and wrapped like a mummy except the arms and legs are individually wrapped, free from his body. I see a woman with blond hair, and human facial features with a black eye in the middle of her forehead which she opened just before another face was shown.

After coffee that morning and thinking about what had happened during the night, I asked Devlin what the name of the being with the third eye was. He told me her name was Alycia, and that I am part of this group, that we are all leaders. I asked him who the girl screaming for her daddy was, and he replied that the girl was me when I was fourteen. I then asked how old I was when I was first taken, and he replied that I was four years old.

That afternoon I worked outside in killer heat but I was too restless to remain in the house, I needed action. I trimmed the Rosemary bush, and started to trim the bush by the back screened in porch, whacking away with pruning shears when I was startled by a little bird shooting out from the bush, screaming bloody murder. I found her nest at the top near where I was trimming. I stopped trimming and hoped that she will return to her babies.

During slow periods at work, I thought about last night and of what Devlin had told me. I did have long hair when I was fourteen. The distance from my bedroom to the front door where I grew up would have been about the same distance in the dream, but was it a dream? And at that time I would have certainly screamed for my Daddy. I thought about being both participant and observer. Nothing was resolved by all of this thinking, absolutely nothing.

Tuesday, 30 May 2006, I am still thinking about what happened Sunday night. Yesterday my left wrist and the outer aspect of my hand hurt, but I didn't think much about it until this morning when I connected the discomfort with beating on the little grey's head. The round back chair that I grabbed in the dream is right by the sliding glass door, and is exactly like the one I saw in the dream, but there is also one of those chairs by the bedroom door, which one did I grab?

I was taken Sunday night, and the pain in my left wrist and hand is the proof to me. That poor little grey, I was really whacking him on his head.
Early Monday morning when I awoke and wrote down what had happened it was, so I thought, post dream status. It was after I had made the journal entry, and went back to bed that the faces of the others played across my closed eyelids. I was lying on my back when I viewed their faces then turned onto my right side, and felt a pressure against my rectal area for quite awhile. I am beginning to remembering bits and pieces. What is not clear is the order in which everything occurred. Why has this been obscured?

Suddenly, as if a switch had been flicked to turn on a light, I began to have recall. The beings had not played across my closed eyelids, as I had thought.

I am in a line with others in front and behind me, as if we are registering for something, like registering for a convention. Each being that I saw was sitting behind a long table, except for the one with the glowing eyes. We were being scrutinized as we moved forward to the next being. There were other beings at the table that I did not describe. I remember not knowing where I was or what I was doing there, and thought it best to give a nonthreatening smile until I could figure this situation out. I smiled and nodded at each being I saw.

As my memory spews forth, it is as if I am there.
I open my eyes, and everything is hazy as if I am looking through a fog. I pop out of my body and see four individual tall greys in the room, and me lying on my right side with one of the four seated holding a large funnel shaped object

at my rectal area; I can feel it and it feels soft. The other three round shouldered tall greys are taking turns looking into my eyes. One of them bends over looking into my eyes and I close them. I remember reading on the Internet how they wipe out your memory in this manner, and I want to maintain some control; I'm not sure what the hell is going on. I watch myself open my eyes, and see a tall grey with his arms crossed standing at the end of the table where I lay, and walk up the side of the table towards my face. His face is close to mine, his eyes become dominant, and I close my eyes and turn my head to the left to avoid looking at him. This repeats several more times with each of them taking turns trying to get me to look into their eyes. Eventually when I open my eyes there is a large eye inches away, and it grows huge until that one eye becomes my entire world absorbing me into it. I am back in my body, and I think to myself that the apparatus at my rectal area has been there long enough, and roll onto my back. I am awake and in my bed.

Devlin says they are coming again tonight but he always says that, I don't believe him. I asked him if he was aware of "fight or flight" and he said yes, that they had underestimated me. I hope I gave them hell but I don't think I did.

Wednesday, 31 May 2006, I slept well last night. There are no new bruises or blemishes this morning.

My mother has become a behavior problem at the personal care home, and will need to go on some sort of behavior control medication. I take her tomorrow for her breast biopsy. She has to be worried about that, perhaps she will settle down after it is over.

At 12:09 PM while I sat eating lunch a short black shadow figure walked past the front screen door and through the wall into the spare bedroom. Where else could it have gone?

Thursday, 1 June 2006, yesterday while at work Devlin told me they were coming last night. At 2:11 AM I woke up, went into the bathroom then crawled back into bed. Suddenly I feel overwhelmingly afraid like a shudder running through my body, and I am so hot and sweaty that I toss the covers off. I reach over to stroke Buster who is lying on his side by my head. It is as if he has been anesthetized. He is flaccid and not snoring; I tweak his sensitive back legs and he doesn't move. I am saddened thinking that he may have died when he began responding by purring and moving.

Saturday 3 June 2006, Devlin said they were coming again last night and that I must "trust". Every night he says they are coming, and I think he does this to make me fearful but it is beginning to have the opposite effect.

I woke up wide-awake at 2:27 AM lying on my back looking for a grey. Buster, lying by my right side, got up and lay down at my right shoulder. A loud metal sounding "KER CHUNCK" came from my left chest area. I looked for a small lit rectangle but saw nothing, and the atmosphere in the room felt fine, so I wasn't frightened. I lay looking around the dark room then caught a white streak zipping across the ceiling towards the wall by the window then it was gone.

Saturday, 10 June 2006, I looked though pictures I had taken last month on the 23rd of May. I had been uneasy hearing beeps and chirps, so I had gotten up and started snapping pictures in the dark going from room to room. I had almost deleted this picture not seeing the face peering from behind the pillow. The face is blue with a red dot above and to the left of its left eye.

I avoided talking with Devlin although he gets into my head and is often surly. If he is a reptoid as he says he is, they do not like humans or so I have read on the Internet. He says that I bore him, and has been assigned to me as punishment.

I did a body check after my shower this morning and found new bruising and pinprick type marks.

Sunday, 11 June 2006, I awoke at 3:27AM or there about, even though I looked at the clock I can't remember the exact time, when the "KER CHUNCK" sounded again. This time it was not on my body but towards the edge of the left side of the bed. I looked around feeling as if there were others in the room with me but could not see them. I went into the bathroom, and when I exited, and sat on the side of the bed, I looked up and saw the vague image of a small grayish being with large eyes floating about two feet off of the floor looking back at me before it faded away. It was small and fragile looking, and I wondered how I could have beat on one of them. I told it I was sorry if I had hurt it. I lay down, and for a few minutes I wondered if they were coming or going before falling asleep.

Devlin said that they were coming for me last night but as said earlier I don't believe what he tells me. He also said that more would be revealed to me as the "time" is almost upon us, and I must pay close attention. Lord Almighty, this is so dramatic. I asked him if we would be working together and he said yes. I also asked how that could be possible when we don't like each other, and he said that we would have to "trust". That's not likely to happen.

Wednesday, 14 June 2006, I woke up this morning with my pajama top on backwards and my hair wasn't messed up. I did a superficial body check finding no new blemishes or bruising.

Periodically there have been nights when I believe that I am holding babies. I have a vague memory of a heated discussion with a black haired woman about allowing the babies to have more activity. I recall telling her that it wasn't normal for human babies to be inactive, and the dreaming of holding babies stopped.

I am growing tired of this. I would like to understand what is going on and why. They have advanced abilities that we have not learned to use. These aliens are not "good" beings; they are scientists who are self-serving and will do whatever it takes to meet their goal, whatever that goal is. We are innocents compared to them. They are able to control our minds and penetrate our thoughts reading them like an open book. They carry us out in the dead of night, and perform whatever procedures they feel they need to do on us to meet their goal. I don't like them. I don't like what they are doing. Why am I still curious about them?

Chapter 12

Friday, 16 June 2006, yesterday out of town guests arrived for a weekend visit. We went to bed around 10:30 PM with everyone falling asleep before I did. The house was quiet, and I could hear the relaxed heavy breathing of sleeping people. My routine was totally wiped out, and I was "keyed" up not a bit sleepy. I read for awhile and then turned off the light, and laid wide awake thinking about the beings when I became aware of a light flashing outside of the bedroom window.

There was no thunder just the flashing light repeating several times. I thought it was either from passing cars or heat lightening and opened the blinds so that they tilted downwards allowing a view of the sky from the bed. The lights continued to flash even when no cars were passing. I couldn't identify the source of the flashes that were coming in threes, and at different levels of the window. Then they stopped. A small white steak of light at least eighteen inches long appeared about two feet from the bedroom wall where the window is located then disappeared. A small white ball flew from the area of the foot of the bed leaving no streak and disappeared then the room became dark. A large lit rectangle appeared on the wall opposite the window. It began to slide along the top of the wall towards the outer bedroom wall. I was amazed watching the rectangle bend at the corner of the room fitting flat against the two connecting walls. Then it flashed in the outer corner of the room where it would have full view of my guests sleeping on the sofa bed in the living room. The door was not completely closed.

The next morning everyone said that they slept well and were full of energy. I wondered what had happened last night because I was sure something had.

Thursday, 22 June 2006, Devlin and I had a brief conversation while I drove to work and again while I was on break. When he has enough of human "talk," he literally shuts me down by slowing my thought process to a crawl, and even though I am thinking, I am unable to complete and send the thought. When our conversation becomes intense I nearly become "free floating," as if I am about to detach from my body, a very strange sensation. He has said that humans are capable of thought sending that can be accomplished with practice, and this is another reason why he does not like us, because we don't thought send.

It is interesting that all of this has become a "normal" part of my daily life, and I'm not terrified as I was at the beginning. The night I was floated out was the most terrifying and most exhilarating experience I've ever had, and I want to do it again only I want to remember what happens. I am having strange "dreams" mixed in with my own and sometimes I'm unable to determine which part are my dreams and which are theirs. My buddy calls these dreams interfered with.

Saturday, 24 June 2006, at work yesterday, I found a sore spot on my right arm that I had not noticed before. When I looked at it, it was a bruise about the size of a fifty cent piece and today it is nearly faded away. I also have three very small bruises on my right thigh in the shape of a triangle.

Last night, I had a sketchy dream of blood being siphoned

from my right arm. I pop out of my body and see my back as I sit on the side of a table facing a wall holding my right arm. There is a bright light above the table. I am back in my body, and I am angry. I hear someone tell me the babies need the blood; I respond that I don't give a damn who or what needs the blood they had taken too much. I could find no marks on the arm this morning.

The evening of the 26th, I saw four small black balls before going to bed. I made an appointment with the ophthalmologist to get my vision checked in July to rule out eye disease.

Wednesday, 28 June 2006, a bridge was constructed and placed on my lower left jaw last August. It hadn't been glued evenly onto the molars causing tenderness by the uneven pressure when chewing food on that side. Eating was no longer a pleasure having to chew everything but a few soft items on the right side. Every time I ate, my wish was that the damn thing would fall out. The dentist told me there was nothing they could do once it was glued in except drill it off. Yesterday afternoon while I was eating, it became loose and I was able to easily remove it! I was astounded, as I thought I would probably go to my grave not ever enjoying a meal again. Well, the absolute amazing thing is today I have a dentist appointment made six months ago. Do you believe in coincidences? I don't. Did the beings loosen it or did it loosen by itself? I don't know and I don't care.

Friday, 30 June 2006, last night a bizarre event occurred. I guess the first place to start is earlier in the day with several short conversations with Devlin. He told me they were coming this night, and that a really big event was going to occur one that I would not forget. He said that it would "end my world". I don't believe him anyway and went about my household chores as planned, read, and turned off the light for sleep about 1:05 AM. On my way to bed I had told Devlin that I intended to take pictures tonight and his immediate response was "NO!" We bantered back and forth while I placed the camera strap around my right wrist with the camera on my chest, and laid in the dark watching and waiting. I didn't see any flying balls, flashes of light or hear noises, so I placed the camera on the bedside table within easy reach.

At 2:35 AM I suddenly awake. I am on my stomach with my face toward the wall where the window is. My vision is as if looking through water, somewhat blurry but still able to see. I am aware that there is something on the wall than the blurriness clears, and I can see that it is hieroglyphics, lots of hieroglyphics all over the wall, written in white with the shadowy wall and window as background. It is a text that I cannot read and therefore understand but I knew "they" were responsible for it. What am I to do with this? There were so many complex figures that I would never be able to remember them. So when you don't know what to do, the best thing is to do is nothing. I laid there examining the figures marveling at their complexity.

As suddenly as the figures had appeared, I felt something to my left. My whole body jerked in reflex with that terrible feeling of fear that starts deep in your gut and shoots out beyond your body then circles back forming a black heavy living snarling beast deep in your bowels. Buster was lying beside me facing the side of the bed where I had felt the presence of the being, and he yowled when my whole body jerked, but he didn't move. I immediately turned over to comfort him. He was stiff so I picked him up cuddling him and giving him soothing strokes. He relaxed and began purring, and I was able to lay him back down on the bed. I looked around the bedroom, got up, and looked through the house but found or heard nothing out of the ordinary. I went back to bed, propped my head up on a pillow and waited.

It's difficult trying to fall asleep when you know something is going to happen, and "they" don't want you to see it but are anxious for you to fall back to sleep. I closed my eyes and new faces began to parade across my closed eyelids. There was a young dainty female mantis with a sweet face and smile. There were faces of young greys and others I didn't recognize, and for once no one looked mean or angry.

I am in a room facing an unadorned large metal curved wall surrounded by others, how many or who, I am unable to tell. A ceremony is in progress. I am in the center and am not afraid seeming to know what is going to happen. Someone behind me says now they will present my robe. I pop out of my body and see my naked self standing in the center of the room with my arms extended out to my sides. I see a one-piece white cloth suspended flat above my head. The cloth is long and has long arms and a hole for the head. When the cloth is sewn up the sides and down the arms a robe will be created like one imagines Merlin wore. I could only see the part of the cloth that would lie next to my skin. I pop back into my body as the cloth is dropping over my head, and I remember feeling the luxury of it as it rested against my body. Somewhere in the moment after it was dropped over my body, I am aware of three golden cords one larger than the other two forming a braided trim around the edges of the bottom and the arms. I am surprised at the gold trim and set in a chair examining and admiring the craftsmanship, and beauty of it. The atmosphere is solemn and serious. I'm back in my bed.

I didn't look at the clock again, but I did talk to Devlin and told him what happened. His response was "Oh my God," then silence. I asked him what is wrong as I felt confusion from him, and he said, "I don't know how to address you now." I asked what does that mean, and he replied that I am a "healer," and he wouldn't talk any more to me. I thought to myself, of course I'm a healer, I'm a nurse.

What the hell? Now what is going to happen? Are they done with me and going away? Was this a staged thing or what? Is the robe invisible but worn all of the time? Will certain others be able to see the robe when the "time" comes? I remember being told that I will heal all who come to me without question or profit, and being taught the words to be said that I have now forgotten.

Forget the profit, I was wondering how I was going to heal others, and what were the conditions going to be that I would be needed to heal anyone in the first place. My mind leapt to a vision of thousands standing outside of my house waiting with lit candles and chanting for the "healer" to appear. Ridiculous!

Sunday, 2 July 2006, nothing happened last night that I know of except that I was over tired and didn't fall asleep until around 3:30 AM. When I finally laid my head down on the pillow I became unconscious.

I had spent hours last night looking up ancient writing on an Islamic writing and an archeological site finding two ancient countries whose writing had the rounded curly cue type of letters seen in the hieroglyphics. One was Kannada from South India, and the other was Sinhala from South Asia. One script that it also reminded me of had been seen many times up North written as graffiti, but the writing on the wall had more dots incorporated with the figures, and was more complex. It was beautiful like looking at a picture rather than a text. There was one very complex and intricate figure that held my attention, and although my eyes roamed most of the writing I focused on the beauty of the one figure. The text did not scroll nor disappear from the wall when my body jerked at the feeling of a presence at the right side of my bed. I used the term hieroglyphics for lack of a better word when I initially wrote about the event but the script was writing not hieroglyphics. Today I plan to look at some of the sites that have alien script on them.

These beings can do incredible things allowing you to think one thing when actually something else entirely is going on. I wonder what really happened last Friday night.

On the web under the Betty Andreasson Luca story, there is an article by Joseph Kerrick entitled *UFOs and NDE* that has a picture of a grey in a robe. The robe in the ceremony was like his except it fitted over the head rather than opening in the front. The gold trim on the robe is less grand than the one in the picture but just as beautiful. I had not seen this picture until last night.

During the ceremony my observing self did not feel this over whelming love and acceptance that Betty speaks of. I have experienced that kind of love during a dream in 1986 involving my father and the women that I had done genealogy on. That particular feeling of love is not found on this earth yet was one I recognized immediately, knew that I missed it, and wanted it back.

Just because you have an "experience," and are overwhelmed with their abilities to control your mind and body does not mean that what they do or say is the "end all". It is important to examine carefully what has happened looking for tiny little clues they, the aliens, leave. It is important that I do not lose "self" during or after these events. It is recorded even in the Bible that we humans are impressed with power and power display, and these aliens have plenty of it. What I need to always remember is that I have power too, each of us do. I have no doubt that there is "The Creator", and because I believe this, I know that I was created by this Omnipotent Creator, The Creator of all things including the aliens. Just because we look different and have different abilities we all essentially have to eat and eliminate in some manner, and so to speak, put one leg in our pants at a time. The aliens are no better or worse than we humans. They are just more advanced, and are more capable in controlling human thought, and in manipulating us. I am not their equal in ability to do these things but I am equal to every one of them in the sight of The Creator. They can humble me, have me screaming in terror and pain, but they cannot ever truly have "me" unless I give "me" to them.

They have the ability to cause you to see, feel, hear, touch, taste and smell what they want you to see, feel, hear, touch, taste and smell. They are powerful in this way. The question that needs to be answered is what is the source of this power? Is it The Creator given or alien developed, and I think it is alien developed.

My intelligence clearly recognizes that The Creator of all things does not need to probe our bodies and perform painful procedures on us. My intelligence clearly recognizes that The Creator of all things does not need to collect ova and sperm, and use humans as incubators for the being's hybrid fetuses. My intelligence tells me that they purposely make issues confusing to us, and even though the purpose of many of them may not be ill intended, they use our weaknesses to their advantage in order to meet their goal, and their goal is their objective. What is that goal? I believe that it could be survival as some think, then again it could be curiosity but no one knows for sure, I sure don't. Survival of the species, the same drive lies in all that The Creator has created be it plant, insect, animal, human or alien. We adapt; we mutate. They are as ruthless as we are or would be if placed in this situation but is survival the situation?

Even though I have a "Devlin" in my head feeding me little messages, and "observers" flying in little black and white balls, and rectangles plastered on my walls and belongings; even though I am floated out of my bed in the dead of the night by two little grey beings who feel pain when I pummel them with my fist; even though my mind is probed and filled with weird unrelated and unconnected events that I cannot account for nor places that I can account for; even though I am "honored" with a solemn ceremony involving magnificent writing on the wall and a white robe, and given the title as "healer"; even though all of this and more have occurred, I don't believe them.

Chapter 13

Monday, 3 July 2006, after I had sent an email about the ceremony to my buddy yesterday, I went into the bathroom to wash my face and get ready for the day. I felt that what I had written expressed how I felt about this whole thing, especially about the ceremony. I was talking to Devlin and he was very irritated with me saying that I was a naughty girl, and should not have told my buddy. I was convinced, based on the memory that I have, that I have done nothing wrong.

I stood looking in the mirror combing my hair when a new voice said to me, "Will you die for him?" This one was as if it were speaking into my left ear. I recognized it as the voice that had spoken on another day when I was in the bathroom looking in the mirror putting on makeup, and now it has said it again while I stood in the same place. The voice told me that I have done something that I should not have done, and that was to send this information out so that the entire world would see it. It asked me again if I would die for him. The voice did not sound angry and was calm, as if it were my father talking with me, trying to understand why I had been naughty.

I asked the voice who "him" was, that I want to know exactly who "him" is. "Him" to me is The Creator or his Son, Jesus, and that I cannot assume that we are talking about the same "him". I asked this voice, "Who are you and why are you asking this of me?" He replied that I have committed myself and they have done everything they could to prove to me that this was not a frittering thing; a "frittering thing"? I tried to make him understand that may very well be true, but I remember none of it because they are bargaining with my subconscious and not my conscious mind. He listened while I explained that my conscious mind is not aware of what my subconscious mind has done or the commitments that it has made to them. I told him that if I am going to die for "him" or anyone else, my conscious mind must know who "him" is and where, when, and why this is taking place, then and only then, will I decide what I am going to do.

I lay down on the bed and closing my eyes, the upper portion of the being that I had seen several times appeared on my closed eyelids. It was the male wrapped in what looked to me like mummy wrapping with eyes of pure white light. I remember him standing behind the group seated at the table watching me, and I acknowledged him by smiling and a slight nod of my head on the night I was taken. He had immediately drawn my attention because of his eyes, and then when I got a close up of him, I remember thinking how different he was from the others, as his body seemed to be wrapped like a mummy with a small piece of the tail end of the wrap hanging from his forehead that I had been so tempted to pull to see if it would unravel. I had also seen him on a ship in one of the rooms I had been escorted to where he stood across the table watching me.

He told me the cloak was a gift, that I could not just throw it away, that I was committed, and that he depended on me to complete my task. I asked him again who he was, and he said that he was Michael, Gabriel and Raphael, that he was all three. The war was about to begin and he counted on me to perform my duties as instructed, and that I am not to worry about what to do as I will know when the time comes. I asked him if there was anyone else besides me who questions what this is all about, and he replied, no, no one. I asked him how could it be that no one questions what is to happen, that they all follow like sheep to the slaughter. No answer. I reiterated that I, me, my conscious mind must know what my body, the only one I have which is where I live, must know what it has committed itself too. No answer. After a pause he said that he would have to consider what I have said but has concerns that I will tell the world. I replied that I have free agency, and if the world should know then I may do that. He said that he could destroy me, and I replied that yes he could, and I would have no defense against his power.

What on earth am I involved with? I don't care how these beings present themselves; this world is involved with another one who is bent on a war, a war with whom? They are going around gathering up their warriors, programming them to do whatever, and not allowing their conscious minds to know what they are committed to. Is this the preparation for the battle that is to be between God and Satan for the souls of mankind, or is this a battle for less lofty ideals? I am at a loss for words to describe how intangible all of this is, yet seems tangibly threatening.

I will wait for him to return to me. I must know whose side I am fighting on and what I am fighting for, to know when and where wouldn't hurt either. Whatever it is there are aliens of many different species involved. Could they be fighting amongst themselves, and using humans to do the fighting?

Tuesday, 4 July 2006, I went to bed around 10:30 last night very tired. Several things happened yesterday.

In the early evening my cats were running around chasing and playing with something that I could not see. They were jumping in the air swatting and chasing it to ledges above them, and having to come to a screeching halt to avoid a collision with a piece of furniture. This is the way it was when I first moved in.

The second thing to happen was when I went to get ready for bed. I had laid my folded nightclothes on the bed before I left for work, and when I pulled the nightshirt off of the bed a round white ball fell to the floor and disappeared. It was the same size and color of the ones I have seen flying around the house. They are still here and they are still watching me.

This morning when I showered and dressed for the day I found new bruises, obviously more is going on then I am aware of.

Wednesday, 5 July 2006, mom has once more displayed "outward defiance" with her caretakers, and they are "writing her up" for the second time. The next time they will ask her to leave. We had talked before about her behavior but she said she had done nothing wrong, and refused to see a doctor. She is a strong willed person, and does not hesitate to voice her thoughts. I will schedule an appointment to rule out a physical problem, and if there is none then I will take her to a psychiatrist. Hopefully medication can be ordered to help her control her behavior. Poor mom, it's sad and alarming to watch your parents decline; you feel so helpless.

Friday, 7 July 2006, well, my mother of eighty-eight years

has been booted out of the personal care home, and I've placed her in a hospital for psychiatric/geriatric evaluation to see what's going on. She is spending the night with me and will be admitted tomorrow morning. I wonder what she must be thinking, if she realizes what has happened, but she doesn't say a word. I think her dementia has progressed to the point that I really don't think she can.

It was that morning before we left for the hospital that I asked her if she had ever floated out of her bed in the middle of the night by something she couldn't see. She didn't verbally answer but her expression said it all; she had. Her eyes lit up than narrowed, the smile on her face was a strange smile, one I had never seen, and I knew she understood all too well what I had asked her.

So it was my mother and not my father but then usually if they, the beings, take one, they take the other, and sometimes the whole family. Why had she never told my sister and me? Why had she never warned us? Was the story of the black finger poking her nose all that she remembered but then no, that can't be true because she was aware of being floated out of her bed by something unseen when I asked her! Would knowing in advance have made their presence easier for me? Was she aware that I was being taken throughout my life? What about Daddy? Was that why we had all of those talks under the stars about life on other planets? Did he know without doubt that there were?

Sunday, 9 July 2006, the beings keep on coming relentlessly. Devlin has been reassigned and is no longer with me; a new one answers. He stammered around and had trouble thinking of a name to use finally deciding on "Macland". I asked him if he was a reptoid as Devlin and the other had been but he couldn't make up his mind finally saying, no, he wasn't then admitted to being "what you call a mantis". He also said that I am his first assignment, and that I am the only one he is to monitor and observe. He is very nervous and unsure of how to answer me giving multiple answers at the same time. Devlin did this too.

Why the change? Am I under more or less control by them? What is going on? They are here enough to let me know they are here, balls, flashing lights and little lights in my eyes at night but at the same time they are gone; they are not standing by the bed. I have so many unanswered questions.

This evening the little black being with the white eyes and triangle tiara ran to mom's bedroom door and down the hallway. It is looking for her again. It has to have intelligence to be able to connect her to that room and to the bathroom she used down the hallway. I told it that if it wouldn't move so fast I wouldn't be able to see it. I don't want to see it, I don't want to know where it is looking or that it is even here. I don't care if it is an alien, or from another dimension, or even ghostly; I want it to go away.

Monday, 10 July 2006, this morning, I took an antibiotic that I've taken many times. Several minutes after I swallowed it, I began to have severe abdominal cramps, followed by nausea, then diarrhea and vomiting. I was unable to decide which I needed to do first, vomit or have diarrhea, then I began retching but couldn't vomit. I was drenched in perspiration, becoming so hot that I thought of getting into the tub to let cold water from the shower flow over me but the abdominal cramping was so violent that I couldn't move. I knew that I was in major trouble, possibly dying. I remembered that lately each time I had taken this antibiotic, I would have some cramping, and the last time some nausea along with the cramping but nothing like this. My lungs began to fill up, and I was coughing up white foam, unable to breath. I lowered myself to the floor hoping to crawl to the phone when the symptoms abruptly abated; they simply stopped as if they had never occurred, and I felt fine although shaky. A voice in my head said, "The next dose will kill you" and that I believed. What had stopped the progression of anaphylactic shock, the beings, my guardian angel, God?

I ate a small lunch, and went to work a little weaker than usual but still able to work. My skin began itching but I didn't break out with visible hives.

Macland said they were coming for me as I had to be cleansed from the poison that I had taken. "Oh," I said, "so you were here and saw what happened?" "Yes," he replied, "we were there with you, and saved your life." That little bathroom must have been pretty crowded, the Queen of England could have been there, and I wouldn't have noticed. Devlin was also talking at the same time, and I asked him why he was there as Macland was supposed to have taken his place. His reply was that I was too much for a novice like Macland. This is like a soapbox opera.

This picture was taken of the sliding glass door on 11 July 2006 at 6:27 PM. The object hanging from the white plastic shelves is unknown. I have not been able to match it to any reflection from the desk area nor do I have a gadget like this anywhere in the house.

The picture below was taken at 6:29 PM. A flap attached to the object has now flipped up showing what looks like a face. When printed, the pictures print out as if behind Venetian blinds although only vertical blinds hang at this window and were open when these pictures were taken.

Tuesday, 11 July 2006, my mind was spinning after I got off work. What can I do about the beings, and how am I going to pay bills without depleting my meager savings, and still provide for Mom as well as my own needs. If she acts out in this hospital, and this would be the place to do it, will medication help her, and where will they recommend placement for her?

The cycle of life. You struggle through your own childhood then you worry about your children while they struggle through theirs, and even when they move out setting up their own household, you still worry. Perhaps, worry is the wrong word because you lack any form of control, but remain, hopefully, a sounding board after they move out. Yes, worry is wrong at this stage, concern is a better word; you are now concerned but do not express it; your role is to listen as your parents listened to you. There are a few years of calm then the worry of aging parents fills that empty worry space, and you hope, you sincerely hope, that your children will be spared this but it is the cycle of life, so they will experience it in some form or another.

I thought about mom, my childhood, than found myself reviewing my own life and the choices made, some good, some bad, and why do the bad stand in the forefront? I've done my share of wrongs, and have no way to amend those things that, at times, set heavily on my conscious. My life would have been different had I made different choices, on the other hand, it could have been worse had I made those choices. The only decisions I do not question or regret has been the birth and true joy of raising our children.

Wednesday, 12 July 2006, Mom has been prescribed

medications that should help her, and will be discharged tomorrow. I have made arrangements for her to live in an assisted living facility because she cannot be left alone or unsupervised. She will have to share a room because she cannot afford the rate for a private room; she can't afford the rate of the double room either. The lady stated she was reluctant to accept her due to her behavior at the personal care home. Has there been a breach of confidentiality?

When I took my break at work, the sun was out in the distance and there were fluffy white clouds against a blue background. I was relaxing examining my hands and arms when there was a flash; there was no thunder and no flashes followed. I watched the passing cars to see if any more flashes would occur, but none did. I asked Devlin if that was them, and he said, "Yep, that was us", who knows? Then I saw that I have a large bruise on the inner left wrist and a needle mark over the vein about one and one-half inch above the bruise. Damn!

Chapter 14

Friday, 14 July 2006, mom is settled in her new home. I had to give the pharmacy my credit card number before they would send her medication. I'm going to be in major debt before this is all over.

Last night I fell asleep from emotional exhaustion waking up about 12:30 AM lying on my left side facing the window. When I opened my eyes there was something on the wall, and when I blinked hard I was able to see writing. I don't think it was the same script as the night of the ceremony, and although it had curly cues, it didn't have all of the dots and little lines. The white and grey figures on a misty background were laid out in a straight line as words on a page. The "page" filled the wall between the corner of the room and the window but I was unable to discern even one figure. The entire wall focused in then became superimposed with a smaller, clearer white page with moderately thick black symbols spaced evenly across it. I glanced at the others, and zeroed in on the last one because it reminded me of a rose blossom then they all disappeared. There was a feeling of excitement or expectation in the room, and I wasn't frightened telling them to come on, let's get this over with, let's go, but they didn't come.

I got up to go into the bathroom then couldn't go back to sleep. I asked Devlin what was going on, and he replied, there was war, that I was needed, and to go back to sleep. Faces that were new to me began to show on my closed eyelids, and I wondered where they came from, and who they were. I refused to allow them to look into my eyes, I didn't trust them. I turned my head away and kept my eyes open eventually falling asleep. My hair is standing on end this morning.

Saturday, 15 July 2006, my buddy believes that I am having out of body experiences (OOBE or OBE). This may well be happening. How wonderful it is to get a perspective other than my own.

Wednesday, 17 July 2006, the astronauts are in the process of reentry, and there is a discussion of the need for increased salt intake due to having been weightless in space for several weeks. The salt helps prevent light-headedness from the increase of gravity. Salt water, Gatorade, chicken soup and salt tablets can be used. Perhaps this is the reason salt was one of the items they said I needed more of but that doesn't make a lot of sense to me since I am not in space for weeks.

Tuesday, 18 July 2006, last night I had trouble falling asleep, and this is not unusual after Devlin tells me they are coming, but I did, waking up around 2:23 AM. When I went into the bathroom I caught a glimpse of a small white ball zipping across the bathroom floor followed by a dark violet rectangle appearing on a slat of the window blind a few feet from my face, easily seen outlined by the darkness around it. I looked through the bathroom door and saw a white rectangle stopping below the bedroom window then disappear. They were here and I knew something was going to happen. I went back to bed laying there wondering if they were going to let me remember but I remember nothing.

Wednesday, 19 July 2006, I worked today and while on break I attempted to talk to Devlin. He was not a happy camper saying that he was sleeping, and I had awakened him. So sorry Devlin! After bantering back and forth, I asked him how many people he was monitoring now, and he replied that I was the only one. When I asked why only one, he replied that the others did not work out; they were safe and had not been harmed. He added they were coming for me tonight, that I needed to get home and go to bed, and that is why he was sleeping. Is there irony in this?

On the way home from work, I saw lightening in one cloud, and not hearing thunder, I decided it was heat lightening. I wondered why on earth I even thought of crediting another meaning to a natural phenomenon. Anymore, it seems that I notice anything that might smack of something unusual or out of place, and then wait. I have grown suspicious and with it possibly a little paranoid.

I walked into the house and readied for bed then fixed myself something to eat. When I sat down to eat, Devlin tells me that I should go to bed immediately. I reply that I will go to bed when I am damn good and ready, and to leave me alone. He did. Midway through my meal the ringing in my ear increased in volume, and I asked him how long is this was going to last? He replied that we were almost completed and it wouldn't be much longer. I was referring to the ringing in my ear; what was he referring too?

My head was on the pillow at the headboard, and Buster was on a pillow turned long way in the bed beside me. I turned off the light around 11:20 and fell asleep immediately. I woke up at 2:10 AM with my head on my pillow next to Buster on his pillow; both pillows were lying long way on the bed and my feet were hanging over the side. What the heck! Was I taken, and whoever brought me back did not know the normal position of the pillow on our beds? Or had I repositioned myself?

Friday, 21 July 2006, today I had an appointment to have my eyes checked and the doctor stated my vision is good. He said he could find no reason why I was seeing little white balls and skillfully moved to another subject.

Saturday, 22 July 2006, I had a dickens of a time falling asleep last night; I just wasn't sleepy. Today I work so hopefully I will sleep well tonight.

I've been finding doors unlocked in the morning that I know I locked the night before. For instance, the front door knob is unlocked, but the dead bolt and the storm door are locked. The dowel placed in the sliding glass door is not in place or the dowel is in place but the door is unlocked. Even though you could swear that you locked them before you went to bed, there is always the chance that you could have missed them. This has happened in the past, but seems more often in the past three weeks. Then finding your pillow and your body completely disoriented in the bed definitely makes you wonder what is going on but then you know.

Thursday, 27 July 2006, last night while I was lying on the bed reading, Buster had jumped up for his nightly behind-the-ear-scratching when something white caught my eye floating in the air near the foot of the bed. It exploded scaring Buster who took off to the other side of me and lay down.

This morning I found fresh bruising in the same place above the inner aspect of my right and left arms above the elbows, as if someone had tightly grabbed my upper arms. The others were just turning yellow and now there are fresh black bruises in the same areas.

Devlin tells me he can see everything that I see and I don't like that.

Friday, 28 July 2006, after I turned off the light I see a bright flash through my eyelids. I am dreaming.

I see a large round table with a highly polished surface like a conference table. There is a dark slightly curved wall facing me; the lit area is only about the table, and the beings sitting at the table look almost human but are not. I smile and nod my head to each of them, and look closely at several who are watching me as I walk to what I think is a chair for me. I set down.

This type of dream is repeated periodically as if I am being interviewed or questioned leaving me with an unsettled feeling that it is a trial of some sort.

Sunday, 30 July 2006, I was tired last night going to bed early and waking up at 1:27 AM. I knew they were coming.

I am in a strange house with Jezebel and Buster. The house is an older one, probably early 1900s, and there is a man to my left who is always just out of my line of vision. All of the shades are drawn, and the windows and doors are locked. I am in hiding, peeking out of the windows periodically, restless and worried. The next time I peek out of the window, the view is not familiar; the street is deserted, nothing is outside on this beautiful sunny day, not a bird, not a dog, not even a flying insect, alarmed I withdraw. Now I am at the front window and I peek out then open the blind so I can see the sky. There is a huge shiny golden spaceship in the sky not far from where I am. Suddenly it is surrounded by five or six dark smaller ships; I know there is going to be a battle. As I watch I think "Good, let them kill each other," close the blind, leave the room and see that a window in another room is uncovered. I can't imagine how this can be since we are in hiding.

I wake up with the word "Die" being said into my left ear. It is definitely one of the little ones who had hummed in my ear on another night. I look at the clock several times but the time won't penetrate my brain. There is faint writing on the wall. I am unable to determine if it is the same as seen before but doesn't seem to be. As I look at the writing, neon colored symbols of blue, pink and green parade across it. I look at the clock again, the time is 3:07 AM, and when I look back at the wall the writing and symbols are gone. I fall asleep wondering why "die" was said in my ear. What does it mean? Who is dying?

Monday, 31 July 2006, I am tuned into a talk show. A man begins to tell his story relating messages he has received regarding the future. As I listen my entire body begins to vibrate, as if every fiber is having a fine tremor, and I have an overwhelming feeling of nausea. I turn off the show and go to bed. A vertical thin rectangle lands on the lampshade and flashes once, then moves to the head of the bed slightly to the right of my head, and flashes again.

I am facing a male being. His face is a few feet away from mine, only the top of his shoulders, neck and head are visible. He has light brown human looking eyes, brown skin and no hair on his head or face. His skin looks to be made of tiny scales and if those scales were removed he would look completely human. We look at each other. His face is expressionless. I don't know why we are here.

Suddenly he erupts into flames. His neck arches backward and his head turns to his left; his mouth flies open flames shooting from it. His neck and head are completely engulfed in flames, and he disappears in a matter of seconds like sawdust. I feel no emotion. I don't understand what or why this has happened or even if it did.

I am floating in outer space where wispy, whirling, thin cloudy like things are around me; it is beautiful and peaceful. I begin talking to the unknown being with me.

I ask, "Did you bring me here?"

"Yes," is the feminine reply, "You need to relax and remain relaxed in order to do your job."

I gave myself over to the universe floating weightlessly, aimlessly. I ask her if this is remote viewing.

She replies, "Your body and soul remain in the bed only your mind is in space."

She shows herself to me after quickly shifting her facial features six or seven times. She is not human and is not any of the beings that I remember seeing before. She is entirely new.

"Thank you for helping me," I say. "What is your name and where are you from?"

"My name is Magzania from Zocar, the third planet from the sun Zaspa."

"Thank you for helping me," I reply feeling myself slipping off into sleep wondering if Zocar and Zaspa even exist and where they are if they do.

Tuesday, 1 August 2006, last night after dinner I went to bed sleeping until 5:30 this morning. I looked at the clock trying to decide if I could go back to sleep for another hour. I am looking at the bedroom doorway, and see three small green balls each the size of a large marble, one after the other, lazily fly across the doorway about a foot off of the floor towards the sliding glass door. I laid my head back down on the pillow, and tried to go back to sleep when I began hearing a low pulsating sound in combination with something else I could not identify. I thought the pulsating sound was similar to blood rushing through my ears but when I raised my head off of the pillow the sound could not be heard. I looked at the clock again and saw that it was blinking. I got out of bed and looked out of the bathroom window; everything was as it should be. I saw that all of the electric clocks in the house were blinking and the TV required a satellite search when I turned it on. There had been a power failure.

Thursday, 3 August 2006, this evening I watched *Close Encounters of the Third Kind*. I had seen this movie when it was first released. We had gone as a family, and not only enjoyed it but came home relaxed and uplifted. This time watching it, I had an entirely different viewpoint toward it, and yet, a part of me wished that the beings were the gentle, wise looking, nearly god-like beings as shown in the movie.

Chapter 15

Early this morning, Monday, 7 August 2006, I woke up seeing yellow writing on the wall. None of it made sense even though it was written in English capital letters and contained #, &, %, and other familiar symbols. I looked at it trying to figure out what it meant, and since then there is something that I am trying to remember, it's there just on the verge of coming through but doesn't. As the day progresses the feeling of trying to remember something gets stronger. What is it?

Tuesday, 8 August 2006, last night I had a dream, well actually two dreams. The first dream was about work.

 My boss called me aside to tell me that the customers were complaining that I smell like cigarette smoke. I know this is a "stress" dream as I am concerned that I do smell like cigarette smoke. It then slides into the next dream.

 I am in a room with chairs and what I think are lockers but I'm not really sure what they are. There are six of us, all female except for one. We are sitting in chairs in a circle examining white, thick, lightweight outfits that fit over the body. They remind me of the white outfits in *Star Wars* only these have skinny arms and legs. The material is pliable, something like plastic, an unfamiliar plastic that behaves like cloth. I am looking into the leg portion of the outfit with the top folded over as cloth does. I am trying to shove my foot into the foot portion of the outfit but I am unsuccessful because my foot is too large. We are laughing because the legs are made for someone who has really skinny legs, legs not much larger then our bones, and even though we try it is impossible to fit into the outfits. Someone haughtily says, "I fit into it." We stop laughing and look up as he walks away from us wearing one of the outfits, then we giggle because we know he wears the outfit all of the time; he is a tall grey

I see two of the women's faces clearly. They are younger than me, one is in her thirties and the other is probably in her early forties. They have dark hair, one that is shorter and curlier then the other, and both have a light complexion. One of them says she hopes that these don't come out as Halloween costumes because her children will want to buy them, and we all laugh again. We are having a casual comfortable get-together enjoying ourselves.

It is at this time Buster, who sleeps on the pillow by my head, gets up and slinks quickly to the other side of the bed crossing over my face. I wake up and look for writing on the wall then sit up in bed and look around the room seeing nothing. I watch a tiny white ball appear above the foot of the bed and disappear then in front of the dresser, and again in front of the window where it disappears. I look at the clock; it is 4:25 AM. I easily fall back asleep until 7:30 this morning.

When I washed my face this morning I see that my left upper eyelid is red, bruised, and slightly swollen. I remember wanting to rub the eye and being told to leave it alone as my hand was moved away from my face.

Thursday, 10 August 2006, there was a full moon last night. I stood at the bathroom window looking at it when suddenly it appeared to be dropping out of the sky onto the earth. I stood transfixed not believing what was happening, than it stopped and appeared normal. Did they put something in my eye that communicates manifestations created by them? What have they done to my eye!!!

It ached last night and today it feels like something scratchy is under the inner upper eyelid that remains bruised and swollen.

Monday, 14 August 2006, I went to bed around 10:30 PM immediately falling asleep. I woke up around 3:00 AM having had a nonsensical dream not remembering any of it. It had quickly ended by an overpowering sensation of fear that is unto itself an unbelievable fear, and I started screaming "Daddy! Daddy! Daddy! " I couldn't imagine what was going on to be so fearful then I felt something wiggle between my folded hands, and I was no longer afraid.

I am lying on my back with my hands, one on top of the other, resting on my abdomen with a hand in between mine. I raised my left hand and traced the outline of the long skinny fingers with my own, and then gently felt the last digit on its right hand from the back of the hand to the tip of the finger and was relieved, I knew who it was. It was the little one. I raised my left hand and stroked the back of his bald round head and gave it a gentle pat. I opened my eyes and looked towards the wall on my left and floating across it was "EEWITHME" written in yellow dozens of times. A white flash occurred on the adjacent wall, the writing disappeared, and I was alone in the room. I went back to sleep, it was 5 AM.

It was as if the whole thing was scripted. I was acutely aware of how fragile his fingers were. They were thin like a thin stick that could be snapped easily with pressure between the thumb and a bent index finger. I remember being surprised that he allowed me to feel the little finger all by its self. His head was bowed forward, and I wondered if he wanted to find out what it felt like to have his head stroked after watching me scratch and stroke the babe's heads resulting in feline ecstasy. Why else would he allow this to be done? Is he curious about us and our way of life as I am about him and his way of life?

I can't explain to anyone the fear that invades and takes over my body, and I know that I am a rogue missile when it is within me but I wasn't last night. There was something touching and rather sad about feeling his hand and stoking his head. While at work I mulled this over having emotions ranging from gut-fear to the earnest desire to know what the heck is going on. I genuinely want to know about the beings.

On Thursday, 17 August 2006, I asked Macland what "EE" meant. He said the greys are "evolutionary enoids" or "EE" for short. Is there such a word as enoid? There is in the world where they live. In our world the closest I have come to "enoid" is "Echinoid" that are sea urchins and sand dollars according to Wikipedia. "Enoid" could be a word in a foreign language with which I am unfamiliar.

Wednesday, 23 August 2006, last night I was very tired falling asleep around 7:30. I began having a confusing preposterous dream, woke up, opened my eyes and saw yellow writing. This time it was not on the wall but on my eyes, and there seemed to be some sort of a film on them. Squinting while focusing on the writing it seemed to be

Arabic or something similar, and was flowing slowly from the top to the bottom reminding me of high school when we were learning to "speed read". Maybe I really do have some sort of an eye implant.

I did not feel a presence in the room yet I felt like something was about to happen. I continued looking at the script then the writing stopped flowing and disappeared. I looked at the clock; it was only 9:45 PM. I turned over onto my right side and saw a glimpse of a white rectangle about nine by five inches land on the book laying next to me on the bedside table plus a few white balls in the room and bathroom. I couldn't go back to sleep.

Have they been feeding information into my mind while I am sleeping and unaware? Now, they have messed with my eyes. Does this mean I will see whatever it is they want me to see? I'm doing that anyway when they are around, but now, can they control my vision from a distance? What else have they done to me that I can't see and am unaware of?

Why are they showing me script that I am unable to read? Am I able to read it subconsciously and be unaware that I can? They have shown me many different types, why? Is some of the writing for the beings in my room? That seems like a low-tech way of communicating to me. What really makes me angry is the inability to stop these things before they occur.

Saturday, 26 August 2006, yesterday I worked. When I got home I rewrote a letter to Budd Hopkins sending a copy to my buddy for her input, then began going through the journal selecting dates when events happened. I became tired and for some reason, anxious and excited, as if I had discovered a revelation. I went to bed falling asleep immediately then was awakened by an unusual smell. It was strong and heavy, almost smothering, and I thought I might vomit, but something told me that I must not do that, as it would undo everything. Everything what? I lay there looking around the room seeing nothing even though I had the feeling that others were there. I fell back to sleep and awoke again at 2:59 AM, the smell was still there. I walked around the house finding the odor throughout, but strongest in my bedroom. Again I fell into a restless sleep with the smell permeating my nostrils. At first I thought I had never smelled this odor before then I realized that I might have a number of times a long time ago.

It was about 1973, a year or so after we had moved into the country house. Our oldest son who was around four years old would lie in bed at night talking. The couch where I sat reading was on the other side of the wall where he lay in his bed, and I could hear him mumbling.

I went into his room and asked who he was talking to, and he replied that it was his friend. Suspecting it was an imaginary friend I didn't think much of it. This went on for a week. Sometimes I let him talk until he fell asleep other nights I would go in and give him some extra hugs and kisses. Each time I entered his room I noticed an offensive odor progressively becoming stronger. Because of the odor I felt this may be more than an imaginary friend, and told my son that I wanted to meet his friend. He replied that his friend was afraid of me, and that is why he left when I came into the room.

I was now worried about what or who my son was talking to each night; something that had an odor worse than anything I had ever smelled. One thing for sure, I knew it was not an imaginary friend, and after stewing about the situation for several days I knew what I had to do. The final evening when I opened the bedroom door the odor was smothering like the one I smelled last night. I went into the room ignoring whatever might be there, and lay down next to my son propping him up on my left shoulder holding him in my arm. I explained that right now he was not allowed to have friends that his daddy and I have not met, that someday he would but not now. I explained that I was going to tell his friend to leave and not come back, and that he should do the same.

I stood by his bed facing the darkness of his room and said, "Leave! Leave now and never come back! You are not wanted here in this house! You are not to visit my son again!" and lay back down on his bed holding him until he fell asleep. That was the end of it or so I had thought, now I have reason to wonder if it was.

Sunday, 27 August 2006, per encouragement from my buddy, I emailed a letter to Budd Hopkins and hope that he will be of some help.

I made a copy of my journal listing only the events without tainting them with my thoughts, and that was hard to do for my thoughts are a part of the whole. Doing this I realized several things, one was that I have definitely been abducted, that I have had contact with some sort of aliens be they from outer space or another dimension, and the last is that I have yet to see a UFO.

From what I have read on the Internet and learned from my buddy, these beings have been educating the young on how to care for the earth. Others have been literally force fed, or as I once heard it described as the "down-loading" of information to the older generations. Apparently these have occurred for many years. Dire predictions have been given to many regarding the end of the world or the end of the world as we know it. Is it that they can predict the future, or is it that they are able to see from experience where the future is headed? Could it be possible they are from the future, and know what the history of Earth is? Their history would be our present and future, but if they were able to change their history then the future as they know it would no longer exist; they would not exist.

If the beings are from another dimension and our dimension is destroyed, how would it affect other dimensions or would there be an effect? If one dimension collapses, do they all collapse? Could that be the reason why there are a variety of beings involved? Could these beings be from different dimensions banded together for a single purpose? Could that purpose be a communal desire to save our world in turn saving each of theirs?

Speculation without fact leads the imagination to contrive many different scenarios.

On Friday, 1 September 2006, I went to bed, read then couldn't fall asleep even though I was tired. I closed my eyes and saw visions of alien faces, human eyes and flashes. I began smelling the little one and I said "EE?" Macland said to hold out my hand, which I did, followed by the feeling of fear charging through my chest. I let my hand drop as I had felt something jump onto the bed, lay down, then jump off. What else was in the room with me?

I blink, and when I open my eyes it is as if I am looking from behind a mask that has been loosely placed over my face. The eyes I am looking through are slanted and shaped like the eyes of a grey.   I am looking through the eyes at a body on a bed and wonder who it is when it becomes apparent that I am looking at myself.

I can see the right side of my head, and my eyes are looking around the room and blinking, then I realize that I am also blinking at the same time. My skin is glowing in the dark, and I wonder if all humans glow like this. Whichever being is in the room is allowing me to see myself through their eyes, and I thought it was awesome. I watched a small white ball fly across the room landing on my right eye, staying there for a second then disappear. My body lying on the bed did not see the little white ball, yet my eye had an instant fading ache, and I wondered if it had penetrated my eye on the bed. Suddenly I am able to see through my own eyes and I fall asleep.

Last night, Sunday, 3 September 2006, I went to bed early. The whole night seemed to be overflowing with strange and confusing dreams filled with meaning.

I am awake and see capital letters made of little white stars on a black background, a "U" and an upside down "U", and I'm wondering what this means. The letters are capitalized, read from left to right, and shown one at a time. "U", upside down "U", "C", "O", "M", "P", and an "L", and I lose interest; I don't care what it says I've had enough. I shake my head, open my eyes, look around the room, and see yellow writing on the wall. I decide I don't want to see this either, moving my eyes and head to another spot, and when I look back it is gone; I am glad. I have decided the upside down "U" means an "N" and wondered if the word says "uncompleted" or maybe "uncomplicated" and I don't care which one, or if it says any word starting with u-n-c-o-m-p-l.

I am dreaming.

I am being shown what looks like an old thin soft-cover booklet entitled "Spy Book" in large black letters. Someone asks, "Do you want to copy the book?" Turning my back to it and walking away, I answer, "No. I want nothing to do with the book or spying."

I am exhausted and my brain is on tilt. I am so restless anymore, and I am having trouble focusing on everything that my mind deems unimportant and almost everything seems unimportant. I am in a battle against beings that have more experience then I, and have resources and abilities beyond my wildest imagination. They come on a night when I work the next day robbing me of needed sleep and energy. They are wearing me down or else I am truly going over the edge and am insane, and have been all along. Maybe this entire past year has been manufactured by my insane brain. Many people who are insane hear voices in their head and I have Devlin and now Macland who are always there. The bloody bastards will not get me, I will fight.

Saturday, 4 September 2006, this morning Macland tells me

that I failed the test. What test?

When I showered there was a burning sensation when the water hit my left lower leg. There is a fresh superficial skin scrape that had not bothered me until it became wet. The area is about 1 ½ inches long, red with fresh scraped skin sticking up. Where did that come from?

Monday, 4 September 2006, I slept all last night, no dreams, and I feel refreshed and ready to go! They have reduced visual images of the balls and the rectangles, and I see only short less bright flashes. Again they have changed their approach to be even more subtle. Maybe this is a different group, a more experienced one but maybe not, there is no way to be sure. There is thirteen more days until the one year anniversary of the spacesuits. What will happen that day?

I picked up mom today and fixed her one of her favorite meals, Yankee Pot Roast with vegetables, coleslaw and coconut cake for dessert. We ate until we were stuffed, cleaned up the kitchen and headed to Wal-Mart to pick up a few items she wanted then she lost interest in shopping, and wanted to go home.

Wednesday, 6 September 2006, a few minutes before I was due off work today, a customer came in needing assistance. Although pleasant, he seemed a little confused and began telling me his life story. As he talked, a white ball flew from his chest area, passing by me and on through a doorway behind me. When I looked back at the man, he had a startled look on his face as he looked at me but continued talking as if nothing had happened. I wondered if he had also seen the ball and suspected that he had by his surprised expression. I began to feel uncomfortable with him, and that feeling grew as he continued to talk. I wanted to run away as fast as I could. He left and I went home.

There were phone messages waiting when I got home including a message from my ex regarding a planned cruise. Yes!! Get me out of here!!! It will be a comfortable trip knowing each other so well; forty years of marriage allows that. There are few surprises left to experience together after forty years, so it will be comfortable. I want to remain his friend; I want to remain a friend to the father of our children. He will pay for the trip because he knows that I don't have two pennies to rub together and he doesn't want to go alone.

I finished reading a synopsis of the alien master plan then switched over to the Cassiopaean Transcript, and my left eye began to hurt. The pain was a throbbing type that increased as I read.

I am angry with the beings, and resent their intrusion in my life. They have interfered in my world, my life, and my belief system. They are deceptive and self-serving using others and me for their secret purpose, their agenda whatever it is. It is ironic, considering that I have accepted and welcomed the visitors from another world. It has changed now; they are no longer welcome, yet I remain curious about them.

Chapter 16

Thursday, 7 September 2006, last night after I had turned the lights off there were two flashing lights, I didn't care. When I was in the bathroom a tiny white ball appeared on the bottom slat of the blind facing me, and fell onto the windowsill then went back to the slat. I tried to smash it with my finger but it reappeared and then disappeared. I use to find this amusing and interesting because I was interested in them but now it is annoying. I got a whiff of "that" odor which became stronger as I lay in bed, and I buried my nose in the pillow trying to ignore it. Both cats lying next to me suddenly shot off of the bed and I fell asleep.

The scrape on my left leg was deeper then it looked but it is healing.

Saturday, 9 September 2006, I got home from work after 9 PM, emailed my buddy, ate dinner although I wasn't really hungry, got ready for bed and flopped on the couch. Nothing on TV was of interest, so I headed for bed to read a book until I fell asleep. I am dreaming.

I am on vacation with my ex. There were many rooms in the place where we are, and we visit each of them. The place is like a mansion, and well decorated. There are people I know, and some family members but I'm not a part of them. I look for the bathroom, and wonder around until I find a little room off to the side that reminds me of the tiny bathrooms on cruise ships. I enter, turn around and leave then stop and go back in. The bathroom is filthy and I have to clean it up. I woke up to "the odor" and knew they were back again.

I said "EE?" and a voice in my head said, "Yes, we are here." I looked around the room seeing nothing, then got out of bed and looked around the house finding the odor strongest in the living room. I went back to bed and slept.

Monday, 11 September 2006, when I showered this morning I found bruises on my upper left thigh. Did I injure myself? No, I did not.

Last night there was writing on the wall of a dark greenish color on a grayish background, actually I couldn't determine what color it was but felt dark green was the closest. The writing was of symbols then changed into another type of symbols, and I heard "EE" say in my head, "We are here." I don't remember anything else, although I was aware of what was going on. Perhaps it will come to me later.

Wednesday, 13 September 2006, yesterday evening I cleaned off the mountain of papers and mail accumulated on my desk and can now see the surface. I went to bed about 1:30 AM, and was at that juncture where one falls into sleep when I was jerked awake by "the odor" that was stronger than it has been. I thought "EE?" and the reply was, "Yes, we are here." I felt a little breeze on my arm followed by a stronger breeze on my face, and my heart began to beat faster while I'm trying to remain calm chanting to myself, "I am not afraid. I am not afraid," and I was told that was good. I fell asleep.

There are four more days until the 17th, the one-year anniversary since the space suits appeared. For several weeks now, I have had this feeling that something spectacular is going to happen on this date. There is a reason why they are giving me so much attention, and I have no idea what that reason is but it leaves me with an uncomfortable feeling, especially as the anniversary date grows closer. Perhaps I'm creating this feeling, could it be intuition or is something in my subconscious trying to break through? I am leery of what is going on; I don't trust them. They are here or at least in some way make their presence known almost every day. I wonder who is in charge of whom? I think the greys are more powerful than some may think.

Friday, 15 September 2006, hooray! I am getting ready to go on a cruise and will return after the 17th, shucks, so sad. There is a new voice in my head, lower than Devlin and Macland's, who says his name is Joseph, and is older than the other two. He tells me there is a job that I must do, and threatens that I will die if I don't do it, and I tell him to go to hell. I tell him I can't do anything that I don't know about, and he replies that I do know about it. These creatures are nuts. First he threatens me with fear of the night, well, that can sure happen easily enough, and when that didn't have the desired effect he threatens my death, and that didn't have the effect he wanted either as I am going to die anyway. These creatures must think we humans are especially stupid and easily cowered.

Sunday, 17 September 2006, after traveling all day my ex-husband and I checked into a motel and went to bed early. I couldn't fall asleep fantasizing the delectable taste of a waffle ice cream cone. I closed my eyes seeing a big brown eye on my eyelids looking back at me. This eye was different because the top of the iris had a "V" shape cut. Joseph began talking, "We are coming tonight." "Sure," I thought and began to give the same long lecture about the value of humans and their inhumane approach towards us; about how we are all created by the same Creator; about what they are doing to us is wrong as well as the way it is done; and that chances of me cooperating with them is next to nothing.

I saw a white blink a couple of times on the ceiling, checked it out and happily found it to be the smoke detector. Then I saw lights moving across the wall at the foot of the beds and found them to be caused by cars on a road running behind the hotel. Relieved I fell asleep.

I woke abruptly smelling that awful smell. It wasn't as strong as the last time, but it was not a whiff either. I thought "EE?" and the response was "Yes, we are here". It's always "we" rarely "I". I looked around the room, saw nothing and fell back to sleep. I woke again laying on my right side facing a four-foot wide wall next to the bed. On the wall was faded bright pink capitol letters forming words as if looking at a page in a book. On top of the bright pink words was faded bright blue capitol letters forming words flowing at an angle across the pink letters. I could read neither. I looked down at my nose to see a white ball sitting on it, and the writing and the ball disappeared. A hologram! Could it be a hologram? Yes, I believe so!

I am home having had a few days of sorely needed pampering and relaxation.

Tuesday, September 19 2006, I went to bed, finished reading a book turning off the light around 1:30 AM, and find I am unable to sleep. Joseph began talking. I rebuked him and he said, "You can't do that." I replied, "I already have." Again he said, "You can't do that." "Joseph, go away and never come back here. Tell your pals the same."

Flashes of light and white balls flew around the room with one of the balls reflected in the mirror. Faces appeared on my eyelids facing and looking at me. They were a mean looking group, and definitely frightening as if from a monster movie. I fell into a light sleep and was awakened by the odor, very strong this time, and seeing nothing in the room I eventually fell back into a light asleep.

As I sit here in the light of a cloudy day, I wonder just what is truly going on, and what the attraction is that they keep in daily contact with me. There are a lot of questions to be answered by them. Perhaps Devlin has already told me what is going to happen when he said a group would be looking for me, and my life will be in danger when they find me. Is this what they have been preparing me for, and are waiting for it to happen? He told me to be watchful and careful. Among all of the lies and deception, is this the one piece of truth? How does the white robe with the gold trim fit in? Will I be wearing it when I am found? Does this "finding" involve humans or aliens? What does my subconscious know that my conscious does not? Truly, this is bizarre.

My sister is planning to come for a visit the first couple of weeks in December. She can hardly wait and is hoping to find out if she has been "taken" too. As we talked, the white and black balls flying around increased, and I felt that they were excited too. She wants to question Joseph, and will be coming at this from an anthropologist's approach. She has no idea what she is getting herself into but will soon find out. She will be able to spend a lot of time with our mom, and mom needs to see her baby, my little sister.

I have not heard from Budd Hopkins.
Sunday, 23 September 2006, yesterday morning when I woke up I saw a symbol in my eye, not on the wall but in my eye, and saw two symbols this morning. Yesterday was a "C" inside of an "O", this morning it was the same followed by an upside down "C" with an "O" inside of it. I do not know what either means. I blinked hard a couple of times and they went away. What the hell have they done to my eyes?

Tuesday, 26 September 2006, I worked today. The customer the white ball flew out of came into the store; this is the first time I have seen him since then. I grabbed my cigs, bottled water, and went out for my break.

I slept well last night waking up at 6 AM seeing writing on my left eye. It was in a yellowish color but not yellow, perhaps there was a little orange in it or red. There were a lot of symbols but I focused on two. One symbol was a little rectangle standing on its end with a filled bar across the top. The other was a small empty circle with nine spokes coming from the outside edges reminding me of a symbol for the sun. What do they mean?

Saturday, 1:45 AM, 30 September 2006, I'm working two part-time jobs to help mom pay for her care. I've worked every day this week, and I am tired, really tired, and I'm bored. My support system lies in another state, the one I moved from. Those friends I could invite to dinner or simply to have coffee and chat; what a pleasant diversion that would be. The people here are pleasant and polite, but not friendly, not friendly in the way I am use to. I am once again a foreigner, an outsider, someone whose pedigree is unknown but I have adjusted to not having close friends; it is lonely, but I have adjusted.

The smell has been very strong tonight, and I have seen many white balls flying around, even blinking before my eyes. I tried to go to bed earlier but there were noises in the living room and with both babes on the bed with me, I knew it wasn't them. It would be so much better if they would just show themselves but they tell me it wouldn't. I think it is interesting that they find it necessary to wipe my mind clean after I'm taken, yet allow me to know that they are here with their balls of light, flashes, and smell. It's probably part of their enjoyment of watching me suffer anticipation of when they will strike and what they will do. I believe that they have a malicious sense of humor while achieving their goal whatever it is. What is their game? I don't like this because I don't understand the game or the rules.

Thursday, 5 October 2006, my sister is still planning to come out the first part of December. I am anxious to see what will happen when she does but most of all I welcome her company. She has a cheery and warm personality, and we care about and love each other. This is what I need, sorely need; someone who knows and loves me.

My buddy sent a blog about a man named Jim Sparks, "http://ufoexperiences.blogspot.com/2006/09/jim-sparks-and-anna-hayes.html". He speaks about a meeting with snake-like-face beings. I found this remarkable as I have seen faces as he described. He saw the entire body which I have not. This man has written a book which I would like to read. I found Linda Moulton Howell's website, and ended up emailing her which she replied with her own article. This article, *MANIPULATION OF TIME BY NON-HUMANS: The Experiences of Jim Sparks*, was better than the blog as it explains what Jim found out and I believe possible. Joseph had said that they are time travelers but was this said because it was thought that is what I wanted to hear? This entire thing is far more complex than any human can imagine; the stuff dreamed of by science fiction writers. What is their purpose in revealing this information? I then ask myself, why am I so suspicious? Why not lean back, relax and learn more if they are willing to teach me? And the answer to that is I don't trust them.

Friday, 6 October 2006, I turned off the light after finishing a book about 9:30 last night. I laid there petting Buster watching white balls flying around, and the quick flashes on the wall above the dresser. There was that feeling of expectation in the room. Eventually I fell asleep with the odor growing stronger and stronger. Did the white balls release the odor or was something else besides myself and the babes in the room? I woke up around 4:00 AM and could not go back to sleep wide awake feeling rested. My last remembered dream was eating breakfast and thought that sounded like a good idea. It was a full moon last night and the sky was clear. Did they come? I think there is a good possibility that they did or they want me to think that they did. Today there is something more that I want to write but I don't know what it is. There is something that I should be remembering, but what?

I took a shower this morning and found dark purple bruises on my arms and legs. I had done some heavy cleaning last weekend, so any bruising obtained from that should not be dark. There are multiple purple bruises on my left upper arm. When I went out of the front door to go to work, I found the screen door unlocked, and I know that I had locked it prior to locking the front door!

Chapter 17

Sunday, 8 October 2006, yesterday, my ex and I took mom out for lunch. She said that she knew what she wanted, ordered, than seeing my platter, she decided it looked better than what she had in front of her, we traded. Even though she ate every morsel on the platter she was still not satisfied. From now on we go to her favorite drive-through, as she knows what she will get there, a double cheeseburger, small fries and a coke, and she will be a happy woman. I want her to be happy everyone needs to be happy with what they are served.

I went to bed and read turning the light off around 11:30 falling into a deep sleep. I hear a noise and become aware that I am dreaming.

I am in a strange house with my mother who is not my mother. Jezebel and Buster are with us, and I learn that someone is going to try to harm them. I remember historically that in some societies cat behavior was little understood with some believing they were familiars, or in some way associated with the devil. With this thought in the forefront, I grab the babes putting them into a closet, and with my gun in hand I stand guard outside of the house prepared to defend them.

There are no streetlights and is very dark. There are bushes in the front of the house and by the driveway blocking my view of the street and neighboring houses. Suddenly two dark shapes are running towards me from the neighboring house on my left. I remember the lesson my father had given me, if you point a gun, be prepared to kill or they will take it from you and kill you. I aim at one of their chests, and fire the gun not knowing if I hit anything. They stop; one of them is bending over holding his left thigh. I can see their faces now as if a light has been turned on. They are teenagers, and the one who is holding his left thigh is my older son and the other is his childhood friend. They look at me, turn around, and run away. I think I should have called out first to find out who they were.

Suddenly I see a tall dark figure coming from the street area and suspect it is probably another teenager. Having shot one of my sons, I don't want to make this mistake again only wanting to scare this person away. I look at the gun in my hand which is a yellow plastic stick reminding me of a child's small yellow plastic ball bat, and fire the gun in the air. The figure stops giving me a surprised look, turns around, and runs away. Again a light is turned on revealing the face, and I see it is my youngest son.

I hear the noise again and am aware that it is me making the noise. I am awake facing the bathroom door, and see bundles of capitol English letters on top of each other. I see "E"s, "W"s and "M"s, and I don't know what it is trying to spell, and I don't give a rat's ass either. I just shot my son and that troubles me even though it was only a dream, an interfered with dream. What was it they wanted to find out? Why didn't they just ask me?

The words begin to swirl around flowing towards a tunnel and are swallowed up by it. I know that this is not just a dream or just writing on the wall because the odor in the room is strong and sickening. It is slightly different then the other odor I have smelled before and even more unpleasant.

I do not smell sulphur that is commonly reported during alien visits. It smells more like human excreta mixed with something else making it stronger and more unpleasant. I lie there not moving watching the dark hole looking slightly larger and larger coming towards me. They are here in the room.

I mentally say, "I am aware that you are here. Show yourself." Instantly there are small bright neon colored symbols of blue and pink jumbled together. They flow across my vision ending at the black hole, but do not swirl into it as the others had, they disappear. The symbols are like the ones I have seen before, and do not know what they mean. I think these are their symbols used to communicate among themselves but I can't be sure. They seem to be used when they realize that I am awake. This has been their pattern. Are they concerned that I will pick up their thoughts? Perhaps, perhaps they are.

"Who are you? You are not the one who has come before. You smell different". I become aware that Joseph is talking in my head, and I tell him to be quiet. The strong offensive odor becomes weaker, and the other odor not as offensive became stronger. It then backed off, and the other odor became dominant again. It is the little one and his friend. I think he is trying to teach me the difference in their odors.

"You know who I am."

"Where did you come from?"

"The mother-ship."

"Did you come for me?"

"Yes."

"I am awake and I want to remember. Take me now while I am awake so that I will remember. I want to remember flying in the air and the mother-ship."

No response. The odor is becoming stronger and suffocating.

"I want to see and remember everything that happens."

"No," it says, "You will not want to remember everything that happens."

"Will it be painful?"

"Yes. You will not want to remember."

"No, I do not want to remember the pain but I want to remember everything else."

"You will remember what you want to remember."

I get up and go into the bathroom. I am able to see the black hole turn into a very dark red blob, and sink to the floor moving behind the dresser where I cannot see it. Then it moves just outside the bathroom door, and is now about two and one-half feet off of the floor. It seems to be a little dark red body that does not have a clear shape yet has depth. I walk past it as I go back to bed and look at the clock it is 2:11 AM, and I know that I am being taken tonight.

I am not afraid.

I am wondering why, in heaven's name, they are focused on an almost 65-year-old woman. What do I have that they need to study? What is it they want from me? Why have they waited until this time of my life? I eventually fall asleep with the strong unpleasant odor knowing they are here, and I don't care. I remember nothing more.

Wednesday, 10 October 2006, I went to work yesterday, depressed, and in a rather bad mood as a result of their shenanigans. The male customer was back in the shop and wanted to talk, fortunately there was a line at the counter, and I was able to avoid him. I had trouble with the computers at work today. Messages popped up when I tried to enter information then when I asked for assistance, the messages were not there even though they had done the exact same thing I had done. A good example where they "toy" with me, and that is not good; I have to eat and take care of mom therefore I need this job.

I turned off the light around 11 PM and slept waking up at 7:30 this morning. There were white balls in the room and bathroom following me around. The dark red blob was standing at the foot of the bed about two feet off of the floor when I went into the kitchen. What can I say? What questions can I ask that I have not already asked?

For two days there is something that I am trying to remember. It is there waiting to be pulled out of the jumble of things to remember but it won't come forward and make itself known. How do I go about releasing it?

Thursday, 12 October 2006, I continue to be upset about the dream I had the other night shooting at people, especially my sons, is not on my list of things to do. They select a subject, set up a scenario, remove emotion, tell you what the objective is, turn you loose, and observe your actions. I am a lab rat. Is it that I am I too compliant or am I being controlled? I don't like what I am seeing in myself.

Friday, 13 October 2006, I believe more than ever that nothing is going to happen that will involve me in the greater scheme of worldly events, such as an ambassador or a healer as they want me to believe. It's all bunk. It is a position of importance placed in my mind because they know I have an ego as all humans do, and a need to feel important, to feel special, to feel needed but to them I am only an experiment. I don't feel important, special or needed after I've been "studied;" I feel used and abused.

Wednesday, 18 October 2006, it is 12:27 AM. I finished reading *Secret Life: Firsthand Documented Accounts of UFO Abductions* by David M. Jacobs, PhD last night then started on a book by John Mack. I had seen tiny black balls flying around me all evening while reading. Earlier after I had turned off the bedside light at 10:30 PM, the odor was the little one I usually smell when they are coming.

Dr. Jacobs writes about baby hybrids being presented to abductees. Again I am reminded of a period where I was holding babies all night and playing" Ring Around the Rosie" with little ones, thinking these children were not normal, and did not play and laugh like normal children making me very sad. I have a memory of arguing with someone about the lack of activity for the children and being told I could not come back.

Thursday, 19 October 2006, I worked last night until 9 PM arriving home about 9:20, ate and went to bed to read. I turned off the light around 10:30, pounded the pillow into a comfortable position, got the babes situated, and still couldn't get comfortable finally ending up lying uncovered on my stomach. The odor was there but not as strong as the night before.

"You are here. I can smell you."

"Yes, I am here."

"Show yourself," I said, as I sat on my knees looking around the room and seeing nothing I fell back onto my stomach. I lay there for a while then bending my left leg, I let my foot drop heavily onto the bed. As it fell it hit something smooth and somewhat yielding. The toenail of my foot hit an object twice as it bounced and skipped further downward hitting it again, followed by the bottom of my foot sliding downward against it landing on the bed. It was not a cat as they were on the other side of the bed. I was surprised and sat up. The smell was instantly gone, and I saw nothing. Whatever was at the foot of the bed got pummeled by my foot as it came crashing down. I heard nothing more and fell asleep.

I am now reading *Abduction: Human Encounters with Aliens* by John E. Mack, M.D. A year ago I could not have read this book. Both, Drs. Mack and Jacob's books have caused me to re-examine what has been happening and when, especially when. There have, no doubt, been times that I have been abducted but didn't realize it thinking that it was a different time. There have been many days that I "needed" to take an afternoon nap that I have always resisted because I don't sleep at night if I do. They lead your mind in a direction opposite of the path they are taking you on.

I think that some of the dreams I've had, such as the one where I am shooting people to protect the cats are "staging" as described by Dr. Jacobs, but I don't know if I've been "mindscanned".

Dr. Jacobs presents the beings as less threatening. I'm not far enough along to see how Dr. Mack will view them. As written throughout my journal I sway from one view to the other, and I would prefer that they not be threatening. I also detect in myself a feeling of fondness for the little one and the babies. Perhaps my tirades on their being a negative force are a reaction to a painful or invasive procedure that was performed the night before and has been blocked as suggested in the book. Who knows? I sure don't have the answers.

I watched *John of God* yesterday. It was very interesting and even though having been a nurse, it made me nauseous. I have been away from nursing too many years and have never been good with living things suffering. What I found interesting is that the scientific world is really looking at his abilities and philosophy. It is all in the way you view things. This led me to think about Christian Science's viewpoint towards illness. Was Mary Baker Eddy saying the same thing using a different approach? Very possibly as hers was to deny the existence of illness recognizing only wellness, the reflection of the perfection of God, and to me, that is similar to *John of God*. Things are as we see them and it made me examine my own views that have switched from a glass half full to a glass half empty since the beings have arrived. I have become pessimistic which takes joy out of life causing one to only exist. I have much for which to be grateful.

Saturday, 21 October 2006, last night I read more of Dr. Mack's *Abduction*. Several of the people presented in the book discovered that they are of two worlds, the alien and the human. I feel of two worlds also, could this be because the beings keep telling me I am one of them? I'm not sure who I am any more.

Since they have been coming I find that I am isolating myself. My fortress is my home better known to me as the "cave" where I seek refuge with the babes; it's us against the world, me against the beings. It feels as if there is a reason behind this that I am supposed to discover by myself. But I have to admit that part of my isolation is due to a lack of funds available to do anything else, such as go to a movie, go out to dinner, go shopping, go sightseeing, to get a pedicure or a manicure. All of the things I have enjoyed and took for granted in the past are no longer available to me at this time.

I finished reading the chapter on "Paul" in Dr. Mack's *Abduction* where he comes to the reality that he is an alien "spy" sent to help them understand humans and their behavior. This set me back a bit. Was I not shown a "spy" book in one of my dreams---Sunday, 3 September 2006? So much in this book is similar to what I have experienced and feels uncomfortably too close to home.

Sunday, 22 October 2006, I found a card for a hypnotist in

one of the books and sent an email receiving a reply. She states that she has dealt with abductions several different times over her years of experience.

Monday, 23 October 2006, last night I finished this months' billing statements when Joseph said, "You need to go to bed." "Okay", I replied. I don't fight them anymore after reading Dr. Jacob's book. I got something to eat, and finished watching a recorded program then went to bed to read the rest of *Abduction*. I turned out the light around 10:30, fell asleep immediately, and was awakened at 6:00 AM by five loud "bangs". I was having a dream that wasn't really a dream, and being shown a list of five items accompanied by a "bang" for each item. I can't remember what was on the list. The "bangs" were not real bangs like something hitting something else, wood on wood or a drum, they were imitations bangs. I was aware that I was half asleep, and laid there for a few minutes wondering what that was all about. I went into the bathroom where a little white ball lay on the bathroom floor. It flew landing on my right upper chest; I went back to bed and slept.

Tuesday, 24 October 2006, mom and I spent most of the day in the emergency room. She was diagnosed with a bladder infection and sent home. The pharmacy delivered her medications, and she was finally able to settle down, drink some fluids, eat a little bit saying she felt better.

I went to bed and read turning the light off at 10:30 PM. Joseph tells me that visitors are coming and that it won't be them, that he doesn't know who they are. I CAN'T STAND THIS!!! Life has enough twists and turns; I do not need their interference in it!

I spent a restless night, tossing and turning finally falling into a heavy sleep. The alarm went off at 6:00 AM. I awoke fuzzy headed not knowing where the hell I was, and staggered into the bathroom. Every bone and muscle in my body hurt. Every muscle was tight and painful, as if experiencing spasms. I blew a lot of bloody drainage from the right nostril. I do not remember any balls of light, smells, sounds or anything else. Joseph tells me that there is more than one group coming, and they cannot interfere. Do I believe him, not for one second? Sometimes what they say rings true, the other times it is malarkey, and mostly that, malarkey.

Wednesday, 25 October 2006, I picked up mom after work. She was exhausted from yesterday's trip to the hospital, looking pale, and unsteady on her feet but said that she felt better. I was told by the staff that she has not eaten except for one can of Boost. She had an appointment with the psychiatrist who said she will improve with some medication adjustments; we were both happy to hear that statement. On the way to take her home, she asked to stop for a coke, so we headed to her favorite drive-through where she not only ordered a coke, but a hamburger and french-fries as well. I am hopeful this means she will begin eating her meals. We then headed to the drugstore to replenish her stock of chocolate Boost. She seemed so much better than when I had picked her up. I hope she keeps eating.

Thursday, 26 October 2006, I think I have a sinus infection and set out the cold air vaporizer that will help to relieve the symptoms by moisturizing the dry air from the hot air furnace.

The staff tells me that Mom has increased her fluid intake that is so important when you have a bladder infection, and her appetite has improved a little.

Saturday, 28 October 2006, the hypnotist and I had a telephone conversation at a convenient time for both of us. She has worked with "experiencers", and was agreeable to hypnotizing me to learn what actually occurred using the bits of memory that I have. Not that she indicated this, but as I spoke with her, I realized how off the wall my experiences have been. They are not the typical abduction experiences. I was disappointed when I learned how costly this service would be. Supporting myself and helping with mom's expenses makes this venture impossible. I had placed a lot of hope on her being able to help me, and I was leery as to what she might uncover but the loss of hope for help seemed to outweigh the fright of not knowing. The feeling of being alone with no one that you can speak with except for my buddy by email, is a feeling of being trapped with "them",

I locked up the house and went to bed, couldn't even read. There must have been fifteen little "fireflies" around my bed and that angered me, I got up. It was as if they were little vultures waiting to swoop in for a meal. I woke up at 2 AM seeing a flash in the bedroom and again at 3:30 AM. I went into the bathroom and saw a little white ball zip across the open bathroom door for about five inches, and another white ball fall to the floor at my feet. I deliberately stomped on it. I woke up again at 7 AM with the inner aspect of my right eye itching that was relieved with a cold wet washcloth then I went back to bed and slept.

The frustration of the whole thing angers me. How is it that we humans have become "studies" for a more advanced civilization? Yet if you think about it, we are being treated as we treat other "lesser" creatures on our own planet. Perhaps they are following our example, and think this is the way it is done here on earth and it is. They are as ruthless as we humans. Such a shame that The Creator did not do better with His creations.

Sunday, 29 October 2007, I spoke with a staff member to see how mom was doing and learned that she had been up disturbing others all night. Oh, oh. We agreed to allow the medication changes time to be effective.

The right side of my nose is swollen and bruised this morning.

Monday, 30 October 2007, a beautiful full moon lit up the sky and the entire neighborhood last night. I called to see how mom was this morning, and was told she slept well last night, and that her appetite has improved.

Today my nose is more swollen and bruised than yesterday.

I am reading *Witnessed, the True Story of the Brooklyn Bridge UFO Abductions* by Budd Hopkins, a fascinating read. I had heard it mentioned but didn't know what had happened.

Sunday, 12 November 2006, I returned from a relaxing four day cruise with my ex, however, each time I go, I think that it will be the last. I get bored on the ship but being waited on makes it worthwhile as does the company of my ex. During the evenings of the last three cruises, I have sat alone on a deck outside of a bar looking at the dark Gulf of Mexico, watching the lights in the distance to see if they move indicating signs of the beings, enjoying the gentle breezes while mellowing out on Margaritas with a shot of Triple Sec while my ex is in the casino. At our last stop we had lunch at a restaurant in Cozumel and without thinking, we ordered iced tea. The tea was delicious and satisfying the price was "Montezuma's revenge".

I was happy to get home to see Buster and Jezebel, and although tired, I had trouble sleeping. I laughed at myself at having trouble sleeping in my own bed but am able to drop off and sleep everywhere else.

Wednesday, 15 November 2006, it is 2:38 AM. I went to bed at 7:30 PM last night and woke up around 1:30 this morning. Hopefully I will be able to go back to bed and sleep some more.

I watched a recorded program about UFO's sighted by pilots and astronauts, and found that I could barely watch it as it verifies they are here. I know they are here but I don't want them to be here the way that they are, if that makes any sense. They are blatant, yet deceptive, and that makes them dangerous because they are capable of doing things that we only fantasize about. My buddy states she doesn't know what they are either. It's a single bag for me, I see them as living beings as we are, with an agenda, and they will do whatever is needed to accomplish it, whatever it is.

Thursday, 16 November 2006, things happen during the night, but I can't always remember what when I get up then later it comes to me but then I can't remember when I set down to write it, like now. There were three things I wanted to write today.

The first one is very early this morning, before 5 AM, I was awakened by a cramp in my foot. I tried to work it out without getting out of bed but it just wouldn't go away. I walked to the bathroom hoping the short walk would be enough to relieve it but it wasn't. I didn't want to get up as it was too early, so I stood by the bed with my eyes closed to see if it would go away. Bam, there was a flash of red by my right eye followed by a flash of white near the red flash, one right after the other. The only thing I could figure out is this is something I don't normally do; stand by my bed with my eyes closed. Maybe they were looking to see if my eyes were open, I don't know. Anyway, I ended up walking throughout the house until the cramp left then went back to bed.

The second thing I wanted to write about occurred since I have returned from the cruise. I was lying in bed waiting to fall asleep and thinking about the little one. I was wondering what he looked like because right now I only know it is he by his odor. I was trying to envision what his size and weight would be wondering if he would be of a weight that I could pick up and carry in my arms because they are the size of a small child. Then I wondered what I would do with his big head, and if I could handle an unbalanced skinny body with an oversized head, and how difficult it would be to carry it as opposed to a human child. I began to smell him; it was faint, but never the less, his smell.

The odor became stronger, and I knew he was in the bedroom; at the same time this funny feeling in my body began, sort of tingling, but not tingling, and my heart began to race. I was surprised by my body's reaction, as I didn't think I would be frightened to see him. It went away as suddenly as it had come leaving me to realize that what I felt was not fright but my body's reaction to their force field, or whatever it is they use. I think that I, and maybe others, mistake this body reaction to fear because the reactions are similar to what we feel when we are fearful, the racing heart and the tingling skin that alerts and induces the "fight or flight" reaction.

I can't remember the third thing.

Chapter 18

Wednesday, 22 November 2006, I have to take mom to see the doctor this morning then I have the next two days off planning to relax and work around the house.

I woke up a few minutes to five this morning while having the second cat dream. The first one I was shooting people to protect my cats; this dream was a situational dream smacking of values clarification.

I suddenly appear in a house I am unfamiliar with, yet know it. I walk outside around to the side of the house, and peer into a neighbor's basement window. The basement has about three to four inches of water in it with debris floating around. The room is small with a large black hole in the back and seeing nothing in it, I assume the black hole is a part of the basement. There are three kittens, two are black, and I don't remember the color of the third one. One of the black kittens is lying on its side looking half dead floating in a plastic tray similar to what one finds in the top of a cooler. The other two are treading in the water and begin to mew when they see me. I decide to rescue the treading kittens and begin to crawl through the basement window. I can almost reach them when the window grows smaller, and I become wedged in it. I work myself out of the window, and rest on my knees listening to the kittens mew. I consider my grandchild who would be small enough to fit through the window with me holding him. I am aware that I am dreaming and want to see where this is going, however, at the thought of putting my four year old grandchild through a basement window that changes size to rescue kittens, woke me up.

I sat on the side of the bed thinking this is sick to be placed in a situation, a situational dream at that, to even consider using my grandchild to save kittens under these potentially unknown and dangerous conditions. The balls were flying around, and I knew that they were playing games with my mind. I don't think they understand my relationship with the cats. I believe they are trying to discover how I feel towards them, the cats, and how far I will go to protect them, as opposed to family members. They caught me off guard with the gun and my sons but not this time.

I looked about the dark room wondering how stupid something so advanced could be, then got up and went to the computer to record what had just happened. Then I mentally sent a message to them as clear and loud as I could as I wrote: Attention beings! Listen to me and understand this once and for all; the cats belonged to my daughter, and I inherited them after she died. You know this. I am protective of the cats because they are something that she had rescued, loved and protected. You have known that I had four, two of which died and frankly, I believe that you had something to do with one of their deaths whether by accident or purposeful intent. Don't you dare touch another cat! If given the choice of protecting my children, grandchildren or any other child or the cats, I would not choose the cats, although I love them.

I am on a roll and unable to stop; I have too much frustration, anger, and resentment stored within me. This is to notify you that I am growing very weary of your constructed situational dreams. Stop them. Stop testing me. What you see in my dreams is not what will happen in real life. Your created situations lack love and emotion and are like watching a robot that is without feelings. Until you are able to place the normal human feelings into the dreams, you will never learn how we think or will react because emotion plays a huge part in our reactions. Your tests are not reliable, so stop them because you will never understand until you start having these emotions yourself. I feel sorry for you; it must be a cold life. Even though you may sense our emotions you cannot feel them; you cannot understand them, and without understanding you are unable to discern our motivations. Leave me alone!

I'm not done and I feel like they are still here, so I continue. I am also tired of you following me around and observing everything I do. I grow weary of this. Some things, such as emotions determining actions, cannot be scientifically studied by those who are deficient in emotions and you, the cold ones, are deficient, so STOP! Take the implants out, stop the ringing in my ear, and leave me alone!

Thursday, Thanksgiving Day, 23 November 2006, last night I had no sooner turned the light out and closed my eyes when there was a bright double flash. Opening my eyes I saw nothing, and when I closed them there was another double flash followed by a single flash. Opening them again I could see a faint whitish figure moving across the front of the dresser then disappearing but I could smell nothing. I closed my eyes again knowing that they were here and something was about to happen. There was a slight tingling in my lower legs; I moved them and the tingling went away. My heart rate was normal and I was determined to remain calm. I closed my eyes and there were two more sets of flashing lights and that is all I remember. I awoke a few minutes after 2 AM then went back to sleep. So, what happened last night after I had written the blistering response to the dream of the night before? They're still here but let me remember nothing. Shame on them! They are so superior yet resist letting me have the slightest bit of usable information. Are they afraid of me? Isn't that an interesting thought!

Friday, 24 November 2006, last night I went to bed around 7:30 stuffed with turkey and all of the trimmings. I read for awhile then fell asleep with the light on waking up around 9:30. I went into the bathroom turning the light off when I went back to bed. The babes shot off of the bed as I began to get a slight whiff of the little one. When I lay down on the bed the ringing in my left ear abruptly stopped, and a lower pitched ring in my right ear began. I closed my eyes and there were two quick flashes. I lay on the bed on my left side facing the window just watching and waiting. There was another quick flash at the top of the window blind followed by a couple of fainter ones. I wondered if passing cars could cause this flickering and flashing on the blinds, so I kept watching and listening for cars. Several more cars passed and I wasn't sure that the cars didn't have something to do with the flashing however, now there were little white balls and a red blotch on the blind. The odor became stronger and my legs felt heavy. I got up watched TV going back to bed around 11:30.

This group comes when I am asleep, but usually lets me know they are here before I fall asleep. I understand that many abductees awaken with them at the bedside without a previous warning such as they give to me. I get out of bed hoping to force them to show themselves yet they resist. I do not understand what our relationship is, if we have one;

that allows them to approach me differently than other humans. What is going on?

Monday, 27 November 2006, nothing happened last night with the aliens. However my oldest son called and my time for "role reversal" has arrived. I know that he loves me and is concerned, or he wouldn't bother. His overall theme was concern for my mental welfare within two areas, one, I haven't dealt with his sister's death and two, the aliens. Apparently my actions have been discussed and judgment rendered. I've told them little of what's going on, and now I can tell them nothing.

I let him talk, "Work it out son," I thought, and while he talked he mentioned several times his "friend" who came out of the closet, and visited every night when he was a little boy. That surprised me as I had thought he had forgotten. That story was told earlier in this book dated Saturday, 26 August 2006.

He finished with his thoughts; we hung up, and I shed a few tears. One never "gets over" the loss of a child, it leaves a hole in your life but time heals, and slowly the hole fills in, or maybe it simply becomes smaller but it never completely goes away.

My son believes that I am a strong woman, and should just banish them from my life. So easily said.

Thursday, 30 November 2006, early last night, I had a dream. At the time I wasn't sure if it was a dream or if it was real. The time was around 1:30 AM.

I pop out of my body and see myself lying on the bed sleeping. I see one of the white balls land on my right eye that I also can see through my closed eyelid. I pop back into my body and feel a zapping of my legs as if an electrical current is shooting through them; I realize that I am familiar with this. My heart begins racing, and I force myself to calm down as I want to maintain control. My body is shifting on the bed; I feel hands on my shoulder moving it realizing that I am laying on my left side and being placed on my back. I think this is amazing. I want to be aware and remember everything. I open my eye and see a cylindrical shaped white light shining down through the ceiling on to the foot of the bed. I mentally prepare myself for the flight up wondering what it will be like as I have been blocked in the past. I think they came straight down through the ceiling rather than through the sliding glass door or bedroom window as I had thought in the past.

The current stopped then started again; I feel my body being shifted again and again; the light appearing and disappearing. I am able to raise my left arm to force my left eyelid open because I want to see what is happening. I am surprised that I can move my hand and arm and at how difficult it is to force the eyelid open. All this time I had thought my eyes were open. I wonder why they keep zapping my legs.

Suddenly I am on the back porch with the babes. The sliding glass door and vertical blinds are no longer there, and the screens and door to the porch are missing as well as the porch furniture. The woman who I know as my "mother" is there, and we are having a conversation when I see Buster and Jezebel are sitting outside in the dark. I express dismay because they will be helpless outside with no claws, cars that can run them over, and diseases for which they have no immunity because they are house cats. I excuse myself and leave to bring them onto the porch, sitting them on the floor where they remain. While I am outside I see my neighbor in her backyard with her little dogs, and hear her calling them to come back inside then she turns off her porch light. Is she part of this dream, if it is one, or has she just returned after being taken?

When I go back inside my mother, standing with her right arm resting on the high back chair in my living room, and I talk. The babes are walking around us then suddenly shoot out on to the porch again. They are excited, and I excuse myself again to go out to see why because the screens and door are missing.

Outside the back door are familiar woods which come within yards of the porch, the small flower bed is no longer by the door; nothing looks like the back of where I live. The babes are growing more excited, and as I watch them I walk closer to where they are standing looking in the direction they are facing. In front of the woods a few feet from us are animals, all kinds of animals. There are birds flying, big healthy rabbits, deer, raccoons and a baby elephant which surprises me. They are larger than real earth animals except for the baby elephant, and they look happy and healthy. The baby deer walks up to where I am and stops facing me, and we look into each other's eyes. It is a sweet little deer, innocent and helpless, and I feel love and understanding flowing from it, and I love it too. I can feel my "mother" standing behind me watching.

My next thought was that I had to go to the bathroom. I knew that I was in my bed, and before I opened my eyes I could smell the little one. I laid there smelling him and realized that it was not a real strong smell but there just the same. I felt a presence by my head and I reached over to stroke its head finding Buster. I was surprised and a little disappointed because I thought it was the little one. I went into the bathroom and back to bed; the odor was gone.

I thought at the time that this had been a dream, but I also thought that it had not been a dream. I was happy that they had let me remember so much and not blocked my memory. I am concerned that I have read so much that now my interpretations could be tainted by what I have read. I had never seen a light shining down through the ceiling onto my bed, nor had I seen little animals before. The being, who I know as my mother, was tall and thin with long dark hair, and did not look at all like my earth mother.

Did they tailor their activities to fit into the context of my personal life? Yes they did. They included everything to keep me calm, and except for that first flash of "fear" that hit me, I was not afraid. Based on what I have read the animals outside, especially the little deer that stared into my eyes, were probably small greys. Were the babes really involved? Was a part of this to let me know that they take my neighbor too? Was the exposure to the feeling of love and understanding in retaliation to my stinging accusation that they have no emotions and would therefore never understand me or any of us? Perhaps all of the above was their intent.

I have never felt my body being shifted in bed; it was done

gently, a portion at a time, an amazing experience. One other thing I remember was that earlier in the afternoon when I had lay down to read and taken a light nap, I was shown a paper with symbols on it. I looked at several different pages with symbols printed in yellowish color written in line after line across each page. I did not understand what I was looking at and got up. Was this in preparation for the night?

What happened last night was more like what I have read. Is this the way it has always happened but was lead to believe otherwise, or have they shifted their ways to match what I think should be happening based on what I have read?

Nothing about them or what is happening to me seems simple, yet it could be. Perhaps I make it complex because I don't understand what or why this is happening inserting answers with which I can cope? Because my summations aren't correct, and the events are beyond my understanding, confusion is created within me. Is that their intent? If I am confused, they have control because they understand what they are doing and I don't. In the end, I have no choice but to do what Devlin has stated time after time, TRUST; and I have difficulty with this. I don't trust them but lack any other alternative when I am with them in their world.

Chapter 19

Saturday, 2 December 2006, I had my third cat dream last night. This situation included my youngest son who was never present, me and an adult male lion. This big cat was sweet, playful, powerful, and as far as I was concerned, potentially dangerous.

I am in the dining room of my youngest son's house with a lion that has a full mane. The lion is friendly wanting to play and be petted. He jumps up placing his paws on my shoulders nearly causing me to collapse from his weight. I'm wondering why my son has this lion in his house, and look around for a cage not seeing one. The lion playfully rolls on the floor at my feet, and I want to put my arms around him and bury my face in his fur but I am afraid of his strength and what his claws can do to me. I thought of the time when our children were little and our daughter had a pet rabbit. The rabbit was litter trained and had the freedom of her room. There were occasions that she brought the rabbit downstairs where it also had freedom to roam, and receive attention from family members. The rabbit and cats soon found each other, and they would play while we watched. One day while playing, the cats began licking the rabbit and as they licked, we saw a subtle change in both. The rabbit froze in his position with his ears back while the cats seemed to become excited. We were witnessing fun play turning into deadly play, each assuming their role of the hunter and the hunted; quickly we rescued the rabbit. I do not want to be the rabbit; there is no one here to rescue me.

I don't understand why my son has left me alone with this huge beast that does not belong caged in a house, that should be running free in the wild from where it came. I have a gun just in case it gets hungry then realize it will be as if a peashooter if needed. I am annoyed that my son has left me alone with this huge beast, and whip out my cell phone to call him. I ask him if he has another gun, a bigger one, and he tells me no but he will send me more bullets, so that I will have a full clip and a better chance to survive. Instantly, from my left, I am handed an envelope, and I thank whoever had handed it to me. I shake the bullets out of the envelope into my hand and see that they are unlike any bullet I have ever seen. They are small with a gumdrop shaped head attached to a thin needle-like rod about one and one-half inch long. As I fill the clip, I wonder how on earth these will be affective.

I am now sitting in a chair with the lion sitting in front of me on the floor, leaning against my knees with his paw in my lap wanting attention. I gently scratch his forehead and behind his ears while calling my son repeatedly about this lion. Eventually I make myself quite clear, "Get your ass home and put this cat into a cage now! This cat should be free, and I don't want to worry that it will have my grandson as a snack."

My dream then transferred to something else which eludes me at this moment. I may remember it later, but I do remember it was totally unrelated to the lion.

As I entered into the second dream I began to realize both were dreams. I woke up and began laughing. The cat dream was absurd and funny, especially the bullets for the gun. The beings just don't understand. A wild lion, although of the cat species, is not the same as a domestic cat. Little lights were blinking in the dark bedroom as I lay there laughing, and shaking my head in amazement of the cat dream and their confusion. They are trying so hard to understand my attachment to cats, regardless of size. I sincerely hope that this dream clarified the distinction between a lion and a housecat. Perhaps they are unaware that when humans become frightened we exude an odor, an odor of fear that animals are able to detect. If this had been real life that lion would have smelled it, gone into action, and I would have been dinner. Surely humans exude the same odor when they are taken by the beings but are the beings able to smell it? Can they smell?

Monday, 4 December 2006, I can remember nothing that happened last night except a new bossy female voice told me to turn out the light, and go to sleep because they were coming, that we had "very important" things to do. I asked her what her name is; she said it was Meadda.

Things do happen around here but I tend to ignore them because they aren't unusual any more, noises after I turn out the lights and go to bed, the cats chasing something I can't see, little balls flying around, and the flashing lights. I've also been seeing little dark things moving around in my bedroom during daylight.

This morning when I got up it was still dark outside, and I usually turn on the bedside light to begin my day, however, this morning I walked directly into the living room towards the computer to boot it up. When I entered the room, there was a lit square sitting on the computer desk at the same level to the right of the monitor then it disappeared.

Saturday, 9 December 2006, I was some place last night and others were there too, but remember nothing. I woke up around 7 AM looking at dark gray writing on the gray ceiling. There was not enough contrast to see clearly what was written, but it was written using English letters. I could make out the word "what", and there was a word beginning with "f", and other letters I recognized. There were approximately six lines of written English words but not clear enough to read and remember. Both cats actively smelled my face and arms, than Jezebel began rooting in my hair and snorting followed by Buster. They have done this before following nights that I think I have been taken. Feeling fine I got out of bed then began experiencing lower abdominal cramping, a severe backache and nausea. I continued my day as planned, but the symptoms persisted throughout well into the next morning.

Thursday, 14 December 2006, I had a lot of anxiety yesterday. I wanted to run away but knew running was futile. If I could get a change of scenery, visit the boys, take a drive into the peaceful mountains, anything that would help get my mind off of the beings but finances are chokingly tight, so I dressed and went to work as scheduled. Implanted in my mind is an impending disaster; a disaster of which I haven't a clue of what it is, or where, or when it will strike. I just feel that it is going to be huge.

Tonight I went to bed following usual protocol, both cats on my right side napping when there was a flash of light in the living room. I got up, looked around, and saw nothing out of place. After turning out the light I could smell one of the little ones. I am having trouble remembering their different smell, and now they seem to smell nearly the same except the newer one is more pungent. The smell became strong as if standing close to the bed. I fell asleep and although waking a few times, I had no trouble going back to sleep. They are just toying with me as usual. Will they continue to do this as long as I respond? What will happen if I ignore them? Will they become more aggressive or will they move on? They are unpredictable. Do I want them to move on? Actually no and yes, I want to know more about them. There are so many unanswered questions and the only way to get them answered is to keep them here.

When I ask the little ones to show themselves the response is always the same, "You will be frightened." Well, of course, I will be frightened because then they will be tangible and will not be able to be blamed on a fruitful imagination. Inexplicably they already are tangible to me.

My ex and I drove north to share Christmas with family and to visit friends. We picked up our grandson on 23 December 2006, to see Santa Claus. The day was his, we did things that he wanted to do, and had a great time watching him enjoy himself. Children have a remarkable gift but you have to be watching for it or it will pass you by. It is the gift of insight into the innocence of uncompromised and uncomplicated sheer joy owned by them at that very moment, and if you are watching, it is yours too.

We stopped at a Chinese restaurant for dinner. Our grandson sat next to me on my left, and his grandfather was seated on the other side of the table. We had ordered and were waiting for our dinner to be prepared and served. The water glass had slipped out of his little hands, and some had spilled onto the white paper placemat. It was a minor spill and easily cleaned up with our napkins. We enjoyed watching him play with a few little toys when he became aware of a wet spot on the paper placemat that was in the shape of a grey's left eye several inches in size. I had noticed it but had said nothing. He pointed to it with his little index finger and said "Their eyes". I said, "Yes". Then he said, "They come, a short one and a tall one." and I said, "Yes". Anger soared through me. How dare they bother this sweet little boy! I hated them.

If his grandfather had not been sitting there I might have carefully questioned him a little. He is only five and would not know what the eyes look like or that there are tall and short ones unless he had seen them himself. I was angry yet not surprised. His two uncomplicated statements answered an unspoken question. How can I protect him?

Thursday, 1 February 2007, there was a full moon and the sky was partly cloudy last night. The pharmacist told me today that people who smoke rarely have dreams, and I would have agreed with him because I rarely had dreams before but since the beings have come I have had vivid dreams.

I am dreaming.

I am in a dark room on a bed with someone to my right who I cannot see. I pop out of my body and stand in the room with a bed to my left where I see myself lying and a door to my right when it flies open. At the same time, I am back in my body and also see the door fly open held by the left hand of a being.

Silhouetted by the hall light behind him, he is short and stocky with rounded shoulders. He is not a grey. He rushes over to where I am and holds me. He is happy to see me, and I am happy to see him. The figure in the room leaves shutting the door and we are alone. I remember nothing after that. Who was this that I was happy to see? I woke up before 5 AM soaked with sweat.

I am reading *Connections: Solving Our Alien Abduction Mystery* by Beth Collings and Anna Jamerson.

Tuesday, 6 February 2007, I have been giving considerable thought regarding the balls especially the white balls. I am wondering if they are able to carry scents. For instance, when I get the odor of either of the little ones has it been released from a white ball giving me the impression that one of them is here? I also read or heard that the balls are actually their ships and I think that is accurate.

The beings have become more secretive in hiding their presence, and I do not understand why this is necessary after such an explosion of activity in September, 2005. I would never know they were here if I had not gone through this experience. I have wondered if I have been "trained" to be aware of their presence because anyone else in the room would not be aware that anything was happening. Why have they done this?

Thoughts from reading: Whitley Strieber in *Communion* tells his alien mother that she has no right to do whatever it was she was doing, and he says her response was she did have a right. In *Connections: Solving Our Alien Abduction Mystery* by Collings and Jamerson, a similar question was asked and the response to the woman was they were their possession. Are we owned by aliens who are entitled to do whatever they want to us? I don't believe that, do you? Captured animals for scientific study are probed and examined then released back into the wild but we don't own them; they are not our possession; and yes, sometimes those same animals are recaptured and studied again. Does this sound uncomfortably familiar?

Since they made their presence known there is never a day when I close the blinds as the sun sets that I do not think of them, and wonder what lies in store for the night, if anything. They have had a definite impact on and in my life but they do not own me.

Monday, 19 February 2007, this morning I woke at 5:00 AM while it was still dark, and felt as if I hadn't slept at all. I am always tired. I got up on my hands and knees, as I had been lying on my stomach and looked to the left seeing a red blob hanging in the air over the left side of my bed. I drug myself out of bed not turning on the light and walked into the living room, a white flash appeared from the wall with the window. This is the way it has been now for a while, they are here watching but it is quiet.

Wednesday, 21 February 2007, on my way home from work last night the voice, whoever it is now, said, "We are coming tonight". "Yah, sure you are," I replied. It asked, "Do you want to see us?" and I answered, "Hell yes." "You will be scared," it said and I replied, "Not anymore."

I followed my usual routine and after working ten hours yesterday I was tired and went to bed. When I was coming out of the bathroom a white ball bounced off of my chest followed by seeing two faces. The only one I remember is a green face with a brown hat and brown coat or jacket, reminding me of a frog then it started shape-shifting then vanished. After I got into bed and settled there were three sets of flashes in duplicate. I fell asleep and remember nothing.

Chapter 20

Thursday, 22 February 2007, yesterday evening I was preparing for bed when out of nowhere the voice said, "We are coming tonight." (This is getting old) "Sure," I said, "you lie as usual." "No! I do not lie!" said the voice. I replied, "You lie all of the time. You just talk and pay no attention to what you say. I believe nothing you say." "We are coming tonight and we are going to scare you," the voice threatened. "You only make my heart beat faster because of your energy field," I replied, "and that doesn't mean that I am scared, it is only a reaction. I am ready for you." He replied, "You have been prepared." Nothing happened that I remember.

I turned off the light at 11:30 and fell asleep easily on Saturday, 24 February 2007. I become aware of a complex dream involving multiple adults and children, all of whom I know intimately but cannot remember who they are.

We are in a building with many rooms, and yet it seems more like a stage setting; things aren't quite right. We are standing around as a group. Most of the people there are children with some adults present. We are watching a tall heavyset man dressed in red wearing a long white beard divided down the middle with each side tapering to a point and curling outward towards his arms. I think Santa Claus but there is something wrong with this one. I am in the position of protector, and know this man is not a good person that he is a deceiver. I attack him by jumping onto his body from the front clasping my legs around his waist, and I'm going to either strangle him with his tapered beard or try to pull it out. From a distance the beard looked white but up close it is yellow tinged, and I have that nasty yellow tinged tapered beard wrapped around my fisted hands.

I am pulling on it trying to wrap the beard ends around his neck but it is too short to strangle him with it, so I decide to pull it out. We are face to face and he looks startled, and I am pleased; he is a bastard. I became aware that I am dreaming.

There was a flicker of white light by my right eye followed by what looked like multiple layers of yellow "chicken scratches" which separated becoming clear symbols. The majority of symbols seemed to be straight lines that followed each other on a page, and my instinct was to read it right to left from top to bottom as the page began to move upward rather quickly. I opened my eyes and could see the same symbols on the wall by the window where I have seen writing multiple times. I tried to lie there as if I wasn't awake thinking that, perhaps, I could deceive whoever was in control of the writing but the writing disappeared, and I found myself awake at 1:33 AM.

I believe that most events occur within my bedroom, as did this one. I believe the lights that land on my eyes are emitted from the balls or are the balls themselves, and possibly, the sounds and smells are from them as well. The balls are able to create the bright white flashes that I see. Are the balls able to morph into a rectangle that I have seen throughout? If this is so, then who or whatever is in the ball is also in the rectangle. Or is the rectangle a different vehicle from the balls? Does the being within the rectangle coordinate the action of the balls? Are all of them, the balls and rectangle, able to project holograms or is the rectangle itself a hologram projected from a ball? When the picture of the box on the bed is viewed, there appears the dimension of depth within it; how is this possible if it is not a hologram or was there actually a clear fronted vehicle on the bed? Are the balls recording and sending pictures of what they see to another source that in turn, for a closer view, can appear within a contained rectangle unseen by human eyes? I am not versed in physics so I am unable to answer any of these questions, only able to ask them.

I speculate they have inserted something within my left eye that allows me to receive dreams, writing, and even pictures but I'm not sure. I'm not sure of anything.

I looked up the stages of sleep on the Internet. Apparently there are five stages of sleep and stage four, NREM (Non Rapid Eye Movement) and stage five, REM (Rapid Eye Movement) are where most dreaming takes place. If these stages are disrupted by interfered with dreams could this be the reason why I am so tired in the mornings?

What is the purpose of the writing; writing that I can neither read nor understand? It seems important to them as they continue presenting it to me. Are the different forms of writing merely a tool used to confuse me, or to create curiosity, or are they searching to see which of the types of writing is stored deep within my memory from a distant past, a genetic carry-over? Is that even possible?

My buddy suggested it might be in preparation for my next life. Do these alien mortals have the ability to know my future death date and prepare me for my next existence? If they are from the future, it is possible they do know my death date, and the reading skills I will need for my next existence. Is it possible information is carried within my DNA and they know nothing about me except what the DNA tells them? Does DNA contain the past, present and future revealed to their scientists who can decipher it?

Wednesday, 28 February 2007, I worked both jobs yesterday sleeping so hard last night that I woke up grumpy and confused as to where I was and which job I should go to today.

Last night I watched a recording of *Digging For the Truth* with Josh Bernstein, the episode about Ramses II. As Josh walked down a street there was writing on the outside of the buildings which looked similar to some of the writing that I have seen on the wall here, lots of curly cues and dots.

Monday, 5 March 2007, I received an interesting email from my buddy dated 3/1/07 regarding an experience she had in the early morning of the same date. The being she saw may be similar to the one I captured on film in my living room; the being that has now disappeared from the picture. It could have been one who came or was sent to protect her from the tornados occurring in her area. Who knows? She felt this being was from a different group, and I wonder if it is the same group that visits me.

Something was here last Friday night as I was falling asleep, I had the distress of fear and knew something was in the room with me then the feeling promptly went away and I went to sleep.

Tuesday, 6 March 2007, last night as I pulled up to the house after work, I saw that there was a beautiful full moon. Joseph said they were coming. Yah, sure, I thought. I fell asleep with no prelude and slept heavy all night waking up with both babes on the bed and Jezebel trying to wake me up; she wanted her breakfast.

During my shower I found fresh scratch marks on both legs, a puncture mark on my abdomen at the waist, and the left half of my face is red as if sunburned. Over the years the left side of my face has developed deep wrinkling. Is this a result of the "sunburn" or is it genetic. My mother's face wrinkled evenly.

Friday, 9 March 2007, I accepted a full time position, so today will be my last day with a group of people I have enjoyed working with. It is a sad day for me but I have to consider the responsibility of mom's and my monetary needs.

Wednesday, 14 March 2007, I wake from a dream.

I am standing in a circle talking with a group of greys. I look down at my left thigh that has caused me some discomfort lately. There is about an inch of wood the diameter of a pencil protruding from the upper, outer left thigh, exactly at the spot that has been hurting. I pull on it and keep pulling until the pencil is pulled out of my thigh. It is at least a foot long, and the end that had been in my thigh is sharp like a sharpened pencil. I see there is no hole in the skin from where the pencil was pulled. I am satisfied that I am now rid of the pain caused by it. Did this have something to do with the dream where I shot my son in the thigh on Sunday, 8 October 2006?

Friday, 16 March 2007, for the past two nights when I have gotten up to go into the bathroom, I have seen yellowish writing no matter where I look or how often I blink. I believe the writing is in my eyes not on the wall. They are not characters that I know how to read and understand but are ones that I have seen often. Last night they were separated and floated around; the night before they were stacked on each other and moving around. Neither night did they straighten out in a line as if printed on a page. They just want me to know that they are here and still have control, the simpering pile of feces.

My buddy sent an email telling me that she was probably taken early this morning. She doesn't remember anything but being pulled from her chair, the wind blowing on her and then waking up in the chair later. It's always traumatic and unsettling for days.

On Sunday, 18 March 2007, I went to bed after 12 AM and fell asleep quickly. I am dreaming.

I am surrounded by darkness standing in a circle with a group of humans and greys, more humans than greys; two of the humans are my sons. We are having a significant discussion that explains everything. I think, "Oh, so that is what this is all about." We shake hands or something is handed to me directing my attention to our hands. I am becoming more aware that this is a dream and am being pulled away from the group. As I am pulled away, I think I must remember what has been said and record it; but the further I am pulled away the fainter the information I wanted to remember becomes, until when I sit up in the bed there is nothing to remember.

What was said that was significant and satisfied my curious mind? Were the two men my sons or was this a "worry" dream about their safety and the hope that they are not being "taken". They seemed to be dressed in dark clothing, at least my one son was whom I could see clearly, while the other stood next to me on my left, so I was not looking at him only aware that he was there. What were our hands doing? Were we shaking hands or passing something? When I thought that I must remember what had been said, that is when I began being pulled back. Was it a dream of frustration searching for elusive answers or had I been given the answers?

Monday, 19 March 2007, while in the kitchen beating batter for a cake, a different female voice began talking to me. The voice asked me questions that I attempted to answer. We finally arrived to the question of who is this, and she replied that she was one of the beings. I again said that I wanted to see them and did not understand why they hold back. I was given the standard answer that I would be frightened and they didn't want that. I told her what I felt was not fear, but a physical reaction to their force field or whatever it is they use. Suddenly there was a powerful overwhelming smell of malodorous feces. I noted how different it was from the two little one's odors and mentally commented on the odor not intending for her to hear my thought. She was indignant replying, "We have a digestive tract too but it is different from yours." What could I say? She and the odor went away.

Thursday, 29 March 2007, I have suspected that there are nights I do not spend the entire time in bed, so I attached a pedometer to the waist of my pajama bottoms last night. It is not there this morning nor is it in the bedding or on the floor.

I went to an ENT specialist and have to admit since I am eating a soft diet and taking allergy meds the ringing in my left ear is becoming less. I am scheduled for a MRI to rule out a brain tumor.

I went to the ophthalmologist to have my eyes examined. She couldn't find a reason why my left eyeball aches periodically and to see her when it does. Well that is near impossible, as it doesn't ache for days on end, just now and then. She said that I have few floaters.

Sunday Morning, 3:36 AM, 1 April 2007, I took pictures tonight in the dark; the following is what happened taken from an email sent to my buddy.

I probably won't be doing this again for a long time as I have just had the living crap scared out of me! It happened during the last group of pictures taken with the lights off. I didn't get many taken because the flash didn't always work. I am walking through the dark snapping pictures, and my ears are ringing like crazy. I turned around to snap the birdhouse chair area, and the camera flash once again didn't go off. I stood there determined to get a picture, and when the flash went off I was blinded. I stood looking towards the floor area that I had shot because I had inadvertently lowered the camera.

When I look up there is a huge hazy white oval about five feet high or maybe a little taller no less than five feet in front of me that. At first I thought it was a result of the flash temporally blinding me. I studied the oval noting its shape and the fact that I was unable to see through it then I became aware that in the bottom of the oval, something is moving! The movement is about a foot above the floor moving in a continuous silent zigzag motion within the bottom of the oval. The motion was akin to that of a small child riding in one of those old fashioned little toy cars propelled by pushing foot pedals back and forth with the feet. I wondered if that was how the oval was propelled or was it an engine of some kind.

I stood there absolutely transfixed unaware of anything else except the vision in front of me. I chuckled saying, "I can see you!" and it started slowly floating towards me. I was trying to figure out what it was----a type of ship, one of the balls that changed shape, some sort of armament---and wondering if this thing has been in my house all along but is just now, finally, going to let me see them while I am awake. I stood waiting for them to make the first move, to materialize.

My mind, a whirlwind of thought, left the wonder of what was before me moving into considering what danger to me it represented, and my imagination took control. I thought the thing moving in the oval was about the same size, maybe a little bigger then that red worm like thing that keeps popping up, and what the hell is it? Is it one of them or something else? Meanwhile it is leisurely getting closer, and all I could think of were red worms turning into blood sucking leeches. My nerves of steel buckled. I took one giant step backward, extended my right arm, and flipped on the kitchen light. I could no longer see it.

I can guarantee that a light will be on all night in this household! Wow, it scared the shit out of me! All my bravado and I head for the light!

It's 3:56 AM and I've had enough white wine that I should be able to sleep. Maybe I will turn out the light after all. You know what perplexes me is what is their purpose in all of this? It doesn't make much sense in human terms. Was this a result of my continued challenges of wanting to see them? It probably was and some being had a good laugh at my expense.

Chapter 21

Easter Morning, Sunday, 8 April 2007. Yesterday I cleaned, vacuuming every room even under the beds. Then I looked under every piece of furniture where the pedometer could have slid but didn't find it. So where is it? I will keep looking.

Friday, 13 April 2007, I turned off the light and lay waiting to fall asleep able to smell the little one. I rolled over onto my right side facing the bathroom door with my eyes closed. I heard the sound of static electricity followed by a click and a bang on the bedside table by my head. My first thought was maybe they had brought back the pedometer. I opened my eyes and seeing nothing, I turned on the light to see if the pedometer was on the bedside table. It wasn't. The smell of the little one intensified, and I mentally said, "Hi, I smell you" and he replied, "Yes, I am here". "Where have you been?" I asked, "I have been sent somewhere else," he answered. "Why?" I inquired. He replied, "We were getting too close, and that is not allowed. I will come when I can."

There were white balls flying around some bombarding my face and eyes. I rolled over onto my back trying to relax becoming hot, kicking the covers off, and fell asleep thinking it was interesting that he had been moved because we were getting too close, and that they do form attachments. I thought of the times he taught me how to resist the fear of being taken, to recognize it as a force field rather than fear; the night that he and the other one changed positions so that I would recognize their difference in smell; the night he placed his hand between mine and I stroked his head; the night I looked through his eyes at myself in bed. I will miss him.

Sunday, 15 April 2007, around 1:30 AM I staggered off to the bedroom with my camera in hand, turned off the light, and began taking pictures starting in the bedroom working my way throughout the house in the dark. The camera was not working properly; the flash was not going off as it should. I thought the new batteries were dead but when I turned it off then back on, I could get one picture with a flash having to do this repeatedly. When they are here I often have trouble with the camera. There were heavy rains last night, so I hadn't expected to capture anything; why the difficulty with the flash? Once when the camera flashed, I saw two red eyes looking back but when the picture was downloaded there was nothing, not even red objects that could reflect red.

The pedometer is still missing.

Tuesday, 17 April 2007, well, guess what! I found the pedometer today! It was lying on a shoebox in the closet. Why would I have put it there? I am one of those people that put things back where they belong, so I can find them the next time needed.

 Nothing is going on here except work, eat, sleep and pay bills.

Sometime after 1:29 AM last night, Wednesday, April 18th, 2007, I sit bolt upright in bed from a sound sleep and looked at the clock then fall back asleep.

Suddenly I am awake with two beings at my bedside. I am surprised and excited that I can see them standing there, and then my eyes close. I yell, "No! I want to see you!" I begin shaking my head from side to side and saying, "No, no, I want to see!" willing my eyes to open and open they did.

I pop out of my body and stand to the left of the greys slightly to the side of myself sitting on the bed. I watch the two little greys hold my arms up and out in front of my body. I am back in my body sitting on the bed facing them. Their heads are much broader at their eye and forehead level than I had expected making their faces look shorter and rounder with a pointed chin. Their faces look streetwise without any feature to soften their looks, and they look determined but not threatening. Their two heads are close together with one slightly in front and to the side of the other as if posed by a photographer. They have big eyes and a nose of sorts, but my eyes are focused on their mouths. I think that they are trying to smile at me, instead they look like they are grimacing with their mouths slightly open exposing their teeth. The tiny teeth are pointed! The reactionary thought that runs through my mind is all they need is blood dripping from their mouths.

Then one is on each side of me with their arms linked through mine that are hanging at my sides. One of them or possibly a third I have not seen peers deeply into my eyes with his eyes becoming my entire world. I vaguely remember flying with one on each side of me.

We are sitting on chairs with me in the middle. I ask the being in front of us, who I can't see, if I can touch the little ones and permission is given. I turn to the one on my left and begin touching the skin on his head and his right arm. When I gently rub my hand down the back and side of his head several times, the area develops a pinkish tinge. The skin is smooth and firm yet slightly rough, a little like a very fine grade of sandpaper but not abrasive. I bend my head down to look closer at the skin on his arm; suddenly it is as though I am looking through a microscope that is magnifying the skin. It seems to be composed of six sided scales. I use the word scale because I don't know any other word to describe what I see, but I don't think they are scales, maybe skin cells. In the center of each one is a tiny dab of brownish color while the color surrounding it is white producing the overall color of gray.

I hold his forearm gently pressing with my fingers and thumb finding there is no muscle or adipose tissue softness under the skin. I am thinking it feels as if his arm is nothing more than skin and an underlying hardness, like bone. It is literally skin and bones. Suddenly he becomes pudgy and soft which surprises me, so I turn to the one on my right and he too has become pudgy. I am thinking this is not right, they have become soft and pudgy like me when they are supposed to be skinny. I was concerned that I had offended or hurt the one I was examining.

I find myself standing in front of them and they are both still pudgy. I see an empty chair between them where I must have sat. They are intently watching me, and I have the feeling they are playing a joke on me but I also wondered if they had had enough of my touching and feeling.

I awake lying on my stomach with a pain in my neck as I am in an uncomfortable position, and have that funny feeling in my head. This funny feeling is similar to waking up with a hangover only different, and although the heaviness and discomfort is there, it soon passes.

This morning I realize that I had not been afraid once, and there had been no odors. There had been darkness behind the chairs as I stood in front of them, so I couldn't tell what was behind them. The chairs looked the same as in the ceremony looking much like our metal folding chairs. I have bruises on my thighs and left leg today.

They come, disrupt your life and leave as if they have never been there then you wait until they come again at their leisure, meanwhile your life is in turmoil.

Friday, 27 April 2007, my buddy believes they let us know in some way before they come and I think she is right. These beings seem involved in our lives. Did the ancients have the same experience and credit them as visitations from angels and visions from God especially the writing on the wall? It would be easy to do. It is such an enigma.

Saturday, 28 April 2007, I had a restless night last night waking up multiple times with the last time at 5 AM; I was hot. I got up to flip on the ceiling fan switch by the bedroom door and as I approached the door, a huge white circle within a circle appeared before my eyes wiping out my vision. I flipped the switch, went back to bed and slept until 7 AM. I looked in the mirror this morning and saw a stranger. I have bags under my eyes, and I not only feel tired but look tired. They are slowly killing me.

Sunday, 29 April 2007, I slept well and woke up feeling

great! It is a beautiful day for working in the garden. I have plenty to do but will need to wait until the pansies die before replacing them with marigolds, and for the Irises to stop blooming because I want to transfer them. I love flowers. The generations of farmer's blood coursing through my veins loves the smell and feel of dirt too.

Monday, 7 May 2007, poor mom fell asleep and slid out of her chair fracturing her hip. She has had a hip pinning procedure, and will need nursing home placement for rehabilitation. My sister arrived early last Saturday morning, and we have been occupied with mom's needs, present and future.

That evening we dug into our meals as if we hadn't eaten in days. So many decisions to make left us not only exhausted but also famished. We had visited local combination nursing homes and rehabilitation facilities based on state survey results. A white ball flew near our table while we ate but she didn't see it. After dinner a black ball flew across the room that she also didn't see but then she isn't looking for them like I am.

We were discussing the "beings" while she looked through my pictures. She admitted that she was hesitant to come because she didn't know what would happen expressing it as "self-preservation". As she talks about her feelings, I am told they are coming tonight.

Both of us had trouble sleeping, got up, had a snack, and went back to bed. The letters came in a jumble, separated then trailed out, and I had no idea what they meant. My closed eyes switched to faces that I don't remember seeing before. There was a flash of light in the room, and I knew they were here but when I opened my eyes I saw nothing, then falling asleep waking up periodically trying to find a comfortable position.

Upon waking this morning, my sister tells me she thinks was "taken" last night. She says she was terrified and screamed for me, begging them to bring me to her instead she ended up in my empty bed then walked to her own. I remember nothing.

Sunday morning at 12:29 AM, 13 May 2007, my sister drew a picture of the being she saw her first night and tried to explain how she felt physically. The ones that came for her were dressed in blue and seemed to have some sort of headdress, a cap or helmet, reminding her of the habits Roman Catholic nuns use to wear when we were kids. She said there were two of them suddenly appearing at her bedside, and that she began screaming for me. She told them that she did not want to remember, and they replied that she had said that she did and admits she had done. Other then the above she remembers nothing except ending up in my empty bed.

Sunday, 13 April 2007, I went to bed around 3:00 AM falling asleep on my stomach. I am dreaming.

I am at a party, I don't know where it is but everything seems familiar, and I know that I have been there many times. Then it dawns on me that I am at the house of a former high school friend with whom I have had no contact since graduating in 1960. There are many people there that I do not know. Her mom and dad are there but I think both are dead now yet I wasn't surprised to see them. I saw a man I recognized as my friend's brother who was a few years ahead of my class, and who I had had a crush on. We made eye contact, nodded our heads in acknowledgement, and went our separate ways.

There are a lot of small children running around receiving attention from everyone there. There are cute babies sitting on the floor watching the people. They are not crying or seemingly frightened. There is a lot of noise, and the pleasant flowing music gives a feeling of festiveness as if at a Medieval Christmas party.

I wonder around looking at the rooms and their furnishings then using the metal handrail, I climb the open metal steps to go upstairs to the balcony surrounding the ground floor. I do not know anyone on the balcony, so I return to the lower level.

I am wondering around and pass through a door finding myself in a hallway with a shiny wall to the left and vendor stands to the right. Everyone is very busy scurrying around doing their thing. They look at me while continuing their work. I am surprised to find vendors in this setting but I don't question it. I finally find a door on the right that seems to be the ladies room, open it, and walk in.

Inside the room there is a tall women with long dark hair dressed in a below-the-knee length black dress with a white frilly apron like waitresses use to wear in the 1950s. She is getting from or putting something into a closet, and looks annoyed when I walked in. There are two closed doors next to the closet, and both doors are the old fashioned wooden ones with a large panel at the top and bottom.

I start for the door to go back out when it opens and a woman my age walks in. She is a little shorter than me and a little over weight. She is pale with blond hair and blue eyes, her make-up is applied perfectly, and she is dressed in a black skirt and a horizontal striped black and yellow long sleeved lightweight sweater. We look each other over but say nothing, and I notice that her facial expression is one of haughtiness. She rushes to the third door shutting it behind her, and I walk out into the hall and into a large room.

I am amused to see my ex-husband is there as he has always denied there could be aliens and spaceships. He is standing with his arms crossed over his chest looking around as if in shock then looking up, he studies the ceiling. I also look up and see a huge dome which must be three or four stories above us, and seems to be made of metal and glass through which the beautiful universe can be seen speckled with stars. The area we are standing in is massive.

There is a man reclining on a fainting couch watching me; I walk over to him and we talk. His voice is different, very low with a different quality then a human voice. His face keeps shape shifting, so I do not know what he looks like. I smile at him and know he is smiling back.

I see a cute human looking baby on the floor, pick him up and cuddle him then carry the baby to the being on the couch. Smiling at me, he says that we will talk later and I nod. I take the baby back to my friend's house, take off his clothes, and he quickly crawls away down the hall. I stand there watching the baby and the people in the area then find I am back in the great room. I wake up lying prone on my bed.

Tuesday, 15 May 2007, for the past two nights prior to going to bed, I have seen white balls the size of marbles flying close to the floor. The voice in my head said they were coming last night but I didn't tell my sister. The next morning my sister said that she dreamt as usual but nothing strange. I had some sort of a dream and did not feel well when I woke up. It was that same feeling I've had before when they have brought me back, and while laying there, I realized that I have had this feeling off and on throughout my life prompting me to wonder if I've been taken far longer then I think. I have a feeling that something is about to happen, not worldwide but personally. I feel as if I am running in circles, in fact, I want to run away and find relief from what I don't know. Thank God, my sister is here to visit with mom because I just can't do it every day any more, I am so tired.

Chapter 22

Friday, 18 May 2007, last night, after I had turned off the light and lay on my right side, a ball hit my left eye and shortly after the parade of faces began. Initially I usually lay on my left side and it is the left eye, the eye closest to the pillow, where I see the little lit ball followed by visions of faces until last night. This confirms to me that there is something in the left eye they use to send their visions. It also confirms the visions of faces I see on my eyelids are sent through the little ball. By what method and by who is the ball guided? I can see no purpose in this other than to let me know that they are still here and trying to influence me. I decided I don't want to see these faces any longer that I don't know if the faces are real or only their creation designed for me. I told them to stop this and let me meet the actual being. Just to clarify, the faces I see are not a still picture; they move, blink, change eye direction, and sometimes, look directly at me as if they are alive and can see me.

Monday, 28 May 2007, 4:49 PM, I worked today and found every down moment was filled with thinking about the dream I had last night.

One of the boys, ages four and six, has an appointment at the children's hospital. I decide that we should leave while it is still dark in order to arrive on time for the early morning appointment. We take a shortcut that will place us there even earlier, and turn off of a blacktopped road onto a dirt road. The road is overgrown with vegetation from the sides and over the top forming a tunnel that we drive through. We come to a curve to the left where there is another tunnel that we pass through. At the end of this tunnel there is a rounded entrance with a ramp leading down into a large round cave.

We get out of the car. I am not sure where we are, but one of the boys recognizes the place and knows who lives here. Sitting around the room are old-fashioned overstuffed furniture. There are tables with lamps and several pictures hanging on the walls. Along one wall there is a closed door with a rounded top, and at the other end of the wall there is a rounded entrance into a round room with a smooth ramp leading down into it.

"Boys," I instruct, "stay close because we have to be at the hospital and will have to leave soon." The boys start running around, and find a friend who is a close friend of the youngest but now seems to be a closer friend of the oldest. I am surprised at this change in friendship and wonder if the youngest feelings are hurt, but he doesn't act as if they are.

A woman walks into the room, and one of the boys introduces her as the mother of the friend. She has long black hair, very pale, and is dressed in a black dress with a white apron. She is pleasant, and excuses herself as she has something to do.

The youngest is with me but I cannot see the oldest. We proceed walking towards the rounded entrance way down the descending ramp and stand in the round room. I hear rushing water, and see a huge wave coming from a large entrance on the left side of the room. I automatically grab my youngest sitting him on my left hip securely holding him in place with my left arm. I am running towards my oldest son who I see in the room soon to be covered with water possibly carried away with the wave into the rounded entrance on the right side of the room.

I am surrounded by water, jumping up and down, and know that I have one chance to save my oldest son. I bounce off of the floor bottom again, and when I break the surface I see an arm sticking out of the water. I lunge in his direction desperately grabbing for him, and feel my hand close around his arm. I know that I have him, and I will not let go of either of them no matter what. The wave passes on through the room leaving my oldest and me standing on the floor looking at each other with me still tightly gripping his arm and the youngest sitting on my hip clutched to my body. I see the floor is dry and we are not wet. We should be dripping wet.

I never quite see the oldest one's face. He has blond hair and is wearing a dark T-shirt with a long sleeved green camouflaged patterned button-down-the-front shirt over it. He indicates that he is fine. "Stay close to me, son. I don't want anything to happen to you," I say, and he nods at me.

I then look at my youngest and take a second look because his face is not natural; he has no expression and is more like a picture of his face. I know it is my son, and I know I have seen that face before but I don't remember him looking like this all of the time. He certainly shouldn't be looking like this after what we have been through. "Are you okay?" I ask. He says, "Yes, I am fine." Both boys should be terrified at what has just happened but they don't seem to be, and I'm not either.

The three of us walk up the ramp into the room where the overstuffed furniture is and the car is parked. I tell the boys that we must leave or we will be late for the appointment but first I have to go to the bathroom, and does either of them know where it is. The oldest takes me to the closed round topped door in the room and opens it for me. I tell them both to wait outside of this door and do not move until I come out.

Inside the room there is a sink and a regular toilet, hallelujah, a regular toilet! As I sit down the seat rotates to the left, and I am looking out into the large room. The car is no longer there, and many women are busily walking back and forth, some empty handed while others are carrying silver looking metal trays. They are pale tall thin women with long black hair and wearing black dresses with white aprons. None of them look in my direction or seem aware that I am looking at them through a wall that does not exist.

The boys and I get into the car, drive up the ramp through the cave-like entrance, around the curves, back down the road with the tree covered tunnel, and are back onto the road to the hospital.

While talking on the phone later that day, I see a picture hanging on the wall that is the same face as the son I saw in the dream. At first I thought it was funny then I realized they knew what he looked like when he was little, and then I was angry. Bastards, they know too much about us!

I knew at the time that these were probably not my boys, and wondered if they were little greys playing their role. There was something not quite right about them but they seemed to be enjoying what we were doing. I was also aware that the dream involved a space ship, and probably black holes, exhibited by the tunnels. I reacted as I would have if it had been my own children. We were role-playing.

Tuesday, 29 May 2007, I woke up lying on my stomach and felt as if my body had sunk deep within the mattress becoming a part of it. I looked at the clock it was 11:29 PM. I went into the bathroom, and when I got back into the bed the clock said 11:19. Impossible, I had to have misread it! I saw a bright white flash followed by a red one and knew they were here and was excited, asking them to let me see and remember. Then I heard my sister's bed creak, and got up to see if they were taking her. I stood in her doorway for a while watching her as she lay on her back sleeping; she was safe. I went back to bed and the flashes reoccurred then I became aware of a humming noise on the other side of my bedroom wall but I did not go outside to investigate the cause. The sound turned into an air-conditioner and a car motor, but there had been another sound which was now gone. I fell asleep.

Wednesday, 6 June 2007, I have awakened within the past two weeks, twice during the night and once in the morning, with my teeth firmly clamped onto a part of my tongue that seems to have an object in it. It has been the same spot and the same size each time, yet when I release it or feel my tongue there doesn't seem to be an object there.

Tuesday, 12 June 2007, I had another dream about cats last night, this time it featured Jezebel, who is my beautiful long legged all black cat. I can't remember the details although I told myself I would at the time, so the story will be incomplete.

I am outside looking at the black sky filled with shining stars. The time is the Middle Ages, and the location is a little village with thatch roofed huts. I am an innocent woman accused of something that has to do with cats. I place a curse on the entire village but mostly on the people who have accused me. The curse involves Jezebel who I know will be killed to avoid the curse coming to pass. I tell them if any cat jumps into my lap I will be found innocent. I feel badly knowing that I have condemned poor Jezebel and all of the other cats in the village. The dream ends, and I wake up at 1:29 AM, hot, sweaty and disturbed. I felt as if I had stepped back into the past, a past full of darkness, ignorance, and fear.

Wednesday, 12 June 2007, I was very tense last night as I lay in bed with my eyes closed. The workday had been one of pressure to conclude the inventory that we had to leave unfinished and will have to complete today. Eventually I began to unwind and relax. There were several white balls that hit my eyes, than a faint red flash followed a few minutes later by a room dazzling white flash. I opened my eyes and seeing nothing, I closed them again. I begun to see something that I thought was outer space, the universe, as if floating in it, and picked up speed zooming towards something. There were faces, objects and geometrically designed objects in clear white bright light. I didn't know what to look at first but the faces drew my attention as they were unlike anything yet seen.

I would zoom up to one, pause then shoot off to another

one. As this was happening, I was not only thinking about what I was seeing, the faces, the geometric designs, and the brilliant light, but how they can get into my mind and control what happens while I am fully awake lying in my bed. I am in two places at once, the physical place on the bed and the non-physical place up here. A huge grey face with its large eyes appeared in front of mine. I fell asleep, and do not remember dreaming.

Thursday 14 June 2007, after turning off the light and closing my eyes I could see curly-cue swirls and some other designs and knew they were here. I heard my sister's bed creaking and got up to check on her. She was stretched out on the bed sleeping, so I went back to bed. When I closed my eyes there was a bright flash of light, and I could see a pattern off in the distance. There was nothing around it, no walls, no ceiling only it as if it were the floor. It was a large rectangle made of bluish-black and white tiles forming a lovely intricate design reminiscent of middle-eastern designs seen in museums. It covered half of the floor while the other side did not have the design but something else that I could not identify, and I remember it as being blank. I was zooming in for a closer look when something black with hunched shoulders, two arms and legs ran across it. I felt a jolt of fear, but it left as quickly as it had come and the scene changed. I was awake and looked at the clock; it was 1:29 AM. There were white and blue balls flying around the room and when I closed my eyes again, I saw curly-cues followed by a baby grey with huge eyes and remember nothing else.

Tuesday, 19 June 2007, I called out from work yesterday due to illness. My sister left to run errands while I laid down to rest and awoke finding a huge dark blue bruise with a surface scrape on the front part of my upper left arm that I did not have when I laid down. This is the second dark bruise like this I have awakened with on this arm. I have walked around trying to match up what I might have hit my arm on to cause such a bruise but have found nothing the right height. Someone at work today said it looked like I had been pinched very hard.

Friday, 22 June 2007, last night I awoke smelling the little one and welcomed him. He is fine and has been busy, and when he left I had the impression that he is never far away, or maybe I don't want him to be far away, and why is that? Why do I feel close to him? Why the hell am I involved with him or any of them?

My sister and I met with a pleasant representative of Medicaid instructing me to obtain a QID trust for mom while she remains in the nursing home. We climbed back into the June heated car, and headed for my bank, Bank of America. After several hours of jumping through hoops, we learned that their legal department still wasn't "happy". We left in confusion and disillusionment. What could be so difficult, we had complied with everything they had requested.

On our way back home we passed a Wachovia bank, did a u-turn, pulled into their parking lot, walked in with high hopes, and our fingers crossed for good luck. A few phone calls were made, papers signed, explanations given, EIN number obtained, Social Security notified by the bank and I walked out with a QID trust account for mom. In our estimation, we had just received the epitome of customer service. It was with pleasure and satisfaction that I closed moms and my accounts and withdrew my meager IRA from Bank of America over the next month transferring all accounts to Wachovia.

We arrived home to learn my grandson requires major surgery plunging my spirits into despair and concern for him and his parents.

I had taken the week off from work to get everything squared away for mom, and it has taken every minute of this time to get it done. Today I ran the papers to Medicaid, did several trivial but necessary chores, and then devoted some time to the clutter of bills on my neglected desk.

My sister is winding up her visit and plans on leaving soon. I will miss her.

Sunday, 24 June 2007, we ate and made every attempt to unwind after a busy and successful week of trying to please all of the powers that be to get Medicaid established for our mother. We cleaned up the kitchen, placing the last dish in the dishwasher when her cell phone rang, and she went into her bedroom to take the call.

I sat on the couch flipping through TV channels finding none of interest when I noticed there was a slight movement by my bedroom door. There is an English oak dresser with dark patina sitting by the door and the end of the dresser did not look right. There was something trying to blend in with the wood but not quite succeeding. I could see the body, arms and legs and a head which size was appropriate to the body size, then the face became clear and I knew it was not a grey. I looked away thinking that I had manufactured this in my head, and when I looked back it was still there. I blinked, looked at the TV set and then back, and it was still there. I watched waiting to see what was going to happen next when there was a movement. It was not a movement that I could see, but rather one that I could feel or somehow was aware when it shot from the end of the dresser to the front of another piece of wood furniture closer to me. I was unable to visualize this little being on this piece of furniture, unable to tell if he had vanished or was camouflaged on the furniture.

Eventually I grew tired and went to bed with white balls flying around. As I closed my eyes white dots hit my eyes and lingered, and I began to see shape-shifting faces. I was taken into space floating among the stars, and in a flash there was a luminous white triangle and I slept. I remember nothing else.

Saturday, 30 June 2007, last night before bed I was told they were coming but the weather was stormy, and I do not remember anything happening. I had been told that we both would be taken as we had to come to a decision. What are they talking about?

As my sister and I talked over morning coffee, she sensed a feeling of electricity or some sort of current that surges through your body, and she said they are here. I could feel it also; my heart was racing and knew that she was right. I fought the feeling eventually getting it under control. We both felt that they or one of them was going to appear before us but that did not happen, and the sensations we were experiencing passed.

My sister is packing to go home and she can't find a gown she had brought with her, a deep green gown with red flowers on it. She said she had worn it the first week she was here, and had put it in the laundry to be washed. I remember washing it and hanging it up to dry. We have looked everywhere for it without success.

Monday, 2 July 2007, last night after closing my eyes, there was a dark red flash in front of my face, and I began to see faces. They were fast moving, and then nothing but blackness when suddenly there was a flash of a green head that startled me. It lingered slightly longer than the other faces had then disappeared. I remember the face as being humanoid exaggerated with big lips. Are they showing themselves to me little by little, perhaps, than when we meet I won't be running down the street screaming from fear? I fell asleep.

Tuesday, 3 July 2007, I got up at 6:05 this morning, opened the sliding glass door so the babes could go out on the porch and lay back down closing my eyes. No visions, then suddenly there was a little white ball just below my right eye. I waited but no visions appeared.

Do I have an agreement with them to be studied or am I an unwitting victim? Do I have a choice? Are there others who experience what I am? Why have they allowed me to be aware? Is it because I have asked? Is it because I am interested and curious about them? This is such an enigma.

Chapter 23

Sunday, 8 July 2007, my sister called today to tell me that she found the gown we had searched for stuffed on a shelf in her bedroom closet. Why wasn't it returned here where she was staying? Was this a subtle message to inform us that they know where she lives?

Tuesday, 31 July 2007, if they have come here to study earth beings then a serious scientist should observe without becoming involved in what they study otherwise the outcome will be tainted. I don't know them well enough to determine which is research and which is involvement on their part, to me it seems a little of both. I probably will always have the feeling that they are watching me especially when I see little white balls and blue rectangles pop up in front of my face. I believe they are as curious about us as we are of them yet they back off like frightened children poking a stick at something strange and unusual. To provoke such behavior lends me to think that we have strengths they do not have that can be dangerous to them. Good, this seems only fair under the circumstances.

Thursday, 2 August 2007, I woke up reading typewritten English letters. There were approximately four and a half lines on the page with a white background. I started to really look at what was written when it disappeared.

Sunday, 5 August 2007, last night immediately after I turned off the bedside light lying on my right side with my eyes closed there were two quick flashes of light and then two curved lights which seemed to fit in the shape below my lower eyelids. I opened my eyes and the light remained a short time then went out. I wasn't sure if there were moving shadows in the room but it felt as if there were. I closed my eyes again and the lights at the bottom of my eyelids came back on and I could see geometric shapes and twirling star-like things, and then I noticed what I thought was a red ball. I zeroed in on the red ball opened my eyes and was looking directly at the red light on the bedside phone. The light at the bottom of my eyes immediately disappeared and I fell asleep.

Tuesday, 7 August 2007, recently in my small town, several people were found dead, possibly murdered, and others were badly beaten in their home.

I am thinking about them, the beings, the aliens, about how they swoop in and out of my life leaving me stunned and in a state of confusion. I wonder if they sit in a corner undetected, watching things like this go on throughout the world, making notes on their little memory pads, or possibly visually recording the entire event for later study and evaluation. I believe that they do have a set of values and morals most likely different than ours because their culture and world is different. They have to have some guiding force for them to exist together confined in a space ship. I also believe they know right from wrong.

I am angry with them because they do not prevent these terrible things from happening when they are aware and are in a position to prevent atrocities. Should they stop such things if they are aware? Yes, I believe they should; this is when the serious scientist should become involved with the humans they study.

They have the ability to scare the living daylights out of people, and to wipe their minds absolutely clean of memory. They don't even have to show themselves. They can produce a dazzling light show, and blast the room with their odor that will distract any idiot who takes a breath. Once dazzled they can invisibly walk up to the intruder and zap him, then carry him up into outer space and dump him in some world where he deserves to be. The intended victims can have their minds cleansed of the event. The beings should be held accountable for their deficiency to prevent terrible atrocities they are aware of when they can do it so easily. I am really angry with them and have made my thoughts known. I want to see the leader of this group and speak my mind.

Wednesday, 8 August 2007, I went to bed, read and turned off the light. There were the usual flashes of lights and one unusual flash followed by a sudden sharp pain inside the top of my head on the right side then fell asleep. I awoke around 2:10 AM having had a dream.

I am with my eight-year-old son, and we are going to do some art and craft work. I am handed a box with different items in it, and one of the items is a dark brownish-gray fat circle like a bracelet. I pick it up and examine it not knowing how we can use it placing it back in the box. The circle suddenly uncurls, and I realize that it is a snake which has now escaped from the box and is slithering loose in my house.

Of all of God's critters I dislike snakes the most. I begin running around weeping and wailing about this snake loose in my home, how it can be anywhere in the house striking when least expected. I am running up and down the stairs of my three-floored house and in and out of the rooms searching for it. I have popped out of my body and can see that my eyes are red and swollen with tears of fear. I am waving my arms and yanking at my hair, yelling, sobbing and wailing for someone to notify the authorities to come and remove it from my home.

I am standing on the third floor at the metal railing looking out over the open level far below. The place is enormous. At my side is one of my sons that is not one of my sons, but he is small like my son. He has run after me as I wailed expressing my dismay over this loose snake, and is trying to comfort me patting me on the back and giving me sad looks. As I stand on the floor of the large room on the bottom level, I wake up.

The bedroom is charged. I feel a presence followed by a wave of fear rushing over me, and I see many little lit balls floating in the room. I push the fear aside determined to face whatever it is, jump out of bed and run into the bathroom. In the bathroom I can hear a humming like noise on the other side of the wall. My impression is something had just walked through the wall where the window is and on outside then the humming went away. I felt my face in the dark, it was not swollen and my eyes were dry. I was angry with them that they had resorted to humiliating me with the snake yet they had given me an answer. They had heard me. I crawled back into the bed. The room was dark and quiet. I felt alone.

This was definitely a dream to think about. I believe they used the snake to represent evil just as the Bible uses the snake in the Garden of Eden as the fore bearer of knowledge; but more realistically, I think they used the snake because they know I do not like them. The loose snake in my home represented evil loose within the world striking at random. The beings cannot be held responsible for the evil in our world, and while this is true, I believe they can be held responsible for preventing evil from occurring against innocent victims if they are aware of it. I believe they placed me in the role of a victim to let me know that if evil should occur, even my own people don't respond to prevent it. It is my people who hold the burden of responsibility for prevention but if they don't know, they can't prevent it, and that is the crux. I remain steadfast if the beings know then they should prevent it.

The next day I could smell the little one's friend, and although I could see no one in the room with me, I knew something was here.

I closed my eyes and thought, "I know you are here."

A voice in my head answered, "Yes, we are here."

"What was last night all about?" I thought.

"Judging; it was to teach you not to judge others."

"Yes," I thought and I understood.

Obviously they did not like the idea of a human "judging" them. Tough.

At first I believed that it was an OOB experience but I was

popping in and out of my body, the victim and the observer, which has happened in the past when I am on a ship; plus I heard the humming on the other side of the wall which leads me to think I was taken.

Saturday, 11 August 2007, I finally dozed off then became aware of a white page with writing on it and five circles intertwined reminding me of the Olympics emblem. The top three circles were black and the first two circles on the bottom were red and blue respectively. I thought it was strange that only the bottom two had colors. The page disappeared and I woke up; it was 1:30 AM, and I felt as if I had not slept. The foot of the bed faces the living room and I am able to see the couch from the left to the middle. In that area was a long rectangle about four inches high and a foot long. It was divided evenly into seven smaller rectangles with every other one lit with a white light, four were lit. I closed my eyes and it was gone when I looked again; then I leaned to my right seeing that it had simply shifted on the couch out of view. I turned on the light and it was gone.

Friday, 24 August 2007, in the early evening we had a badly needed rainfall with lots of thunder and lightning vivid against a steel gray sky. The electricity was flickering off and on, and finally went off. The front and back doors were open and the wind was blowing through the house feeling superb as we had become prisoners in our air-conditioned homes. It was dark in the house, and I wondered if I could capture anything on camera, so I grabbed it and began taking pictures

In one of the pictures of the back porch is the head of a

smiling snake with its body curling downward, a snake's picture so close to the dream about not judging is remarkable.

I remembered having had another snake dream. I was standing at a chest high table with someone on my left talking to me about a snake lying on the table top. He wanted me to touch it. My vision was blocked so that I could see only the body of a grayish brown, fat and healthy snake. I remember standing with my hands tightly clasped behind my back thinking that I must not let them know how much I dislike snakes. I nodded my head as he talked thinking don't let them know, don't let them know, hide it! I guess I didn't hide that fear well enough for on 24 August 2007 at 5:35 AM, I took a random picture that shows a smiling snake floating on the sliding glass door and then, of course, there is the snake-bracelet dream.

Sunday, 2 September 2007, every night for several weeks after I turn the light off, I lay in bed watching the dark and every night the same things happen. There are the little white and blue balls, a blotch of red, flashes, an occasional rectangle, and so forth. I have noticed that if I awaken during the night the same things occurs, even early morning when it is still dark. It is like a rerun each time with a little variation, but nothing attention grabbing. I have come to the conclusion that they are here by some sort of remote device, a watching and performing device but they are not really here. Perhaps they just don't want me to think that I am free of them. I believe that they slip in and out leaving me to think they are here every night, and that I am unaware of the real from the staged. I think that there is a "shift" of some sort in the room that lasts for an instant;

a brief shift of light when the room becomes absolutely black. At times when I have been certain that something else is in the room with me, I have seen this "shift". Is this a dimensional thing, a being coming from one dimension to another? Is this just one group or is there a variety of groups able to slip in and out by various means? Is the shifting a sign of a portal?

Monday, 4 September 2007, I am dreaming.

I am with my "son" and a man and accept that they are my youngest son and ex-husband. We are with a group of other families and people who are walking around in and out of rooms and different buildings, looking at things that I cannot remember and that do not seem important. I am wearing a white button down cotton blouse, and a full skirt with large pockets hidden in the side seams; an outfit and style that I have not wore since I was a teenager in the 1950s. The only thing missing is a chiffon scarf tied in a square knot around my neck.

I am constantly feeling the object in my right pocket that is a bottle of pills in a box. The "police" are looking for this bottle, and are searching everyone; we are trying to look innocent, and avoid being searched. I know this bottle of pills belongs to me because I have a prescription for my headaches, they are not illegal but if found on me, they could accuse me of something illegal. I feel rather smug about how we have maneuvered around being searched, and keep my hand in the pocket feeling the box. I am aware that this is a dream, and now, as I have often done in the past, I watch the dream to see what will happen.

I am aware of the strong smell of the second little one; it is powerful and nearly suffocating. I tell the man with me that I need to use the bathroom, and we search the building, finding it I go into the room. I do not use the bathroom instead I stand in front of the mirror fixing my pony tail and slyly slip my right hand into the pocket to reassure myself that the box is still there. Now it is not a box of pills for headaches but a box with an inhaler for which I also have a prescription. I shrug my shoulders because I really don't care what's in the box as long as I still have it in my pocket. It belongs to me.

I leave the room and stand with the child and man. A blank screen pops up in front of us and shifts so it is facing me. On the screen a black being that looks like a grey with white eyes and black pupils wearing a black band around his head is looking at me. He sternly says, "You should not have …." The screen did not surprise me but the black being did as I did not remember seeing a black grey before, and I had flinched as he started his sentence. He stopped mid-sentence looking surprised, and he and the screen disappeared. I placed my hand in the pocket and the box was gone. I knew that I was innocent but why was I feeling guilty? Because I was being sneaky! The odor lingered for a short time then it too disappeared.

Thursday, 13 September 2007, early this morning, I become aware I am dreaming.

I am with two people, one small and the other tall, both are at my side throughout. There were also close friends that I could identify and family members, in and out of the room passing through. We are in an old setting, not a bygone era, but the building or whatever we are in, is old. Something is wrong with someone and I am supposed to fix it.

A short heavyset woman with blond hair wearing a dark colored dress brings in a baby wrapped in a blanket. The baby is clutched to her chest, and she is visibly upset and tearful. The baby is laid on a table in front of us and the blanket is removed. It is a beautiful baby, perfectly formed but there is something wrong with its intestines, and I am supposed to fix it otherwise the baby will die.
I do not remember the abdomen being cut open nor do I hear a baby cry, and I think this is not normal, everything about this is not right. I look down at the baby and see a small incision in its little belly. I can see the intestines and the problem spot, and make a teeny tiny slit in it, problem resolved. I rewrap the baby---who is not in any visible discomfort and wide awake not having received an anesthetic--- in the blanket, and leave the room. I am brought back to the baby who is once again lying on the table with the blanket removed. My best friend, pale and tall with long black hair, is walking in and out of the room, checking on things. She glances over at me as she walks though, and I am comforted by a feeling that she is being supportive.

I stand looking at the baby suddenly remembering that I have not stitched up the incision and I am upset because I should have done so immediately. I ask for suture material and am handed a green linen bundle. I check the tape seeing that it has been sterilized because this is the way instruments came packaged when I worked in the OR back in the 1960's. When I open the bundle I find a long rusty needle holder and no needles to thread, so I look for packaged suture thinking the needles might already be attached. The tall one hands me multiple strips of thin flat plastic with thread sticking out of both ends reminding me of a strip of paper with those little colored Candy Buttons we use to buy when we were kids. I have no idea how this is used, but thank him, laying it down within the opened sterile package.

I can't remember what size silk to use for a baby. I suture the small gut with two tiny stitches, and worry there will be leakage that could cause peritonitis and death. I prepare to close the peritoneum and see that it is intact, and I wonder how that can be possible after exposing the gut. I slide the thin fascia across it knowing this cannot be sutured.

I am handed the rusty needle holder by the tall one, and I'm trying to determine what size silk to use to close the skin and which stitch to use, intermittent or running. I realize I need another set of hands to hold the skin in place while closing. I am unable to yank the thread off of the plastic strip and I have no needle anyway rendering it useless. What had I used to stitch the gut? I begin fretting about the need for an antibiotic because none of this surgery has been done under sterile conditions but I don't know which antibiotic or dose should be given to a baby. Nobody has worn gloves or masks and the needle holder is rusty! The baby lay on the table smiling at me.

Suddenly I am as a small child who has done something terribly wrong, and find myself trying to hide this terrible mistake that I have committed yet must assume guilt for the entire episode. Why had I tried to perform surgery on an infant when I am not qualified to do so? Why had I let the baby lay after the surgery rather than closing? Why did I not use sterile procedure? Why was the needle holder rusty? Why was the silk suture attached to a plastic strip and unable to be removed? Why were there no needles? I was feeling as if I had willingly committed bodily harm for I was sure the baby will be harmed forever or worse, die. Why had I done this, I'm not a doctor!

I awoke that morning with a feeling of heaviness in the front part of my brain as if I had drunk too much wine the night before.

Two guilt dreams following my accusation of their lack to assume responsibility to do the right thing when they are in the presence of wrong being done. I must be taught a lesson and they have done so in interesting ways. I'm not perfect either and I too, can get caught up in circumstances where I think I am doing the right thing, but in the end I have not. This is quite a reaction from an accusation made against them by an inferior being, a human being. So we role-play in situations devised by them and they stand at my side and assist me in my role of arrogance, incompetence and poor judgment. They are allowing me to show them and myself that I am not such a stellar person. Or is this what the past couple of dreams are about?

The reason doesn't matter, the two dreams are finished and the role-playing for them is over but a lesson has been learned. They set me up and I let them.

Chapter 24

Thursday, 27 September 2007, I am dreaming.

We are in a small bungalow. There is one small child, the one that had been with me in the flooding cave and is wearing the same face as the picture on the wall, a neighbor boy, my "mother" and a family member. I don't know why we are together.

We go outside to wave goodbye to the family member who is driving away in a yellow convertible with the top down, when suddenly a huge explosion shakes the ground. The shock is so great that I see the car jerking from side to side on the road but the driver continues on down the road as if nothing has happened. I can't understand how she can be oblivious to the explosion and the danger she might be in. The rest of us turn and run back into the bungalow.

I spew out instructions while pointing at the basement door, "Get yourselves, the animals, as much food as you can, clothing, blankets, matches, candles, water, first aid kit and anything else you can think of that we might need into the basement, and stay there until I check out what is happening."

Everyone begins to run around grabbing the animals and items we will need taking them into the basement, meanwhile I go out through the sliding glass door onto the wooden deck in the back of the house.

The house is built on the side of a mountain with an unobstructed view of the skyline of a huge city in the distance. I see no trees or greenery of any kind anywhere. I can see lights on in the high-rise buildings and I find this strange because when the driver drove off a few minutes ago, the sun was shining.

Suddenly a huge burning round ship falls out of the sky landing on some of the tall buildings creating another huge explosion shaking the ground, followed by the firing of missiles and more explosions. I search the sky and see an enormous round white lit area aimed at some tall buildings, and know that these buildings are next to be destroyed. We are in an alien war.

I know we are in Miami, Florida because someone tells me we are, and I stand there thinking Miami, Florida, Miami, Florida, Miami Florida and wonder where in Miami, Florida there is a high hill like the one this house is on. I think of Miami, Florida being flat located on the Atlantic Coast but I do not see the ocean. I am speculating why it would be destroyed like this, and how in the hell did I get here to Miami, Florida? The dream snaps off and I wake up, it is 4 AM.

Later I remembered that during the above dream something tight had been placed on my head. There was a tight band running from my forehead around both sides to the back of my head, and whatever it was holding onto my head, was heavy. I reached up to readjust it and a small grey appeared in front of me telling me not to touch it. I could also see a tall grey standing nearby. I am popping in and out of my body watching myself, the little one and the tall one. I am also aware that I am still lying in my bed or think that I am. So where am I? Am I in the bed or sitting somewhere else with a tight band around my head with me popping in and out of my body watching this happen; the three of me. I escape my body only when I am around them but I could feel the pillow and bed, or thought that I could. How can that be? Was I with them or was I in the bed?

Two years have passed since I saw the space suit standing in the bedroom doorway.

Two other dreams:
The first dream is of landing next to a large white city sitting in the middle of nowhere surrounded by what I assumed was white desert sand. It looked to be one very large building with tall, thin, round turrets within and around the building reminiscent of a fairyland castle. There were empty ramps without guardrails, curving upwards around the turrets that had windows, and each turret was capped with a cone shaped roof. I find myself reluctantly getting into the vehicle, and watching the city grow smaller as we flew away.

The second dream is of being on a planet with enormous green and brown plants. There was a group of us, and while several of the group wanted to look around further, three of us did not. I thought if the vegetation was this large how large were the creatures that lived here; we were like small animals standing beside the plants as large as small trees. The three of us sheltered ourselves under one of the leaves to screen us from the hot sun while we waited for the others to return.

Monday, 1 October 2007, it was a beautiful full moon last night without known visits or remembered dreams. I have awakened the past two mornings tired, and this morning I could hardly move. I am on edge feeling as if something is about to happen, and I'm not sure that I am prepared. Maybe this is simply the result of knowing that I am not in as much control of my life as I would like to be.

My sister called and we talked about the beings. We both have come to the conclusion that there is a possibility they may be from a different dimension as opposed to being from outer space, although I believe they have space traveling abilities but I waffle back and forth about where they are from, I can't make up my mind. She tells me that there has been little communication with the beings as opposed to when she first left here, and that she has had several dreams of which she could remember nothing except being told something very significant in one of them, and then it was wiped from her memory.

I've had some interesting faces presented that I felt were significant thrown in here and there in a hodgepodge manner. It is the way my body reacts to these faces that I believe that I may have seen them before in a different context. One was totally covered in white fur with arms and legs like a human and seated on a large log. He had a face but I do not remember what he looked like. The other was also male of blackish-brown and I was shown his face head on. It began with a close up view of his right eyebrow area that was unevenly and deeply ribbed. Then I was pulled back until I could see his entire face that was fat and although he had a nose, mouth and eyes, it was grossly disfigured according to our standards. His face then morphed into a human head shape and turned towards his left revealing a human type ear, and then he vanished.

Thursday, 4 October 2007, there have been a few times in the last two weeks while lying in bed watching the dark that my heart beat suddenly quickened. This happened twice one night before I fell asleep, and I fought the feeling that comes with the quickened beat knowing that something was present. I have the impression that I continue being taught how to overcome the feeling of being taken; is it the little one doing this?

Saturday, 6 October 2007, yesterday was a very busy day at work, and I came home exhausted. I stood motionless at the kitchen counter in the dark for a while to see if there were any balls, red blotches, blue spots or ripples. Only one blue rectangle about the size of a half-inch appeared and disappeared in front of me. I saw nothing else but had wondered if the action is triggered when the lights are turned on and then off when I go to bed, and except for the blue rectangle, I would have been satisfied with that thought.

My back and feet were aching. I changed into the always-comfortable nightclothes, had a snack and looked up stuff on the Internet accompanied by the overwhelming smell of the little one's friend. I went to bed, read, turned off the light and the odor was back double strong. I spoke in my head to him, and he answered back that he was visiting and the little one was all right. He also said that they would be back to take me and, of course, I never believe them because they say whatever and there is no way to prove or disprove their statements. He left and I slept well until Jezebel bore a hole into my right ear at 8:30 this morning; she was hungry.

Sunday, 7 October 2007, I settled down at the computer to read a web site that is a theory presented by Martin Cannon called *The Controllers: A New Hypothesis of Alien Abduction* that I found interesting, plausible, and shocking if true. Have I been dealing with humans who work with aliens, or is it just aliens? I thought of the human odors that I have smelled and the dirt found in the bathtub. This theory is more frightening then to think there are aliens kidnapping people.

In one of the writings one of the little ones was referred to by government people as EBE--Extraterrestrial Biological Entity. This immediately reminded me of the experience with my favorite little one on Monday, 14 August 2006, when I saw writing on the wall "EEWITHME" and was told that EE meant Evolutionary Enoid.

My sister called to tell me about her dream. She does not write them down and tends to forget them, so she asked me to write it down for her. She was sitting out somewhere on a rock with a male who was attractive with short curly black hair, light brown skin, and beautiful brown eyes that she described as his best feature. They began talking about archeology that led into religion, and it was then she noticed that in the background there was a shadow man who just stood there. Their conversation was stimulating and out of the blue, she asked him what his religion was. He looked at her and at that moment, his ears began to grow becoming pointed at the top, then his face shape-shifted except for the beautiful brown eyes. The ears were the prominent thing she was focused on because they looked to be of skin and cartilage like our ears with visible veins, then he and the shadow person disappeared.

Friday, 12 October 2007, I am in misery, not dying from pain, but certainly uncomfortable that seems to be my gall bladder. I am nauseated all of the time, feel like there is a soft ball under my right rib cage, heady not dizzy and have an annoying side effect after I eat. Lomotil was ordered and the doctor said she would prescribe something for the nausea that I look forward to receiving.

Tuesday, 16 October 2007, I saw the surgeon today and will have a colonoscopy done because of the need for Lomotil.

I've been putting it off for years, but he won't do the surgery without it as he suspects there may be two problems. The little bastards keep telling me that they are here to watch me die, maybe they are right.

I went to bed last night exhausted, read awhile and fell asleep. I couldn't have cared less if an alien was there. Early this morning while it was still dark, I was awakened as the bed was vibrating, and I was getting whiffs of the little one. I laid there letting it vibrate and when it stopped, the cats began nudging me to get up. This is not the first time the bed has vibrated while living here; it use to vibrate up north as well, only there, sometimes I could hear falling rocks as if there was a landslide deep underground with the sound carrying through the waterbed.

Thursday, October 18 2007, I was not sleepy at all last night. The last time I looked at the clock it was 3:30 AM, and it was around then that I turned off the light having finished the book I was reading. I lay in the darkness looking around aware that there has been little activity lately. Both cats and I were snuggled up together on the same side of the bed, comfy and cozy. I closed my eyes and suddenly opened them again seeing a light shine through the window then streaking across the bed to the dresser wall. There were three quick consecutive flashes coming from the wall shortly followed by two flashes coming from the wall at the foot of the bed. A bright light coming through the window shined briefly on my face then faded downsizing to the size of a marble and hovered not changing in size. I watched it for a while waiting for something to happen, then closed my eyes again and chanted to myself to relax, relax, relax, and I could feel my body relaxing while my brain was grossly awake and aware.

I was wondering if they were inducing this relaxation or if I had done it to myself, as I felt rather unworldly. For a brief second I thought something had touched my right shoulder, and waited to see if my body was going to be moved but nothing happened. Abruptly images leapt into my mind, and I was watching thick designs floating and moving around over and under each other. They reminded me of fat pretzels in a square shape and realized that this could be very hypnotic, and guarded myself not to become lost in them. They changed into thinner and different shapes as I relaxed even more trying very hard not to let them know how awake and alert I was.

Suddenly a square appeared in my head followed by four more floating designs as a background for the square. Each design had a creature in it that did not look human although I recognized them, but it was the square that caught my eye as it was a black grey with white eyes that seemed to turn red and then was gone. I was wondering if the eyes turned red because that is what others have reported, black greys with red eyes, and I changed them to red, or did it really have red eyes? The eyes had looked white with some redness, the same as humans have when their eyes are bloodshot.

As I got up and walked into the bathroom I wondered if this was going to end the session. There was a brief light flash at the bathroom door, and I thought I saw the little black one with the white eyes but wasn't sure; I knew that I needed to act as if asleep because they were watching. I walked back to bed and closed my eyes while crawling back into it when there was a flash in front of my face. As I lay down on the bed I quickly glanced at the bedroom curtains and could still see the marble sized light shining through.

After I was comfortable on the bed different images popped into my head. One grouping seemed to follow another. I marveled at their patience, and wondered if this was a set sequence then wondered if they realized how awake I was. One set was of geometric designs and were the neon colored ones I have seen before. I was very relaxed and could hear myself breathing heavily and slightly snoring yet my mind remained aware of what was happening. I tested the waters by moving a little as one has seen others do while sleeping, and the pictures continued. My nose and the area around my nose began to feel thick and heavy, and I began to have a little trouble breathing through it. I wrinkled it and the sensation went away then returned a short time later feeling heavier as if my nose was being gently pinched, so that I would have to breathe through my mouth. I rubbed at my nose as if something was bothering it, a fly perhaps, and the sensation was repeated. By this time I was aware that they wanted me to breathe through my mouth, and I was not going to open my mouth. I rolled over onto my left side and saw that the light was still shinning through the curtains. The pictures eventually became lighter then disappeared, and the light shining through the curtains faded away leaving the room in darkness. I felt that they had left, and fell asleep not waking up until 10:30 AM.

So many questions! Did they leave once they realized that I was not in the state of consciousness they desired? The length of time they took and the varied symbols they used was amazing as they went from one to another as if it was preprogrammed. I wondered if these were codes telling my brain what to expect or just a simple hypnotic technique. The entire episode probably didn't last more than 10 minutes but seemed much longer. In the end it was the nose trick that told the story that I wasn't asleep. Why did they want me to open my mouth?

Tuesday, 23 October 2007, last night while I lay in bed with the lights off there was a faint flash at the foot of the bed followed by what I call a "ripple" in the room. It occurred to me that it is also like a black flash seemingly identical to a white flash only black. I watched the area of the curtained blinds where the light is seen shinning through, and saw what looked like the black shapes of tall well formed men. There were five of them who silently walked in through the window as if it were a doorway and turned to their right. There is not enough room in that area to hold five large men or women for that matter or even five children. I dozed off waking up again at 10:10 PM and sat up on the side of the bed.

Pictures had been flashing through my mind. The last picture was of an attractive young human man with light brown hair and a pencil moustache. He looked familiar then I recognized him.

The picture of the young man remained, so that I could get a good look then another picture flashed up next to his. I do not ever remember where a picture remains to allow me to get a really good look, and never do I remember another picture being shown at the same time, side by side. The second picture was the full length of a thin grey in front of a dark background. I could not tell how tall it was as there was nothing to compare it to but its demeanor was one of bashfulness as one would expect in a teenager, and I thought I knew this one too. It was wanted that I should believe that they were related, half brothers sharing a single parent.

I sat on the side of the bed and could see a white ball on the floor over by the dresser. Suddenly a small white rectangle appeared where the ball had been. It was probably three by four inches, white with pictures on it. I couldn't see the pictures clearly, but it looked as if there were faces and signs on it. I could see that there were four columns with items in each column like postage stamps. While I strained trying to see the items clearly, it vanished. I turned on the light and got out of bed.

Chapter 25

Wednesday, 24 October 2007, I pulled up the plantation blind on my bedroom window and looked out to see if there was something high enough that could beam down through the bedroom window at night. Yes, there was one of those tall cement poles used for power lines. The poles were put in and the power turned on around the same time the beings began coming. When I assumed the position on the bed that I usually lay, the top of the pole was way too low. I examined the area of the curtain and tried to visualize the direction the beam would have to be coming from in order to hit my face. It looked as if the beam would have to pass through a small space between the bent arm of the gutter and the eve. The only way I could visualize that happening is by something suspended in the air from which the beam is emitted. I closed the blind and the curtain, and hung a thickly woven alpaca wool blanket I had bought in Belize over the window.

When I went into the bedroom that night to go to bed I could smell the little one. He acknowledged my greeting then asked me why I had hung the blanket over the window. I didn't want to answer that question because it was none of his business, simply replying that I wanted it there. He told me that I didn't need it there and again asked to know why I had hung it. I replied firmly that this is the way I want the blanket hung and the questioning ended. I went to bed, closed my eyes and slept. As I write this, I wonder why I didn't tell him that I wanted to block their light, and that I wanted them to leave. Was I leery of how they might react or what they would do? My behavior was passive-aggressive, was this because I didn't trust them? I did not.

Friday, 26 October 2007, I turned off the light around 12:30 AM after finishing the book I was reading, and rolled onto my left side facing the window covered by the wool blanket. I wondered if the light beam would shine through the blanket, watched it for a while then began seeing more than usual little diamond sparkles around the room. I relaxed and a face popped into my head and shape-shifted eventually settling on the face of a lizard-like being with yellow eyes and black pupils. I told him to go away and he smiled at me, not a pleasant smile. I told him he was not wanted here and to leave, now, listing the reasons why he should leave. He slowed down my thought process until the words I had placed in a sentence to say were scattered all about leaving me trying to collect them and place them in order. There was thought transference from him of words that gained speed until they became a blur causing my brain to feel a pressure as if something was being forced into it thinking that it might explode. My last thought was that we humans were being used as storehouses for information.

I am being shown a drawing of a wing shaped structure named "Skylark". The picture is upside down, then whisked away, and slapped down on the table as if whoever is doing it is impatient and irritated. There is a person standing on the other side of the table from me as well as one standing to my left but I unable see either of them. I can only see the left arm of the being on the other side of the table that is covered in a dark blue sleeve and the human hand as it slaps the drawing on the table. There appears to be large rooms in the drawing, and I am not sure if it is a building or a space ship. I get a good look at the structure upside down as well as right side up. It doesn't have a lot of rooms, and doesn't look like anything special to me but what do I know about
250

these things---nothing. I say, "Yes." to acknowledge what I was shown. A female walks into the room covered in silver metallic looking clothing that accentuates her femaleness. She is bald with a narrow face and a slender well built body, and is all business. There is something about her ears leaving me with the impression that they were long and floppy like a dog's. I couldn't tell if she was human, but I didn't think she was. I asked who she was and was told her name was Sats-star or Satch-star. I wasn't sure which by the way it was pronounced.

I woke up. It was only 3:01 AM and was dismayed; I didn't feel as if I had slept at all. I mentally said, "Why are they here? I don't want them here?" The voice replied, "We cannot stop them." "But you told me that there were three of them here to protect me!" He said, "They have left." "Damn!" I said to myself.

I felt a heaviness or pressure over my upper right abdomen where I have been having the discomfort and it began to ache. I lay on my left side and something was happening in my mind but I don't remember what, when I felt a painless punch in the upper right abdomen causing my entire body to jerk and jump and wondered what the heck that was. There was a bright light above and behind my head on the pillow, a flash followed by darkness then my mind became busy with other thoughts.

I woke up at 8:49 AM with a headache, dizziness and nausea, a doozy of a hangover without the booze. The odor of the little one was strong not only in the bedroom but throughout the house and then faded away as I busied myself making coffee and feeding the cats. I do not remember anything else at this time but as the day goes on more things may surface.

Wednesday, 31 October 2007, I smell the little one a lot lately, so strong that the odor could singe my nostrils. There is something here that the cats chase around vigorously and "plays" with one cat at a time. I've also been hearing noises at night, pings, etc. and the bed in the guest room creaks as if someone is laying on it. Something is here that is quiet or leaves periodically.

Sunday, 4 November 2007, when I drove home last Friday evening after I got off work, an airplane with its wing and taillights blinking drew my attention. As I watched, a lit ball-like object shot straight up from the bottom of the middle of the plane, flew in a straight line towards the tail disappearing after passing the tail. It was sudden and very fast.

Wednesday, 7 November 2007, my sister called to tell me she will be coming for a visit next month and I am so pleased. She briefly told me of a "situation" dream she had had, waking at the end to see a little one with the arm of a tall one around it, both smiling at her as if they were pleased.

I go in for surgery Friday. My side feels like it is housing more than it should and I will gladly be rid of it.

Monday, 12 November 2007, the surgery went well and I was home by noon feeling no pain.

Saturday, 17 November 2007, I was very tired last night yet restless and unable to sleep. When I turned off the light and lay on my back with my eyes open, I thought I had forgotten to take off my glasses. I felt my face, the glasses were not there yet I am able to see a clear outline of the glasses as if they are still on my face. In the center of the glasses is a dimly lit square while the area around it is pitch black, around the black is the rim of the glasses with a light glow surrounding the glasses. The light must be located in front of them. If I move my eyes or head it all fades away then gradually reappears back into view. After moving my head several times, it stopped.

I looked up at the ceiling and saw the shape of a large human form with two arms, two legs, a torso and head swimming around the ceiling fan in a counter clockwise circle using the breaststroke. It is as if he is on the surface of a body of water, and I am on the bottom looking up at the surface. I am aware of other activity in the room on the ground level and each time I look around and then refocus on the ceiling, the figure continues swimming around the ceiling fan.

This occurred twice and at first was unsettling. I am aware that they do things like this to distract me while something else is happening but I am unable to watch two or more activities at the same time without moving my eyes to see both and they know it. How clever they are.

I rolled onto my left side and closed my eyes. A light appeared and I was able to see the pink veins in my eyelids then there was a dim flash as if it was coming from the pillow area above my head.

I find the whole thing bothersome any more. I see nothing accomplished and find myself becoming impatient and annoyed with their antics. It is as if a game to them. Their shenanigans do not entertain me as they once did when they first began. I want more information from them and none is forthcoming. And though I am interested in them as living beings, I have distanced myself returning to human life and for the first time in many years I am in the Christmas Spirit. There are aliens around, so what; they probe and study, so what. There is not much I can do to redirect or stop them. I apparently have no input into the situation and they do what they want but that doesn't mean that I approve or willingly co-operate. They will slip up and I will be ready.

Sunday, 18 November 2007, I don't remember what time I fell asleep. I didn't look for anything prior to closing my eyes, just drifted off into a welcomed sleep. I am dreaming.

My sister, a small boy and I are in a room, a living room I believe. There is an overstuffed couch sitting further away from the light gray wall than would be normal, and there is a door to the left behind it. The room has no other furniture except for the couch.

Everyone is smiling in anticipation of what's to come. My sister walks in front of me and directs the little boy to stand in front of the couch. She then talks to me in a low confidential voice as we stand facing the child. He has blond hair and a sweet chubby face and is watching us intently. I become annoyed with the child based on what she is saying, and know that I must discipline him. I do not want to do this. I can feel the anger rising up in me as she talks and am debating if I will have to spank this child. I look closely at my sister. She is tall and thin with long black hair that makes her look extremely pale. She has no nose. This is the same woman who says she is my mother, and I recognize that we are role-playing, again.

My "sister" steps out of view to my left and slightly behind me. I turn to the child, walk over to him and start to question him about what happened. He is standing with his back to me facing the couch, and when he turns around there is excitement in his eyes and there is a cute little smile on his face. I look closely and I realize that he is the little one and the smile is a grimace because he can't really smile. I shrug thinking to myself, this is another of their dreams and if I spank him I could really hurt him because he is so fragile. I don't want to hurt him, I am fond of him. My sister has a surprised look on her face as I turn and walk away. I wake up, look at the clock and see that it is nearly 5 AM. I go back to sleep.

I have choices in role playing! I didn't do what they wanted, walked out, and I woke up in my bed! What were they searching for that they could not witness by observing a real family. It should not be difficult to find a parent swatting the back side of a kid now and then. I wonder if they wanted to see if they could feel my emotions as I spanked the little one or was it to study my emotions as I spanked him, maybe both. Clearly the intent was to spank him, and the little one was excited to be spanked which demonstrates to me that corporeal discipline of their children is foreign. Why do I feel guilty for walking out of the room? Was it because she looked surprised when I did, as if I had let her down?

Several nights later while setting on the couch I saw a flash on the ceiling by the ceiling fan. Seconds later it flashed behind me to my right and again by the ceiling fan several more times then again behind me to my right. I could see out of the corner of my eye that it was a rectangle. This continued for about five minutes and I was excited as this was something new and I was hoping that someone would step out but that didn't happen. I read then turned off the light after 1 AM.

I am gasping and struggling to breathe lying on my back knowing that I am suffocating thinking why aren't they coming to help me, where are they? A man and my mother had been with me but they have left the room, and there is no way I can attract their attention. As I lay in the bed I can hear myself making noises as I breathe; at the same time I have popped out of my body and watch myself as I lay on the floor gasping for air. I am back in my body on the floor and see a pale skinny female with long black hair bend over me, quickly grab my arms by the wrists pulling them over my head dragging me across the smooth metal floor and out through the doorway. As she is doing this, I think that maybe the inhaler would help and it is handed to me, and I pop back out and watch myself take a couple of puffs sucking in the mist.

I am awake in my bed and deeply sucking in air. My tongue feels extremely dry and is glued tightly to the roof of my mouth, and I'm having difficulty releasing it. I remember that I have awakened the past two nights like this; my tongue glued to the roof of my mouth. Those two times it felt as if my tongue was securely sealed to the roof of my mouth and had been surprised that it was not swollen due to the suction needed to release it. Once again I am aware of being in three places at the same time; I am in the bed, I am with them, and I am popping in and out observing the one with them.

This picture was taken 19 November 2007 at 3:53 AM in my bedroom; the large orb is shaded blue and white.

Chapter 26

Monday, 19 November 2007, I have thought of little else but the dream of spanking the little one, the strangeness of it, and still have no answers. It seemed so real until the little one turned around and grimaced. If it had been a human child would I have spanked it? No, I am beyond spanking. I've seen a few kids that might benefit from a swat to let them know they have gone beyond the limit but have thought reasoning with them would be more beneficial. Discipline starts in the home and then carried through elsewhere, and if discipline is lacking in the home, what can a parent expect when they are taken in public? I've also thought that maybe it's the parent who needs the swat, an encouragement to pay attention to the ones they have brought into this world, a reminder to accept responsibility for their child's behavior.

The beings were so excited, and who was behind us in the room? I did not look behind me, never even thought to but knew that someone was there. They are strange beings to want to do this; they don't really understand us even with all of their studies. They don't understand our extremes or how we get to them although my "sister" was certainly making every effort to make me angry. Are they so emotionless or maybe they experience different ones? Do they feel a fondness for the ones in their care, or is it simply a sense of responsibility?

I read on one of the websites that everything one woman believes she truly needs is placed in her path, and I have found the same, even money that I need to support mother and myself. How are they able to do that or should I even credit them for it? Perhaps it is The Creator's blessings as I have been taught and believe. What are they taught about The Creator or are they taught anything. I was told by them they do not believe in a God but in The Creator.

I wonder if they have pets.

Tuesday, 20 November 2007, last night unable to sleep, tossing and turning, I got up around 3 AM to get something to eat in hopes that would settle me and it did. When I crawled back into the bed and lay there with my eyes closed, the "glasses" appeared.

Within the rectangle in the center is a light gray area with little dots that swirl around turning blue as some separate from others. I see a mass of small clouds reminding me of popcorn, scattered in a circle swirling around, we are at the top, a part of the clockwise swirling mass.

I pop out of my body and see myself sitting alone at an angle on a curved window seat looking out of the large curved window. We are in a ship which has begun to swirl around in a large circular downward motion towards the large black hole in the center, and continuing to swirl we enter into it then straighten out. The sides are black and ribbed reminding me of ribbed grafts used for aortic abdominal aneurysms. The ship is moving fast following the bends and curves of the tunnel. There is not a lot of room for the ship to pass through without hitting the sides, and at times I can feel slight vibrations as if we are skimming them. I wonder if the sides are solid. I recognize that whoever is driving this ship is a master at the wheel.

The ship abruptly exits the tunnel and suddenly stops. Slightly to the right of us is a massive living ball of reddish orange constantly undulating and throwing off reddish orange blobs of various sizes which I hope do not hit us. I realize we are just out of reach of a sun. We abruptly turn to the left entering into another ribbed tunnel until at the end there is a white-ladder-like structure that the ship lands on riding it downward then suddenly upward and out into blue sky with white clouds.

Wednesday, 21 November 2007, last night I turned off the light at 9:30 extremely tired after my first day back to work following surgery.

Saturday, 1 December 2007. The odor of the little one is very strong this evening and I say to him, "I want to remember what is happening and I am not allowed; this isn't fair. I don't think that this was part of our agreement. You continue to observe me but you are not sharing. Who is the small one with the large nose, pointed ears, red short sleeved shirt and requires a huge body guard, and where is my mother?" I do not remember the answers.

Sunday, 2 December 2007, last night the full moon was covered by lightly scattered clouds through which a limited number of stars were visible from where I stood. When I look at stars, they bounce and waver forcing me to find a stable spot, so that I can tell if something is indeed moving. I bent over and rested my chin on the windowsill hanging on to both sides of the window frame with my hands.

I focused on one star which I thought was a part of Orion's belt but I couldn't see the entire belt from this angle to be certain. As I stared at that area I began to see small white dots zipping around, some blinking then disappearing. I wasn't sure if I was actually seeing moving objects or if they were small stars in the background wavering due to cloud movement. I continued watching then began to see what looked to me like small white objects being shot at each other. Since when do stars shoot at each other? I was mesmerized. One exploded with a huge red flare and the shooting continued then stopped. I remember dreams of alien wars and wondered if what I was seeing was real or imagined or simply planted in my mind. I watched another star to its left and after awhile, I again saw little white objects shooting through the sky. Was this another staged event for my benefit entirely in my head or did I actually see UFOs? I think it was staged; I have to believe it was staged.

Wednesday, 5 December 2007, I fell asleep after reading last night and didn't pay much attention if anything was going on. I was tired after working nine hours and fighting a cold waking around five this morning to multiple white balls floating around. I went into the bathroom with one of the balls preceding me then disappearing. Knowing they are here makes it harder to fall back asleep. I tried to pretend that I was asleep but had difficulty controlling my eye movements as I didn't know if they should be moving or not deciding on not.

There was a large white flash followed by the blue rectangle then there were multiple little white balls seemingly in my eyes. My hand game appeared in front of me, and I began playing. The numbers were not quite right but I played anyway. The numbers became picture cards of people or beings making me angry; they had taken a simple game that was mine and messed with it placing it in a dream. I found a very long sharp knife in my right hand and began stabbing the picture cards rather than punching the buttons and threw them on the card pile until the playing cards were gone. "Get away from me! Get out of my life!" I mentally yelled.

Suddenly there is another flash and a white circle appears followed by an amazing red geometric shape with a blue and white cloud background that is exactly the background on my computer desktop. The color red is not red, as we know it but slightly different, an intense red. The design seems to be made of tiny straight lines, and the shape seems to be a square stretched until the shape is no longer a square. It is lying flat and I am looking at it from the flat side. The shape changes into another one with a different color but I am not ready to move on, I want to continue admiring the red shape.

The face of a male being appears. He is medium brown with fierce eyes and multiple wrinkles on his face; I have seen him before. He has eyes, eyelids, eyebrows, a nose and a mouth like a human but he is not human. I don't remember if he has ears or hair, but I know that he is my teacher for the lesson. Meanwhile I am thinking that I must continue to pretend sleeping and see what else they are going to do. A design appears which is nonsense made up of letters and that is the last thing I remember until I awake around eight this morning.

They know when I am not totally asleep and no matter how hard I try, they manage to "hypnotize" me into sleep with floating things that I am attracted to watch. Yes, I have the choice to get up because I am not asleep but if I do, then I may miss something that I would want to know or see such as, in this case, the teacher's face. Obviously they are intruding into my life and heaven only knows what they are feeding into or taking away from my brain, thoughts / knowledge / beliefs / emotions, etc. I would call this an in-depth study for sure. It makes me uneasy to know that I have little resistance to them and that I am getting nothing in return, most importantly, no knowledge about them. My curiosity is the umbilical cord that keeps me attached to them.

Later this month I am going to visit family for Christmas, and I am excited. I am in the Christmas spirit, and have decorated the house with holly, pine branches, pine cones and sundry Christmas items collected over the years.

Friday, 21 December 2008, I was standing in the back of the store looking towards the front after restocking and straightening shelves. *Jingle Bells* belted out over the intercom, and I noticed that near the front of the store were three small Christmas trees perched on the top of the shelves. One of them had huge lit balls that were blinking in time to the rhythm of the music. The colors changed from all purple then all red followed by all blue and so forth, finally ending with one red light at the top of the tree on the last beat. I was transfixed watching the light display in sync with the rhythm of the music. For the rest of the evening I glanced at the tree to see if it would repeat the light display to the beat of the rhythm of any song but it didn't. It did not light up again nor had it lit up before.

My ex and I left driving north to be with our children the

next day. This year I have been in the Christmas spirit for the first time since the loss of our daughter. Laughter and joy fills the heart and clears the head.

Saturday, 12 January 2008, last night while my mind was open and in limbo it occurred to me that my ability to be a body on the bed, to be in their presence and to also be an observer is something they are unable to do. It was a revelation when this thought hit me and was profound, an epiphany. I lay there wondering if this could be true or was it just my own imagination seeking answers. I wondered if they were even aware that I popped out of my body because none of them ever looked at it, me, when it happened.

There was a tiny white light shining through the curtains not in the same spot as in the past or as large as it has been, then the "glasses" appeared over my eyes with a bright light behind it. I was shown beautiful abstract art of black, grays and white using the bedroom window as the focus. The designs were simple yet captivating, one unique figure after another shaded perfectly. Occasionally things moved such as the window blind slats moved back and forth and sideways then flapped as if in a great wave of wind blowing in through the closed window, and a clock with distorted hands appeared on the wall. One form seen was a wavy river of air or water flowing from the window into the bedroom. I enjoyed these visions and thanked them for the lovely art.

I was restless and weary yet charged with energy. What had I just witnessed? Will they go away or remain, yet each return to bed brought new fascinating entertainment. Was this a reward or was this a way to distract me from erroneous epiphanies? Do other people become three? People speak of OOB, but I have not heard anyone say they become three.

Up and down, unable to sleep, I again returned to bed lying on my back with my head slightly propped up on the bunched up pillow allowing full view of the room except for the wall at the head of the bed. A light was shining through the window blind, very small and not disturbing but there. Two small lights appeared from it and floated off onto either side then vanished. I gazed around the room and a different form of artwork began. I could see this with my eyes opened or closed, it didn't matter, and found it was impossible to keep my eyes closed. There was a subtle smattering of multiple colors, gold, blue and red, of small things floating around unable to distinguish what they were. There were multiple comet-like objects streaking across the ceiling with little curly-cue tails of different sizes. There were multiple little balls twinkling like diamonds, and transparent orbs of different sizes floating around with some coming close to my face. Everything was moving around and I watched fascinated. The room was alive! I got out of bed.

At 5 AM I went back to bed and finally dozed. I suddenly become aware that my pillow is moving; the bunched up pillow is being flattened out on the bed! There is no odor, and my eyes pop open hoping to see the little one, instead I see nothing but what should be there? How do they do that? How can they move the pillow and not be seen or even a presence felt? I think I had been taken and the art display was a distraction.

Sunday, 13 January 2008, on my days off, I visit mom; this afternoon I went to see her. She likes to sit in the hallway near the nurse's station watching the activity, and I pull up a chair to sit with her. She seldom talks, but her eyes are alert, responding to what I say to her. I wonder what she is thinking.

I found the lock on the door knob, the dead bolt and the screen door were all unlocked when I left the house to visit mom. I remember distinctly locking all three after a neighbor had visited late yesterday afternoon. How did they become unlocked today; need I ask?

Tuesday, 15 January 2008, today was one where I should have stayed in bed. I had a dentist appointment at 10 AM, and they were behind in their schedule, so I was behind getting to work. I rushed home to change clothes, replace my makeup, and hurry on to work. I looked for the key to lock the dead bolt and realized the key ring was lying on the kitchen counter; my house is like Fort Knox minus the guards. By 2:00 I had paid a locksmith to unlock the door and was flying down the road headed for work. My sister and I had done this same thing last July that had prompted me to have spare keys made, and were any of them in my purse, car, buried in the yard somewhere, or given to a neighbor, of course not.

Thursday, 17 January 2008, I got off work at 9 PM carefully making my way to the car leaving footprints in the pristine white snow. It was so quiet, no cars, no human noises not even the wind blowing; a silent fantasy land glistening under the parking lot lights casting a soft yellowish glow. The slush in the streets was frozen at the edges of the slippery tire tracks. Relying on the lessons Dad had taught me while driving on snow, I slowly maneuvered the car home remembering to pump and not stomp on the brakes.

It felt good to snuggle into a warm bed with Jezebel beside me and Buster under the blanket. I turned out the lights and saw different layers of English letters moving around, the letters L-O-V came to the forefront individually but wasn't sure of any others that followed. White balls were flying about the room and faint gray, white and black designs appeared. I was surprised as I was under the impression that when the weather is bad they do not come. They are capable of more than we credit them because we give them the same limitations that we have, unless they never leave or whatever is left can be controlled by remote.

Sunday, 20 January 2008, yesterday evening I drew a few pictures of things they had shown to me and some of what I have experienced, unfortunately my artistic abilities are limited, see pages 237 and 238. As I walked to the bed I made a decision not to read as usual. My head had barely hit the pillow when the "glasses" appeared, and did not fade out as they usually do when Buster moves around or if I move my eyes, especially if I move my hands.

Buster was on my chest pressing his nose towards my face when the light behind the glasses changed to a dark reddish glow. It was as if he was checking me out but I hadn't felt his cold nose on my face as I usually can. The light behind the glasses then lightened, he leaned in towards my face, laid his head down remaining in that position. I stared straight ahead with my peripheral vision taking in details around the room, to the sides, above and below the "glasses". In the glasses I watched a swirl of multiple tiny white dots as if watching stars in the sky, and began seeing the wormhole I had dreamt about as if I was again traveling through it and then it was gone. The tiny blue rectangle appeared and a red blotch exploded over the glasses creating red waves around them. I knew they were downloading, and began to have a pressure headache followed by a white flash when it ended. I slept peacefully until after 8 AM.

My buddy sent several articles about the huge ship seen flying over Stevensville, TX on Jan 8, 2008. How can people not believe that living intelligent beings other than humans exist? Maybe they feel safer not believing.

Chapter 27

Friday, 25 January 2008, I went to a computer training class yesterday then stopped to visit with mom. She was refusing to have her hair done but with some encouragement she consented. No matter the age, we women look in the mirror admiring and patting our new hairdos, and I had to smile watching her do exactly that. She is doing really great. I dropped by the library after visiting with her, picked up some books then went to bed early sleeping heavily until 1:00 AM. I am dreaming.

We are in a mountainous region and it looks like it could be on earth. I exit the vehicle's front passenger seat door standing next to it looking at the small village across the fast moving muddy river. On the other side, just before the river bends left, I see four one story wooden shacks on stilts sitting close together with fishnets and other fishing items hanging from the porches. Several people are walking around, and one of them climbs into an old car then drives out of sight to my left on the light colored dirt road between the shacks and the river. Behind the village a steep mountain covered with green trees and thick green foliage rises upward. There are steep pointed mountains around the bend of the river to the left of the village on both sides of the river. I think to myself that I don't know where I am or why I am here.

A man says I should not worry that we are going to someone's house for a bar-b-cue. I open the door and climb into the back seat behind the driver. I look at the driver and see that it is my sister, and I am surprised because I didn't see her on the trip to the village. There other person with us is sitting in the front passenger seat, and although I cannot see him, I know who he is and that he should be there. I am not worried.

The vehicle flies across the river onto a deeply rutted dirt road. The road is narrow with many sharp curves and my sister is driving as if she is in a race at the Indianapolis Motor Speedway. We are surrounded by beautiful lush green foliage as we follow the road deep into the mountains.

Suddenly my sister is no longer in the driver's seat and is setting in the space between the two front seats facing me with her forearms resting on her knees; the other person with us is no longer in the front passenger seat but in the back seat with me. My sister has a mischievous look on her face, telling me that we will be there soon, that someone very special is coming, and that she hopes that I will enjoy myself.

I smile and nod my head in acknowledgement to what she has said; but I am wondering why there is no driver at the speed we are going, and what will happen to us and the vehicle without one. That thought had no sooner flashed through my mind when we hit a huge hole and the vehicle dipped and bounced. My sister who is facing me does a backward summersault, and is thrown forward landing with the front of her body plastered flat against the front windshield. She has blown up like a balloon with little appendages extended outward looking at me and smiling. I am shocked at what has happened then see that her smile is not a smile but a grimace, it is not my sister but a grey, the little one. I begin laughing until the tears run down my cheeks because the puffed up being looks hilarious plastered against the windshield, and we all laugh.

We need to slow down and we need a driver before someone really is hurt. I am in the process of climbing into the driver's seat when the vehicle abruptly slows down and turns left into an unpaved driveway and stops. Another vehicle pulls in behind us from the opposite direction.

We are in front of a one-story small ranch styled house with a picture window. The house is covered with white vinyl and red brick and surrounded by thick green foliage. In front of the open garage door is a man wearing slacks, a short-sleeved shirt, and a long white apron cooking on a charcoal grill. We walk up to him. He proudly points to the pieces of meat that are cooking on the grill then as he turns them over, one falls onto the ground. He bends over, stabs it with a long two-pronged fork, stands up, and thrusts it into my face as if to gain my approval. It looks like a pork chop that has been marinated in a red sauce then dipped in dirt; everything looks normal. Smiling, I nod in acknowledgement and am impressed with their attention to detail.

He tells us to go on in. We enter the house and are standing around talking when the people from the other vehicle enter. I am only paying attention to the woman who is walking in front of the two men behind her. She is very short, looks plump, and is wearing a camel colored buttoned down coat that hangs down to the floor, and looks exactly like one that I own. She is wearing a red, purple and black woven wool hat shaped like a lampshade on her head with the brim pulled down hiding her face. The hat reminds me of the colors and weave of an alpaca wool blanket I had bought in Belize, the one I had hung over my window. I find her get-up amusing and smile at her.

Everyone in the room is standing around watching us; I sense tension. We are now in another room that seems to be a sparsely furnished garage on the other side of the house. She is standing on my right with the top of the hat just above my elbow. I know that this is not my "mother", I wonder if it could be the little one or even one of my grandchildren. Whoever it is, I am delighted to see her.

I watch her as she stands there dressed in the ridiculously heavy coat and wool hat in this warm tropical climate, and I can no longer hide my amusement. One of the men nods his head signaling to me that it is okay to speak as if he had read my mind. I look at the figure in the crazy getup, and smiling I say to her that the hat she is wearing looks like a lamp shade, and crack up laughing. Everybody starts laughing. Suddenly I am sitting in a chair, and pull her onto my lap giving her an affectionate hug telling her that I was only teasing, as I had seen her become tense. She relaxes and leans into me laying her head on my chest allowing me to hold her tightly with affection. We are content.

Towards the end of the dream I become aware of my heavy deep breathing. They are very deep breaths through my mouth as I lay on my left side. I wake up as I hold her on my lap falling into another heavy sleep then waking up as if drugged.

Sunday, 3 February 2008, I went to bed early, turned off the light and the "glasses" immediately became visible on my face. The frontal portion of the glasses was blocked and black. The babes did not seem to mind the light on the other side of the glasses, and I have wondered if they see it. I lay in the dark, the lens cleared, and I thought I saw a tiny light shining through the blinds that did not move. I got up, grabbed a heavy coat and went outside in the backyard to see if I could spot the source of the light.

It was a beautiful clear night sky with brightly shining stars. I looked for anything that could shine in through the window at the angle where I can view it while in bed and found nothing. Thoroughly chilled I went back inside and opened the curtain and blinds then lay in the bed looking out of the window to see if I could see the beam. There was quite a bit of light shining through the window, and I had just about given up, convincing myself that this was all in my imagination, when a bright ball the size of a ping pong ball flashed to the right of the window in the darkened corner. A few minutes later there was a bright flash up by the head of the bed to the left of the window. I lay watching to see if anything else was going to happen then got up, closed the curtain and blinds and went back to bed. At 1:15 AM I awoke after having a strange dream. I am dreaming.

I became aware that I needed to shave my legs. The hair is so long that I bend down and began braiding it. Suddenly I am in a two-story house with my husband and infant son. The other children are not here, and I wonder where they are but I'm not worried. I am tired from endless house chores. I see that my husband has not turned off the light when he came up from the basement. I finish with the last chore and go down the doublewide stairs to turn off the light, so that I can go to bed. I stand on the lowest step and see a hall on my left, two doors on my right, and one door straight ahead at the end of the short hall.

Suddenly I am outside on a flat yellow grassy-like field surrounded by nothing. In the distance I can see three figures. One is a tall, full figured woman wearing an old-fashioned floor length black dress with a little ruffled flounce in the back below the waist. She has on an old fashioned brimmed hat with a maroon ribbon tied under her plump chin. There are two children with her, a girl jumping rope and a boy facing the girl with his back to me.

I approach them noting the woman has a pleasant face and is smiling at me. She begins to talk, but I do not remember what she said because I am not interested in her. I nod in acknowledgement passing her striving towards the children. The woman follows me explaining why they are here, but I am more interested in the children and study the girl to see if she is all right.

The child is the size of an eight or nine year old with a long braid resting on each shoulder. She is wearing a tan pinafore with puffed sleeves and a white petticoat underneath, long white stockings and black shoes. She has stopped jumping rope and is holding the ends in each hand watching me approach. The rope falls onto the ground to the back of her, and the boy moves behind me facing away from me.

The girl and I look at each other, and I become aware that her face doesn't look like a real little girl, as her skin seems to change and become faintly creased and old looking. I look into her eyes and see not those of a child but small, calculating, cynical eyes. I had the impression the child was displeased with me. She continued to watch me as I turn from her and walk away; she is eerie, and I don't want to be around her. I wonder who she is and how she had become this way. I wonder why the boy turns his back to me, I never saw his face. I had wondered if the children were okay, but they seemed to be fine. Actually I didn't believe they were children. I wondered if the woman was the mother or a governess. I continued walking leaving them behind, and was back in the basement standing on the bottom step.

At the foot of the stairs I enter the hallway to my left. There are three rooms on my right and two on my left with another hall at the end turning to the left. The basement is "U" shaped.

I do not look into any of the rooms although I can see that there are lights on in some of them. I pop out of my body and see myself standing alone in the hallway in the middle of the "U" with a bare light bulb hanging down from the ceiling above me. There are too many lights on in the basement, and things don't seem right suddenly becoming frightened.

I round the last corner on my left where there are two rooms to the right and none on the left facing another flight of doublewide stairs leading up. My husband is at the top of the stairs pacing back and forth holding our baby who is wrapped in a white blanket. I call to him, asking him to come downstairs to be with me because I am frightened. I wake up wet heavily sweating.

Chapter 28

Tuesday, 5 February 2008, I am trying to figure out where the children and older woman fits in. They are unlike any other dream involving the beings. I have had a Middle Age theme dream in the past, and now, this one seemingly in the late 1800's early 1900's. Was this an interfered with dream interfered with by another entity? I think it is time to search for a hypnotist as everything seems to becoming mixed in with each other when it use to be separate and clear cut---my earth life versus the beings.

Thursday, 7 February 2008, I went to visit mother this afternoon. As I drove to the nursing home, a feeling of heaviness descended over me, and I had a vision of myself dressed in a white gown swinging a long broad sword over my head with my right hand; I am a warrioress. Every down moment held this vision.

Mom had been placed in bed for an afternoon rest, so we were able to sit and visit face to face without the distraction of activity going on in the hallway. She knew who I was, and I told her what was going on in the family. I end up doing the talking because she can't remember long enough to carry on a conversation yet when you tell her about the family, mentioning names, her eyes brighten and she seems to understand but I don't think she remembers.

After the visit I drove home, made a few business calls then laid down to read one of the library books I had selected. My head started pulsating until I thought it would burst. Unable to concentrate, I got up, worked on the computer, did dishes and the feeling finally went away. I don't know what is happening to me, perhaps I am psychotic but I'm afraid to find out. I don't know how much is me, or how much is them interfering with me, or if I am imagining these past three years.

I watched two new UFO programs and I found myself becoming anxious. It is one thing to have alien interfered with dreams and partially remembered alien events, and totally another to speculate on their existence when I know they actually do exist. What will happen when people learn the truth of the beings existence, to those who don't believe and to those who think they are of the devil? The world could become chaotic with everyone differing in his or her opinions and denying fact. We could destroy ourselves out of pure fear or band together in unity as never before.

I don't seem to be startled by any of the dreams anymore; I just muddle along taking each thing as it happens, then think about it ad nauseum for days on end. Life is becoming tedious, and I want to throw off everything that clings to me, to run away and hide.

Monday, 11 February 2008, I contacted a hypnotist and clairvoyant who is also an abductee and saw her yesterday for a session. I can't afford this, financially I am struggling but I also am at the point that I cannot mentally afford to not do it.

We talked about forty-five minutes with her asking a lot of questions I tried to answer as best I could. I had originally wanted to find out about two dream episodes, the being that burned in front of me and the ceremony. I would give her no details because I didn't want her to lead me and without the details, she refused to ask about them. It was a lengthy session of being in a hypnotic state for three hours and fifteen minutes. Surprisingly it was exhausting, and I was beginning to think that she was never going to release me. Several times I was going to just break it off but it would have taken too much effort, and strangely enough during the whole episode, I was wondering if I really was hypnotized.

I drove home with a headache and could hardly think, went to bed around 8 PM, and the glasses appeared as well as some faces, ignoring everything I promptly fell asleep, woke up at 11 PM, drank a glass of water, and slept through until 7 AM. I have gotten more done today than ever expected, and I am not wiped out.

I do feel better. Maybe it was the safety of knowing that I had the freedom to talk about the beings without being judged. I brought forth things that I had not realized that I myself had created, for instance I learned about "Iron". "Iron" had formed iron bands around my heart, and when she asked it why, the response was to hold my heart together because it had been broken. Amazing what we can subconsciously do to cope with harsh reality. She explained after the session that the iron bands around my broken heart were a way that I was coping with my daughter's death, and not a particularly healthy way. As I brought forth other entities it was enlightening to learn that many things can attach themselves to a person, even things that have no idea why they are there. I also learned the dream involving the short woman in the camel colored coat and lampshade hat was me; I held and comforted myself. She is supposed to send me a summary today via email.

Thursday, 14 February 2008, I went to work today knowing that we have a new computer program to conquer. Fortunately or unfortunately, we are all in the same boat, nobody knows the ends and outs yet, so we will muddle through, hopefully with the good will of customers, until it becomes rote.

Below is a portion of the summary from the hypnotist:
You are processing your experiences vividly since so much has happened, leaving you feeling vulnerable. It's a way for your emotional body to protect itself.

The second energy (from your dream) was Nanna from the 1200's and wanted you to understand your complexity...that you are many experiences (people). The children were there just to get your attention. She wanted to warn you of danger. Nanna warned that if you continue you will find your life is barren. Her presence was making you experience mental solitude, the feeling of being old and complacency about your life.

The Little One was an ambivalent energy whose job was to do the bidding of the Old Ones. Its job was to befriend you and keep you open to bring in more ET's. Its energy was neutral and its vibration, although you felt it was high, was destructive because it only cared about 'them'.

This is also true of The Old Ones. The Old One said it doesn't care what we think. It is self-serving in every aspect. It said you were important to them. That is because you are a willing participant.

Destructive energies disguise themselves as friends, companions and nuisance. They are destructive, self-serving, boastful (it was self righteous). (End)

She had told me that I have a "bright light" which attracts entities but I don't really understand what this means except that this must be the reason that wherever I have lived, strange things begin to happen. I have always felt, and believed that I have a "protection" yet when she started peeling away entities like layers of an onion that had latched on, I was surprised. I hadn't realized that they actually attach themselves to you thinking that they simply "hung around" in the same living space.

From what she has said, I have been duped. How many people can say they have been duped by aliens? Yes, I have been a willing participant at least initially, and even though I want them to go away I still remain curious about them as living entities and, perhaps, that is all it takes to keep them coming back; but I don't think my wishes one way or another makes any difference to them. I also don't know how much her own experience has colored her assessment, and that isn't a fair statement regarding her professionalism, but it can't be ignored either. I will not be able to afford another session. The price was two weeks of my pay.

Friday, 22 February 2008, I slept well last night. This evening I went out about 9 PM to take a short walk, and on the way back as I got to the corner where the street light is, I heard what sounded like a humming but wasn't a humming, and saw a fairly large object's shadow on the street below the streetlight. I looked up and around but did not see anything flying that could make a moving shadow or hum. I'm told a Great Horned Owl lives around here perhaps that is what caused the shadow.

Tuesday, 26 February 2008 all day yesterday I worked on genealogy that I had lost interest in since they started coming. Twice I laid my head down on my crossed arms on the desk, and saw a black rectangle with several greys looking at me and each time the greys were different. I am still a zoo creature.

It is quiet here and I like it. There is no question that I have been used by the beings but I allowed it to happen or did I? I do not know how I could have stopped it. They always seem to have a plan and in control of every situation. My part in the "dreams" remembered is minimal, plus only a portion of the "dream" is remembered and out of context not knowing the before and after. Then too, I'm not sure all of them were dreams. It's true that I had deduced on my own not to trust them and I don't. But in reality, I did not jump up and down waving my hand in the air to draw their attention either; they were just there and I was curious, still am. Is it possible that we are using each other?

Thursday, 28 February 2008, while I was in bed reading there was a bright flash in the living room. When I turned out the light the glasses came as usual except the light around them was brighter. I had my face covered with my hand and over the hand was the top sheet. I began praying and visualizing a white ball of protection surrounding me as the hypnotist instructed. I fell asleep and slept heavily.

Chapter 29

Friday, 29 February 2008, I am aware that I am playing some kind of game. At first I think it is the hand held game I play but this is far more difficult. The game board is four across and four down involving numbers and pictures. I am trying to match them up or put them in some sort of sequence, and seem to be doing all right, then I start to miss them one after the other. The last choice I make shows a picture of a brownish grey with what looks like little scales on him. It is a portrait shot from the waist up with his hands on his hips and a smirk on his face. I wake up and set up in bed in time to see a white ball fly out of the bedroom into the living room. I look at the clock; it is 3:13 AM. I did not sleep well the rest of the night.

Sunday, 2 March 2008, I worked on genealogy without much luck. I wanted to talk to my sister and after numerable attempts I still could not get through to her. My ex-husband has been ill and says he feels better today. We are of an age when anything can happen that will absolutely change our lives forever; it's rather frightening and just confirms how little control one has over their life no matter how healthy you've been. Then I got a call from the committee president saying we will have our monthly meeting tonight at my place, and my place reeks of cigarette smoke that I have to get rid of before 7:30 PM.

So when I went to bed I was unable to sleep, my mind wasn't going to shut down. I read and kept getting up. At 2:30 AM I turned off the light again, and finally dozed off. Several times I surfaced to hear myself snoring and adjust my head only to wake myself up again. The last time I surfaced I opened my eyes and there were white wisps dancing on the wall by the window followed by two white orbs that seemed to enter through the wall behind the head of the bed then disappear.

I thought to myself I don't want them here, and I sure don't want to see their trickster stuff, so I closed my eyes. Instantly as if a switch had been thrown a rectangular "screen" appeared. It was a deep lemon yellow with raised white fuzzy edged writing on it. The writing was not in English making no sense to me, and began moving to the right. I opened my eyes and the writing remained, the clock read 5:18 AM. I turned onto my right side, closed my eyes and the rectangle snapped back into place, and continued to move. I opened my eyes and saw the writing remained then closed them again, and it sped up moving at such a fast pace that it was a blur. I sat up in bed and yelled, "I want no part of this!" and got up, went into the bathroom barely making it to and from because of dizziness.

When I crawled back into the bed, the lemon rectangle and white writing reappeared zooming by. I opened my eyes and looked around wondering if this was all done by remote control, and they did not realize that I was awake and aware, or maybe they did and didn't care. I could see the wispy white strands and what looked like a white three fingered one thumb hand on a long white bent arm then something that made me think of a face. My heart was not racing as it usually does when they are around, but my head felt funny. I closed my eyes again and pages of designs appeared followed by their attempt at cartoon characters, followed by the lemon rectangle and white writing. I think I slept.

If they can capture my attention with designs and cartoon characters then they have me, and I am sucked in like a boat caught in a whirlpool. They are relentless but I'm not really fighting them yet.

Monday, 3 March 2008, Saturday night there was no glasses, no lights, balls or flashes. I slept uninterrupted.

Thursday, 6 March 2008, I went to bed last night, rolled over onto my stomach, and did not move or wake up until Jezebel nose dived into my ear at 6:30 this morning. I have slept this way for the past two nights; it is wonderful! When I went onto the back porch to have my morning cigarette and coffee the sliding glass door was unlocked but the bar was in the door. I know that I locked the door as well as put the bar in place, so what happened during the night, am I sleep-walking? Without a night vision video camera in the bedroom I don't know.

Thursday, 20 March 2008, I am now smoking only outside, not even in the car. Next Monday I start working at the job I formerly had and I am happy about this. I will miss the people from this job but there are rumors of downsizing, it is time to move on.

Every night when I go to bed I wrap myself in the bubble of protection suggested by the hypnotist, and then I start wrapping the family, one by one, to protect them. After the third night I had trouble concentrating becoming suddenly aware that I was thinking about other things; one second I am wrapping a person in a bubble, and then I am not. I believe it is their interference; they do not want the protection bubbles placed which means the bubbles must work or maybe, they don't want me concentrating on anything other than them.

It is quiet around here since I saw the hypnotist; they are still here but not as obvious. I find myself thinking about them, about the weirdness of what has happened, and wonder if it was their intent to alienate me then wonder if they have done this to others.

Am I free of them, or perhaps, they are simply regrouping, and reorganizing their approach? I wonder if they understand our free agency and what it means. I wonder if they can over-ride it, control it or even remove it, so that we will do as they wish becoming a form of zombie. There is no guaranteed behavior or reactions when dealing with humans, at least not as long as we have our free will.

Tonight when I went outside to have a cigarette I watched the stars dance, zigzag and bounce around. Unexpectedly I saw a hazy orb slowly fly over the street and was transfixed to the spot. Hot damn! Is anyone else seeing this? I moved my head to see where it went, and realized there was a cloudy spot on my glasses. It's funny how I really want to believe that these beings do exist even though I know that they do, I want tangible non-dream proof. I still don't think I am afraid of them yet when the hypnotist asked me how I knew I wasn't, I told her I really didn't because I can't remember. I do remember being cautious, trying to prevent them from knowing what I was thinking because they are mind readers, and we are not skilled in preventing others reading ours therefore we're "sitting ducks" for their mischief.

Thursday, 27 March 2008, I had sat on the back porch smoking a cigarette with the babes who were intently studying the night looking for critters. I came in, puttered around until they came in then darted to the sliding glass door locking up for the night.

I turned off the light then lay on my back with the covers pulled up over my head because it was chilly. Even though my eyes were closed there seemed to be a glow in the room and the glasses appeared on my face. There was a white symbol of some kind at the corner of my left eye but was unable to get a full view. I pulled the linens down and the light, the symbol and glasses instantly disappeared but after a few moments the glasses reappeared. I began praying and envisioned being wrapped in the protective bubble and the glasses disappeared. I began in the nightly wrapping of my family individually in the protective bubble and while doing this, I fell asleep.

This morning I woke up with Buster lying close to me and surprised that Jezebel wasn't on the bed. I got up, fixed coffee, and fed the babes. Buster went over and sat by the sliding glass door; this is not like him, he is the first at the food dish. I went to the sliding glass door, and there sat Jezebel on the porch. She was not frantic as I would have expected, strutting in not the least bit upset. I petted her apologizing for her being left out all night. When I touched her the fur was warm and upon inspecting the porch there was no feline mess. Had she been out all night? No she hadn't; I had let them both in before closing the sliding glass door. How did she get on the porch?

Tuesday, 8 April 2008, last Saturday I took down the country blinds then hung a thick drop-down window covering in my bedroom window and over that, I hung blackout drapes. I constantly feel that someone or something is watching me through the window. I am unable to see light through the blackout drapes when standing outside. Feeling watched through windows is not a new feeling to me. When living in the country house, the children and I had this same feeling when watching TV in the family room at night; none of us liked to sit in that room alone after the sun set although we did.

Wednesday, 9 April 2008, I am trying to cut down on my smoking and my strategy is if I make smoking inconvenient enough I will eventually quit. I sit on the back porch or sometimes sit on the bench on the front porch if it isn't late at night, and stand in a shadow at the corner by the front door when it is late.

Thursday, 10 April 2008, I worked until 9 PM yesterday evening, and picked up a cheeseburger and fries on the way home. After gobbling those down, I brewed coffee and sat on the front porch bench unwinding from a busy day.

It was a clear night, the stars seemed to be twinkling more than usual and one seemed to have little white specks shooting off of it. I was looking for more of the white falling things that I had seen the other evening instead occasionally I would see slight arcs of wide smoky things. I moved my head around trying to recreate whatever reflection might be occurring off of my glasses but was unable to replicate it. There were three of them, whatever they were, and high up then disappearing. Jets were flying in different directions at various heights, and I was tracking one when it suddenly veered off to its left, flew backwards towards my area then swooped down in an arc and vanished. Thinking damn, what the hell was that, I wondered if it was a UFO or simply my imagination, it had happened so fast. Shaking my head I gladly went inside.

Friday, 18 April 2008, during a program of the *UFO Hunters* they interviewed airplane pilots. One of the pilots described a UFO in the shape of two diamonds with the tops sitting on each other so that the top and the bottom were pointed, and had lights surrounding the broader middle. I looked back through the journal but was unable to find the date when a small similar shaped object with red and green lights encircling the center was in my bedroom just inside the top of the bedroom window. It took my breath away to see this object recreated on TV.

Last night after turning off the light a lit rectangle appeared on the pillow next to my head. It looked as if there was movement inside of it but when I looked in its direction the rectangle disappeared. This happened twice.

Monday, 28 April 2008, I worked on the computer for a while yesterday while listening to the original *The King and I* on TV. I had forgotten how much I enjoy the music, and stopped what I was doing to watch the death scene as entranced as when I first saw it. Now that the old actors are gone I appreciate even more their stellar acting abilities. Jezebel was setting on my left, and I was stroking her when a white ball about the size of a golf ball flew right by my left eye to my left then disappeared.

After I turned out the light and wrapped the protective

bubble around everyone I sensed that something else was in the room. My heart started beating faster and I began to feel fear but not fear. It went away coming back later then left again. I fell asleep.

Thursday, 1 May 2008, I am really stressed today. I woke up this morning with only Buster on the bed. Sometimes Jezebel sleeps on the other bed but I found her on the back porch again. She shot in like a bullet when I opened the door, and although she didn't seem upset, she was more talkative than usual. How did she get outside? I had checked the porch before I locked the sliding glass door last night.

Saturday, 3 May 2005, I stood in front smoking and star gazing around 10:30 PM; a large smoky plus sign appeared in the distance above the houses. Following that was a thick arc over the house across the street. I can't write every little thing down, it is too much to remember and then who cares, what do I do with the information anyway?

Monday, 5 May 2008, I finished reading *Confirmation* by Whitley Strieber yesterday, and then I wrote him a letter that I will email today. I told him about the waking up with a bruised left eye and the creature burning in front me. Maybe he will answer, maybe not.

Tuesday, 6 May 2008. There are so many thoughts running through my mind about Strieber's book. One of the things mentioned in it is the possibility of man directed and missioned. That is a possibility as there was a time that I did smell human odors, and I am still seeing "shadow" human shapes in and outside of the house. There is also the night

I watched a male "shadow" figure swim around the ceiling fan as if the ceiling was the surface of a body of water plus the five that walked in through the window. How angry and betrayed I would feel if this is manmade. Could it be possible?

Tonight when I stood outside at the front door smoking I thought I saw a huge shape above the houses down the street. It was a mist like oblong shape with a rose color on the bottom present for a second and then it vanished.

I have ridden in their ships, seen other planets, and felt we were selecting where we will live. I feel that I selected a green planet, and have been told that my family will be intact; no one will be left behind. I have been told to trust over and over again, and it makes sense if I and my family are to depend upon them for our preservation. From watching UFO programs, regular people from all over the world have been selected and alien contact made. My problem is I neither believe nor trust them. They are scientists and scientists study targeted projects.

Wednesday, 7 May 2008, Jezebel woke me up this morning by thrusting her nose into my ear; she wants me to get up and give her breakfast. While sipping the first cup of coffee, I noticed my nightshirt seemed uncomfortably tight at the front of my neck. When I investigated I found the shirt on backwards. I'm well practiced in putting my shirts on with the label in the back. When and how did this happen?

The past several days I have felt, not excited exactly, but more like expectant, looking forward to an unknown something.

Chapter 30

Friday, 9 May 2008, I am dreaming.

I have pressure in my lower abdomen, and feel something between my thighs. I know this isn't right and that something is wrong. I am calling for help and a woman, who is tall with long dark hair dressed in a white wrap around, comes to my side. I am writhing around on the bed trying to get comfortable, to figure out what is wrong when she says, "Let me look between your legs." I spread my legs and pop out of my body, and look between them seeing a round white plump head sticking out of me. The eyes are closed and puffy, the nose and mouth are there but not prominent, there is no hair or ears and it makes no noise. I am back in my body lying on my back and the woman pulls the head and body out of me. I watch her with the baby and she says, "Oh, it is dead". I am sad and disappointed that it is dead, and I feel sorry that it has not had the chance of life. Suddenly she yells, "Look! It is alive!" I look at her holding the baby who has now grown into something with long white thin flailing arms and kicking its legs like a human infant. I can still feel the pressure in my lower abdomen; I wake up to go to the bathroom.

I set on the side of the bed with my feet on the floor having the impression that there is movement in the bedroom doorway but I am distracted by the white ball floating towards me from that direction. I watch it because I am curious to see if it leads me into the bathroom or follows me but it does neither, it disappears. I see a flash of eyes just beyond the bathroom doorway about four and one-half feet off of the floor. I blink, look again, and they are gone.

I know that they are here, and I'm waiting for one of them to show its self to me. I lay down on my right side with my eyes shut and there is a bright pink flash in front of my face, and I immediately open them seeing nothing then roll onto my left side. I feel my brain descending into the depths, falling as if I am going to pass out then it stops. A vision of a thick black snake, body and face, flashes on my closed eyelids. The face has intelligence but the idea of a snake, any snake is repugnant, and I deny what I am seeing. I fall asleep.

Saturday, 10 May 2008, my mind is unsettled with thoughts, so many thoughts.

How many varieties of ETs are there? Who keeps track of who sees what, and what the circumstance is when ETs are seen? It's nebulous. I can relate what I've seen or thought to have seen but did I really see anything at all other than what they wanted me to see?

What if there are multiple groups of ETs visiting earth, others besides the greys, reptoids, snake people, Nordics and mantises. I hear discussed "their agenda" but what if there are unassociated groups each with individual agendas or maybe groups with no agenda other than a look-see of earth?

If there are different groups working together as some people believe, I have to ask how it is that they can survive peacefully in a confined environment, avoiding disagreements and upheaval among themselves. We humans can't survive peacefully in our own neighborhoods, our own work place, even in our own homes. How did the different species become involved in a mutual undertaking? Are they from the same planet?

Some have speculated that they are interested in our DNA due to the "scoop scars" left on people but we all know DNA can be obtained by noninvasive means. What is the purpose of the scoop? Identifying our DNA makes sense to me if they want to know where we are on the "chain" and how we are related to each other, and maybe, just maybe, to them. I would love to know a definite answer because I believe that we could be related to them but then that's what they want me to believe.

Others think they have come from a dying or dead planet and we are their last resort for the survival of their own kind. How did they decide who left and who stayed? Was it done by lottery?

Some think they are connected with God and others that they have come here to save us when our planet is destroyed. Why do they need us when they have our DNA, sperm and ova? What they do seem to lack is knowledge about how we think, how we make decisions, how we handle our emotions, and how our emotion effects our decision, at least with me; do they target this area with others?

My buddy has received instructions from them since the age of six. She believes they have been coming for thousands of years. If others can make this statement then maybe that is the one known truth.

Mother's Day, 11 May 2008, I received a beautiful bouquet

of flowers today. I love their fresh scent. I'm planning to visit mom this afternoon and will take her favorite chocolate candy. She is doing well.

Yesterday I started writing but found myself getting all tangled up, and unable to express my thoughts in a logical and reasonable way. I need to do some more thinking about this because nothing that has happened is reasonable and logical in my world, so it is difficult to say what I want to say and make sense.

Monday, 12 May 2008, there were unusually high winds all day yesterday and this morning, the wind chime that sounds like a cowbell rings most of the time. The sun is shining and the temperature is about 68 degrees. The foliage is fresh and a little raggedy from the high winds but still beautiful. Last night nothing happened that I am aware of however, when I stand up, Jezebel runs like hell to get out of the room. Hmm, makes me wonder. She's a jittery cat, but usually not this bad.

Thursday, 15 May 2008, I am nearly finished reading *Breakthrough: The Next Step* by Whitley Strieber. He spends half his time asking them to come and when they do he runs like hell. I can sympathize. I believe the aliens somewhat tailor their visits to correspond with the interests of the human they visit an example is their art productions for me. I am left with the impression that this book seems to focus on the soul, esoteric studies and beliefs, and how the beings visits are possibly linked to these views. Anyone that has been taken searches for an answer.

I believe the beings are doing exactly what they are here to do---study us like bugs on a leaf.

Sunday, 18 May 2008, these beings will do whatever is necessary to push for the outcome they desire; and humans are lilies being picked indiscriminately without impediment from their own species. Instead, the picked lily is discriminated against which is equivalent to a defenseless person found guilty for the outcome of someone else's poor judgment. As long as the alien existence is denied nothing will change. There are many of us who don't need our governments to confirm the aliens are here, we already know that they are.

Some people search for the meaning behind their visits. I believe they will give whatever it takes to make each individual happy, to keep them doing their bidding just as has been done to me. The hypnotist said I was a willing participant and that was a true statement but less so now. I am a skeptic where they are concerned, and no matter how hard I want to believe they are God-like or God sent they are not, I don't trust them.

These beings are extremely advanced with technology that we do not have nor understand, and that needs to be respected. I need to wait for a while before reading more on this subject as my mind becomes overwhelmed and cluttered.

I've had some time to mull over the dream of the birth of the baby grey. I think that I am not one of them, only a vehicle for birth of their own because this baby was not human, and the body I saw was that of a young woman, my body when I was much younger. At the same time as convincing as the dream was, I have to ask if this is what they want me to believe happened in the past when in fact, it did not; I refuse to believe that it did. Last night I went to bed and slept.

Monday, 19 May 2008, I find myself connecting the beings with Noah, how absurd. Yet is it beyond the possibility that the ark was a space ship transporting the animals two by two to a new world, earth? Was man already here or brought here as well? Was man one of the animals? Many of the beings I have seen have animal shaped body parts such as ears, skin and shapes yet most body shapes are the same as man. Were the animals placed on this planet with an equal beginning to observe those that would survive and advance? Do they come to check on their experiment? My mind runs rampant searching for explanations.

Thursday, 22 May 2008, I worked last night until 9PM, stopped for a Big Mac meal and gorged myself when I got home. Fixed a cup of java and stood out front sipping it, and enjoying another last cigarette of the day around 11pm.

There were flashing balls in the sky and one streak of something that looked like a blast of something big, a missile perhaps. I saw some of the thin white things streaking down from the sky and the thicker ones that the other night showed three at the same time and last night even more different, but I can't remember how. I decided that maybe they weren't due from reflections off of my glasses. I also somehow knew that the beings were coming, and was resolved not to show fear in case that I had in the past.

I went to bed, read for a short time, turned off the lights, and rolled over onto my side prepared for sleep. I lay there feeling tremendous anxiety and knew it was due to them being present. I fought this feeling with deep breaths, focusing on mind over matter, and my body relaxed.

I began to see faces, the first being the face of a very stern looking grey that I recognized followed by several others with the last the face of a baby grey I see often. I tell them that I want to see what the other beings look like receiving the standard reply that I will be frightened. I respond that I did not expect them to look human, and if I don't feel threatened I won't be frightened. There were three quick flashes of light and five faces began appearing one after the other. I remember flinching with the first one as it appeared suddenly and was frightening to look at. I said that I didn't know how to "read" their faces, and had heard that the eyes are the "gateway to the soul", and before I could complete my thought I was seeing just eyes. I realized that even then I had no idea if these were good or bad beings.

There are two more quick flashes and I am looking at what I call cartoon pictures. There are five frames each with the same character, the first four the man, looking more male then female with an over-sized nose. I have seen cartoon pictures twice before, and they must be done by the same artist because they have the same character done in a simplistic style. I have not understood them in the past because I never got beyond examining the artwork. Someone told me they did this to relax me, but I'm thinking that this time they may be telling me something. I wondered if the cartoons were a "picture" thought being sent from one of them. I also wondered if it was a picture thought, why they could not send the picture showing what the actual subject looked like. I tried sending back a picture thought asking if this is what they were doing, and before I finished with the thought, which by the way was hard to do, the reply was "yes". Later I wondered if this is how they see us, as cartoon characters with big noses.

I was shown each frame individually and could not look back at the previous one. This is what I remember seeing:

First frame: The man is sitting up in a bed with white sheets. He has on a button down pajama top.

Second frame: The man is sitting up in the bed. The number "3" is drawn in white on the man's left chest then the number "4" is drawn in white on the man's right chest.

Third frame: The man now has only the number "3" on his chest.

Fourth frame: Both of the numbers are gone and a white dagger or bolt of white light is piercing the man's left chest.

Fifth frame: the man is lying flat on the bed.

I fell asleep.

I had no idea what the cartoon meant or if it had a meaning except that I went to sleep. I certainly didn't feel threatened if that was their intention by using a white dagger or bolt of white light in the left chest. No one in the immediate family was 3, 4, 43, 34, 7 or 77. It was a relaxing cartoon and I left it at that.

Chapter 31

Friday, 23 May 2008, today I saw the ophthalmologist and with correction, I have 20/20 in the right eye and 20/25 in the left eye.

I sent a thought picture of myself with a yellow zigzag circle around my left hip, my lower back, and neck with the message that they ache, help me. I waited to see if there would be a response. I became aware that I was looking into a room with six men sitting at one end of a pool table. The picture was dull and hazy. The table did not have pockets in it then thought it might be a billiard table as there was a ridge around it. It looked as if they were dealing out cards, picking them up and looking at them in their hand. I watched for a while, and making no sense from what I was seeing I got up, and fixed something to eat.

Saturday, 31 May 2008, last night a dull and hazy cartoon appeared. I cannot remember the first frame.

The second frame showed a space ship with two large windows. I was standing on the ground looking up at it. The ship looked like two saucers upside down and held together with graduated ridges from the center to the top and the bottom. I became aware that there were greys looking through the windows at me.

The next frame is a close up of the two greys in each window looking at me.

I do not remember the fourth frame. By this time I was anxious and wanted to flee, so I got out of bed.

I visited with mother today. The nurses say she still likes to set in the hall entertained by the antics of the other residents, and to watch the staff. My mother had been a nurse and a good one from what I understand. I wonder what she is thinking as she watches.

Sunday, 1 June 2008, I have been restless for two days and can't set still or concentrate except for short periods. I am tired and listless with sleep offering no relief.

Last night around 11:30 PM I stepped out front for a cigarette. A fat white streak landed almost in front of me. That has never happened no matter how I move my head around to create a reflection off of my glasses. It was rather startling. When I came back in I could smell one of them and although familiar, I didn't know which one it was. I fell asleep.

At 2:05 AM I woke up to go into the bathroom. On the way in I saw blue over by the computer desk that fitted over half of the monitor, and thought I saw writing on it. When I came out of the bathroom the blue was still on the monitor but the writing was no longer there instead there were white circles all the same size which were moving around like a screen saver. I wanted to have a closer look instead I went back to bed sleeping soundly.

Tuesday, 3 June 2008, today is mom's 90th birthday and we are going to party! I decorated her room and we celebrated with birthday cake, ice cream and her favorite chocolates. She was all smiles and really enjoyed herself.

Having read, heard or told that if you ask them, they will

show you your "beginnings" in dream form, so before I fell asleep I asked to have a dream of my beginnings that I would remember.

I am dreaming.

I can see that I am wearing a short white skirt, and running from house to house looking for someone. I am a young man in my late teens or early twenties with a light complexion and blond hair. I pop in and out of my body and am the person and the watcher of the person. I became aware that I need to go into the bathroom and began to drag myself from this dream. It was as if I was under an anesthetic, moving in slow motion, struggling to open my eyes, set up and get out of bed. The odor was prevalent for the little one, and when I glanced at the clock it read 2:04 AM, and I thought to myself this is their time.

I staggered into the bathroom feeling annoyed because I didn't get to finish the dream. Where did this dream take place, and I thought, perhaps Italy, Rome maybe, based on how the boy was dressed. I looked up towards the bathroom door, and could see white symbols in different layers changing and floating around. I didn't have my glasses on, and being half asleep I could not read them distinctly, but I believe they said EEWITHME. I could feel a lightness and excitement then became annoyed because I felt drugged, my brain was foggy, and I wondered why it always seemed to be this way. The symbols disappeared and he and the odor left. I slept.

Thursday, 12 June 2008, I have been very sick. The doc thinks that I have a sinus infection and possibly asthma. I think that I will not make it through this. If they are coming I've been too sick to notice. Several years later I was to learn that I have an allergy to the beautiful Magnolia blossoms becoming ill when they bloom. I now know when they bloom because they smell like dog feces to me.

When I got up in the middle of the night to go into the bathroom a white ball floated in. I said to it, "Land on my hand," and held out my hand palm up. Then I realized he might think that I would grab him so I turned my hand over and said, "You will be safe now. I can't grab you." The little ball settled on my wrist. The other night the same thing happened only this time it landed on the wrist and then on the middle knuckle of my hand. In both instances the ball was not a crisp white but rather blurry, so I wasn't sure if the ball itself landed or if it sent a hologram letting me think it had. Whatever it is, it is intelligent.

Monday, 16 June 2008, today I think I might live. I have an appetite, and food has a slight taste but no odor yet.

My little grandchild had major surgery today, and I don't know how, but I knew when he went under the anesthetic. I guess the easiest way to explain is to say I felt it. I lay down on the bed, and tried to do OOB but that didn't happen, seems I can only do it when with the beings. What did happen was that I had a vision of him curled up on his left side sleeping, floating in a golden bubble sitting at the top of a long golden stem. The stem was like a light beaming up from below him towards his back. The hue reflected was golden and I felt, no, I knew, the ancestors were with him, protecting him. This vision remained with me most of the day until a little after 2 PM I heard the call, "Nana, Nana!"

I had told him to call me when he needed me. I lay back down on the bed asking how I could help him. He told me to sing a song, and that I did then continued sending soothing thoughts. He was quiet for a while then he asked me to hold him, I did. I tried to get a look at his face but it was fuzzy allowing me to only see his little mouth and a small part of his right chin. I knew when his parents came into the room and told him to be with them, as they need him too but to call me when he needs me again. My son has sent a picture of him sitting up in the bed. His face is uncovered but I hadn't been able to see it.

Saturday, 21 June 2008, early morning I had my coffee on the back porch with the cats; they love this time of day watching the other creatures forage for breakfast. I moved to stand up and both cats nearly had apoplexy. Buster was walking to a new position and he literally fell to the floor onto his side. They were frightened by my movement! What happened the night before? What is happening here with my animals?

Monday, 23 June 2008, my grandchild is home recuperating and denies pain. Thank the good Lord.

I turned off the light around 2AM. I couldn't get comfortable and every time I turned, poor Buster had to move. We did this little dance until there were flashing lights and little twinkling balls throughout the room. One of them landed on my eye and a cartoon of four frames appeared.

The first frame was a large brown wooden table with thick legs. There with a lot of small items sitting on it in no specific order. An apple sat in the middle of the table.

The second frame was the same table with four apples sitting on it, two across the top on the left and two down the right side.

The third frame had no apples on it and I remember being somewhat alarmed.

The fourth frame was the same table with many apples scattered around on it. So what does this mean or does it have a meaning?

Friday, 4 July 2008, they were here last night, and I had had a feeling they were coming because the flashes were different. There was the same argument with the one in my mind, probably Macland, about the superiority of aliens versus humans. It always comes down to the same thing----- respect for living beings alien or human or whatever.

I am dreaming.

I am in a room with three beds with white sheets. In each bed is a patient that looks like the cartoon man. In front of me is the medicine cart. I bend over to pull out the individual patient drawer of medicines and a meal tray pops out. I deliver the tray to the patient and go back to the cart. Each drawer I open, a food tray pops out and I deliver it to the patient. I go to the next room and see that it is much larger than the last one. This room has men, women and children in beds with white sheets. I pull out a medicine drawer, a tray pops out, and I deliver it to the patient. I serve each patient, running back and forth from cart to patient. Eventually I realize this dream is very strange and not at all what it should be. Trays should not be coming out of the medicine cart. I wake up.

I opened my eyes and looked toward the bathroom door. In the upper left hand corner of the bathroom doorway a ball of letters floated then broke up forming words. The words enlarged to about three inches but I could not decipher them. They kept moving seemingly to float back and forth, up and down. The first impression I had was they said "EEWITHME" but I gave up trying to read them. The ball of words floated about a foot away from me then disappeared. I sat up in bed and began talking; I was happy to see them.

There was movement in the room, and I could see glimpses of eyes and faces but nothing materialized to show itself. I rolled onto my back then onto my left side, and it was like turning on a switch. Faint scratchy-like letters began to appear and float around. I was out like the light.

Friday, 11 July 2008, last Wednesday night around 1:30 AM; I stood out front smoking the last cigarette for about the 10th time. I was too restless to fall asleep; my thoughts were jumping in every direction. I glanced over towards the houses scanning the area where I had seen the huge object with the rose colored bottom. One at a time, four white squares appeared creating a large square then they seemed to fade leaving only two faint ones in view, one on the right at the top and one on the left bottom of the large square that they had formed. Out of the large square a faint hazy sphere emerged and flew above where I was standing. One at a time, three more flew out. They were not going fast. The fourth one stopped above me then disappeared.

For some reason I wasn't excited or scared, I finished the cigarette, went to bed and finally fell asleep. I woke the next morning in a grumpy mood that followed me all day; I haven't slept well the past two nights.
Was this "square" a portal? Can they create a portal wherever they choose?

Tuesday, 15 July 2008, I laid down about 8 PM last night to read and fell asleep. I woke up at 11:30, let the cats in, locked up, and went back to bed then woke up again at 2:20 AM. I lay in between the layer of sleep and wakefulness when I heard a six note mechanical sound that came from outside my bedroom door. The sound was similar to the mechanical sound heard several years ago when abruptly moving the envelope from the computer desk to the trash basket. I went to investigate finding nothing out of place or any beings. I looked at the clock as I crawled back into bed and it was 2:30 on the dot.

Wednesday, 16 July 2008, I went to bed fairly early last night. I have been tired and grumpy, so figured I need to rest and relax then maybe I'll fall asleep. I grabbed a book from the bedside table, and lay on my back with the book propped up on a pillow on my chest. There had been many pictures on the wall at the foot of my bed, but last week I took them down leaving only four hanging. Looking at the page on the left of the open book I could view the wall at the foot of the bed, movement attracted my attention. I watched a long rectangular light, the length of the picture closest to the outside wall appear by the picture frame then vanish. I watched that spot for a few minutes but nothing happened, so I moved the pillow and book slightly to block their view of my face from the wall. I know this will not stop them but it lets them know that I am aware they are there. I have seen rectangles slide along the wall as easily as the light from a flashlight moves along a wall, and have even seen the rectangle bend to go around a corner. They have to get bored as hell watching me. Why on earth do they do this? I thought I was crazy, maybe they are.

Thursday, 17 July 2008, I came home from work last night exhausted, read for a short time and fell asleep. I am dreaming.

I am lying on my right side with my knees drawn up to my chest. Someone behind me is telling me that he is going to have to do it 15 times to each side of the vertebra. My land, I am thinking, that's 30 times and he said it would have to be done a total of four times, that is 120 times to each vertebra! I pop out of my body and look at myself lying on my side, and at the sitting being leaning forward examining my back. I remember nothing more.

Chapter 32

Thursday, 31 July 2008, yesterday was a hassle. I spent nearly 45 min, on the phone with a Medicaid woman then hustled off to work without time to eat. I left work at 1PM still without food, jumped into my 12-year-old car, and sped my way to the Medicaid office to learn that my mother's payments will increase due to an increase in the little royalty she has. I don't mind paying Medicaid for mom's care, they deserve payment but they could care less about her taxes or that she is paying off a huge loan made in good faith by her grandson to help her long before the need of Medicaid. I left with a massive headache, exhausted and frustrated. I kept my big mouth shut for fear coverage would be canceled then both mom and I would be in a simmering pot of stew.

Today I got everything set in motion that needs to be done. The nightmare stories I had heard are not rumors. The noise I hear today is the grinding of my teeth.

One cigarette after another, plenty of fluids because I was dehydrated and a good book, *Plague Ship* by Clyde Cussler, thank the good Lord, I finally drifted off.

I was half awake realizing that I needed to go into the bathroom, urgently. Somehow they can trigger whatever in my body to make me want to go to the bathroom because it seems like all of their visits and dreams correspond with bathroom visits. Perhaps it's because while growing up before we went anywhere, mom would always ask us if we went to the bathroom. It's deeply ingrained in my sister's and my daily routines, we still follow the old instruction as given in childhood, perhaps that is why. With my eyes closed and positioned on the side of the bed to stand up I am presented with another cartoon. I opened my eyes and the cartoon is still there. There are two frames.

The first frame is of a bicycle sitting in front of a doorway. I thought the bike looked familiar and realized that it was like a blue and white bike I had as a child, and it even had the basket on the front handle bars.

The second frame is of a familiar hallway with open doors down each side, and I realize my mother's room is off of this hallway in the nursing home.

"They know too much about me," I grumble out loud, "and this is just not acceptable." The clock said 3:50 AM when I crawled back into the bed. There were balls flying all over the room, and I didn't give a hoot. There was a feeling of excitement, of expectation but I shared none of these feelings; I was annoyed!

This morning I put all of the Medicaid requests in order and got the ball rolling for some and completed others by 11 AM. All of the errands are now run, and I am ready to meet with them again today.

While driving home from the meeting I began to see the humor in the two frames and something deeper. The humor was they had dug up pleasant memories of my old bike that I had ridden all over the small town I grew up in, and connected it in to my mother who is now in a nursing home. The bicycle represents the past when my mother had cared and provided for me, and now I must do the same for her, the past and present in two poignant frames. They must have standards and morals to come up with this cartoon at least they know what I should do that is morally right on this earth. And I did it.

Thursday, 7 August 2008, last night I had two pairs of slippers by the bed for my four feet, a blue pair and a white pair. When I woke up this morning, there was one white pair, and only one blue slipper. I have searched everywhere and cannot find the blue slipper. I have even looked outside around the building, and cannot find it.

Sunday, 10 August 2008, this morning there was an orange piece of square paper lying on the floor by the bed. It had "inspected by 23" written on it. I have purchased nothing recently, and I do not know where it came from. There is also a piece of white paper lying between the screen and the grate on the left side of the back porch door. It is a bar code from "GAP" and was not there before. I have bought nothing recently from the GAP that would still have an "inspection by" or barcode label on them. Now where did these come from, and how did they get here?

I went outside to sit for a while this evening and glanced around, there was a large beam of light shinning down from the sky onto an area where there are houses and then it was gone. It wasn't a tiny little thin light it was large but I could see nothing in the sky.

As I was falling asleep last night around 11:30 multi-colored letters and symbols appeared in a little patch over by the bathroom door, and although I was aware of them, I didn't care and fell asleep.

Monday, 11 August 2008, I was up a little after eight this morning, took a shower, and found a two inch scratch on the outer upper left leg with bruising. I did not have it when I went to bed, so where did it come from? It is deep enough to have some scabbing developing, and it would have hurt when done, so I would have remembered doing it.

This all bothers me as it is not consistent with their past behavior. I don't think it is the same group even the faces that flash through my mind prior to falling asleep are not the same. One reminded me of the dog family, and the others were mean looking little greys. The only consistent thing that continues is the little white ball that seems to follow me around and makes its self visible to me. It is more easily seen in the dark but I do see it during the day too. What the heck is going on, why the changes?

Wednesday, 13 August 2008, it is 4:32 AM and something very strange has occurred. I was aware that I was dreaming or was I?

Instantly things are confusing in a way that I cannot describe, and I am not sure how I know but I do know that they are here to take me away. I do not even know if they are actually in the room touching me or if it is the initial phase but they are here. I begin yelling "NO, NO, NO, NO" over and over and as I yell my voice changes into a deep male mechanical sounding voice. My throat hurt as it changed to make this different sound. I begin thrashing around in the bed but they or something now has a hold of me, trying to control me, and during this struggle I am having difficulty breathing. My breathing stops then becomes ragged as I fight to breathe; I know that I might die if this doesn't stop. If I can wake up the person in the bed next to me, they can help me and I am reaching over to pinch them.

All of this is going on at the same time, my yelling "NO", thrashing in bed, trying to pinch the person in bed with me, having difficulty breathing while determined that they are not going to take me. I wake up. It is 3:51 AM, there is a red word on the wall, and I am aware of symbols but I don't care or even try to read what is there; I am focused on trying to breath.

Jezebel and Buster lay on the bed undisturbed. The bed is not a mess and there is no one else in the bed with me. The smell of the little one or any of the others is not in the room, but there are white balls flying around. I felt powerful, very powerful that I had defended myself and prevented them from taking me. It was instinct, my basic core instinct and I, my waking, plotting, planning self, had nothing to do with it. It was my basest of preservation instinct, fight, kill. I have a fresh scratch on my stomach that itches. Did I really stop them and who was the other person in bed with me? What really happened?

Tuesday, 9 Sept 2008, Sunday evening while standing on the front porch having the last cigarette of the day and scanning the sky, I saw a huge rectangle opaque in the middle appear at the end of the street in the same area I had seen what I thought was a ship with a rose colored bottom. It lasted about six seconds then was gone. It couldn't have been much longer than thirty seconds when an opaque orb flew down the street from my right darted to the left of where the rectangle had been then vanished. I saw it again going towards where the rectangle had been then vanish. Was it the same one or were there two?

Several weeks later I was standing on the front porch scanning the sky. A large cloudy area appeared at the end of the street close to the area where I had seen the ship with a rose-colored bottom and large rectangle. It was dark in the middle visible for a few seconds and then closed. It couldn't have been much longer than 30 seconds when an opaque oval flew down the street from my right stopped and set in front of my house then darted into a hole that appeared in the cloud and vanished. Shortly after another oval arrived and sat briefly then it too shot off entering the dark circular opening at the end of the street and disappeared. The opening closed. A third oval flew up and set in the same place as the others. The ovals have been large enough to hold a moderate sized person in a sitting position, and each appeared to have an occupant. I am awestruck by what I am witnessing when I see a head in the oval hovering in front of me, turn, look in my direction then shoot forward into the dark circular opening where the others had disappeared.

I didn't wait around to see if other ovals with occupants were going to follow because I was worried about the one that turned its head and looked at me. I knew it had seen me, and I wondered if the others had as well. I ground out my cigarette and shot through the front door locking everything possible to lock wishing there were more locks, turned off the lights, and headed for the magic covers on my bed. I didn't go out front for the last cigarette of the day until 2012. If they are flying down my street to enter into a portal I don't want to witness it.

I was reading the History Channel's website on UFO's. One contributor said that the greys were insects filled with liquid. The one I was allowed to examine did not feel that way as I could feel what I thought was a bone covered with skin, but there could have been liquid within the "bone". I have no experience with insects and have never seen a grey with a broken appendage, so I have no way of determining what they are filled with, it could well be true.

I have read the greys absorb nutrients through their skin as well as the function of elimination. This sounds efficient but also somewhat confusing, and I wonder if they have or even require kidneys or something equivalent? Certainly the odors from the greys are stronger at times, and because of what I have read I attributed the strength of the odor to when they may have last "eaten". If this were true, there would be no need for kitchens, kitchen staff, food waste disposal and dining rooms; even toilets would not be required or waste storage tanks. But what about the other beings and the humans I have seen? Does absorption and elimination occur in the same manner for them? Were the Evolutionary Enoids genetically designed to function this way? I think the answer lies in from what did an Enoid evolve.

Thursday, 11 September 2008, yesterday I showered when I got up and found my back was stinging when the water hit it. When I got out of the shower I looked in the mirror and saw that I had a large number of small-darkened areas all over my back from waist to shoulders. Along the left side of my spine were four small round areas that seemed to be evenly spaced and felt were in the area that had burned while showering. I checked again today, and the spots remain while there are none left on the right side.

Reviewing the journal I had written on 17 July 2008 of a grey's assessment of having to do something to my back. Today, 24 days later, I have marks on my back. Is there a connection?

I could go completely crazy trying to make reasonable sense out of what is happening. Whatever the answer to the question is, it doesn't really matter, this is how I am surviving, and yet it does matter because I want to know. I am betwixt and between.

Thursday, 18 September 2008, I went to sleep around 1:30 AM, and woke becoming aware that I am watching the beginning of a movie where the title and credits are being shown. It is not quite like humans prepare this portion but very close. Although the words seem to be written in English they are not registering in my mind, so I am unable to read what is written. I see a few drawings and two bright yellowish objects in the upper left portion of the pictures just out of sight. I know that if I shift my eyes to get a better look at them the entire program will disappear. There is a red object towards the bottom right, and although I can see it, it doesn't have any meaning for me. It is a soundless musical and I am delighted with the dancers reminding me of the Fred Astaire and Ginger Roger's movies I had been watching earlier. I knew that whoever had created the mimicking of a human musical had done it for me. I wonder if the beings dance. The entire show lasted about 30 seconds as the items flashed before my eyes one after the other. When it was over I applauded the creator for his efforts.

I lay still while faces shifted, never becoming clear, marched before my eyes. I became aware of the top of a ledge from which a head began to slowly rise up, and stop just below the eyes. My first impression was the eyes were piercing but not menacing, my next impression was, "Oh, he is shy!"

He was very black, a soft midnight black, blacker than black. The shape of the top of the head was a rounded point. The eyes were startling as they were a crisp white with round black pupils. I knew that this being was the creator of the entertainment I had been shown and I thanked him. I wondered if he hadn't created all of the cartoons that I have been shown. I will call him the artist. The clock showed 3:08 AM. I slept.

Sunday, 5 October 2008, I fell asleep early yesterday evening then woke up around 11 PM, finished some chores I had started earlier in the day, answered some emails, and went back to bed about 3:30 AM.

I become aware of the "feeling", the "body panic reaction" when they are going to move you. I am lying on my left side, and feel my body quickly placed on my back. As they flip me onto my back I say, "I won't hurt you". There are two of them, and they are small. I don't think they are the greys but I'm not sure because I can't smell them. I feel my body gently lifted, and we fly to what I think is the bedroom door then turn towards the front door. I remember my buddy say many times that she has been taken through the wall, so I say, "No, no, I want to go through the wall. Please take me through the wall". I hear a sigh up by my head and feel our direction shift towards the guest bedroom where we quickly pass through a wall. I feel a brief sensation that I cannot describe nor remember and hear what sounds like static.

We are floating upward, there is a light, and I am aware there is something above us assuming it is the ship. I am aware that the light is guiding and protecting us because the air temperature is not cold nor is there a breeze. I say to the being on my left, "Let me hold your arm. I want to hold your arm" which he allows me to do. I place my left hand on his right arm and gently rubbing his small arm twice I realize he has hair on his arm. I am surprised because I have never felt hair on them before, and doubted that the being was a grey. The hair was not thick like an animal such as a cat or dog, more like the hair on our arms but slightly courser.

Suddenly the ship is above us and I am surprised at how far we had to travel. I am told to get ready to get on board. Everything happened quickly and is somewhat muddled. The room is similar to the one I described earlier when I was tossed in it like a rag doll. There are three others there waiting for me, and I can see their shadowed figures from the light showing through the open door behind them. They are tall and thin wearing white robes, they are the old ones. As we prepare to enter through the door I am stopped and told by one of them that I will remember nothing more. I am disappointed and know my protests will make no impression but I am pleased to have been allowed to remember this much as it is the first time. I wake at 5:02 AM.

It is very easy to confuse a "routine" visit with them and my life here on this earth, everything seems intertwined, their world and mine. The human quandary is to make sense of what happens based on current knowledge and experience, but when I am with the beings I feel like I know everything and nothing at all when I am on Earth. Are the beings totally separate from us or is it possible that there is more depth to what is happening to me and others in this world.

It has been three years since I first saw the space suits in the doorway.

Chapter 33

My ninety-year-old mother had a fall and broke her other hip, stabilized then lingered for a few days while a hospice patient. Then suddenly declining, she passed away. I was there when she died. The nurse in me said everything is going smoothly while the daughter in me was horrified by what I was witnessing. This old woman in the bed is not just any old woman, she is my mother. I wasn't prepared for her death even at the age of ninety, and even though I had watched her decline, I wasn't prepared for the end. Her body received ceremonial preparation required by her religion, and was cremated on the 30th anniversary of our father's death. My sister pointed out that we are now orphans and we are.

My ex-husband has a girlfriend, who he has never mentioned and that's okay, he's a bachelor. But since I didn't know she existed, it was out of the blue when I received an invitation from her to attend a function with the two of them even telling me what they will wear. I declined; my mother had been dead for only a few days, and I needed solitude. I was disappointed in my ex because he hadn't mentioned her then realized that she must not know that I didn't know about her. How confusing life can become due to the lack of communication.

I am stressed to the max between the sudden death of mom, the beings, taxes, Medicaid, probate court, wills and lawyers and bills, bills and more bills, and now this. I have hit my limit, and I do what I always do when frustrated and stressed, I either clean house or bake. I clean house.

I head for the attic. I have kept everything from my childhood, and my children's childhood then moved on to include the grandchildren. I am a sentimental hoarder, and have sixty years of stuff preserved, lovingly wrapped, boxed, labeled, and carefully stacked in the attic. The attic is filled with boxes. I sort through each and every box, removing all family heirlooms and special keepsakes trashing the rest. I watch sixty years of my life ride down the street in the back of a garbage truck. When I die the boys will not be burdened with mom's junk that they would have tossed away anyway. I feel good, really good and I feel clean.

I give the wall to wall furniture I have amassed over forty years critical assessment, made my selections, and called Paralyzed Veterans of America who were more than happy to accept the antiques. I dusted, rearranged furniture, vacuumed and on the seventh day I rested. I feel really good and I'm content.

No wonder the beings want to be with me 24/7, who knows what will happen tomorrow.

Saturday, 11 October 2008, I started reading a book written by Jeanne Marie Robinson entitled *Alienated: A Quest to Understand Contact* sent to me by my buddy. I turned off the light at 1:30 AM, and went to sleep then woke up at 3:01 AM. I had been dreaming a "war" dream.

I am battling, fighting and killing with my sword. My sons are beside me, and I can see their shining steel swords raised in the air as we push onward surrounded by men also carrying swords and flags. There are white saddled horses some with riders battling on our side. We are in the

Middle Ages, and the battle is physical and bloody. As I awake I am aware that it is a dream and wonder why I am dreaming this awful bloody battle scene as I urgently get up to go to the bathroom. I can smell the powerful heavy odor of one of the little ones, they are here and waiting. I turn on the light. I feel drugged. I mull over turning off the light versus leaving it on deciding that I will not sleep at all with the light on, and I was tired. I woke up around 7:30 AM, unsettled but I didn't know why. I was more tired than when I went to bed.

Thursday, 23 October 2008, I am dreaming.

I am standing by someone on my left who is showing me a head lying on a chest-high table, and I wonder if this is someone my sons and I killed during the battle I had dreamed. My attention is drawn to a large amount of dried dark red blood on the head's right side as if it had been bashed which I assume was the cause of death. The fact that it was just the head did not bother me although I wondered how it was attained and what happened to the body. Above the jagged cut on the neck where the head had been severed, the head is covered with reddish-orange fur with a hint of gold. The scalp portion of the fur is long and matted. The hair on the face, ears and neck is approximately a quarter inch long laying flat without ruffled areas. The closed eyes are human sized and there is a human appearing nose, mouth and ears; the expressionless face looks as if he is sleeping.

I am listening to the being speak about the head as I look at it. I have many questions about it with the first being who is he and the second how did this happen although I think the being is telling me this information. I do not consciously hear what he is saying because I am absorbed in my own thoughts, and I think, why am I here? Instantly I become aware that I am lying on my back on top of the bed covers with my hands lying on each other on my abdomen. I fall back to sleep.

Sunday, 26 October 2008, I had a great day yesterday. I got so many things done even planted little pansies that bring so much color on a dismal cold winter day. I worked on genealogy, family members living in Pennsylvania captured by Native Americans during the Revolutionary War. It's always exciting to find out who you are. I have decided to give the oldest grandchild her ancestor's story plus a book on Mary Jamison who was captured by Native Americans telling her story, *Indian Captive,* before she died in her 90s. I think it will make a great Christmas gift, I hope she will appreciate it someday if not now.

When I finally turned off the light there were four blinking white balls. Of course, then I didn't want to fall asleep and miss something, so I played opossum. I hadn't lain there long when I could smell a being, a powerful strong odor, and it wasn't one that I was familiar with. Jezebel jumped off of the bed and ran out of the room while Buster continued to lie beside me. I began seeing faces that shape-shifted and then boom, one that didn't. It looked like a lizard, a young one, and there was intelligence and mischief in his eyes. He was darker then a lime green and had bumps on him of different sizes. I didn't see any teeth but then he didn't open his mouth. I didn't like what I was seeing, so I mentally called for the little one who always comes, telling him that someone I didn't know was here, and that I didn't trust him.

I continued my thought sending of where are you; I need you! Shortly after, I began seeing tiny red lines that formed the simplest of pictures. They seemed unconnected but then would form a figure then sketches of faces. The color changed to yellow forming faces then they turned white and I could feel myself relax.

I heard laughter in my head then him saying, "You are such simple creatures that can be relaxed by such simple means." I didn't like what he said, but it was a true statement and corrected him by replying, "We are innocents not simple," and he laughed again. I tore into him concentrating on our innocence compared to him and the other beings. I opened my eyes and could see curly cues floating around the room and red oval shaped blotches. I rolled over onto my left side and saw that it was after 1 AM. That is the last I remember until I woke up this morning.

Monday, 10 November 2008, today I am unsettled and expecting, expecting what I don't know. I continued thinking about them, and how they keep those of us who they have contacted in a constant state of anxiety and readiness. What the hell are we waiting for? It seems to me like a waste of energy, time and emotion since they give us nothing of significance to mull over.

Tuesday, 11 November 2008, I am dreaming.

My family and I are together; I think we are on vacation. My ex-husband is even here looking dazed not quite knowing what to do. We are in a huge complex, buildings within buildings with many levels. It is all white and absolutely massive.

There is a discussion about who is going to stay where but there isn't enough room where we are for all of us. I tell them I will go to another hotel which I know has room and they can stay here. I am a bit annoyed, and leave looking back at them standing in the doorway watching me. I am alone and in somewhat of a huff. I realize I have been here at least one other time as I recognize everything I see.

In my hand I find I am carrying what looks to me like a dark brown wooden yardstick. There are small white people following me, and trying to get me to turn back but I am determined to find a place to stay, and refuse to go back. I begin running and dodging around the corners of huge white block like structures that is part of the décor. One of the little ones jumps out at me and I whack him with the yardstick. The battle is on and I find I am enjoying this whole thing of acting like a child running and whacking and playing. I whack another one. It seems serious yet it isn't, we're playing. Now they are shooting little round black pellets at me but every one of them misses, and I continue running and dodging and whacking. The pellets come out in showers. I do not feel that they are trying to hurt me after all it is a game but I am sensing serious undertones. I round a huge white block with my yardstick raised ready to whack and defend myself while at the same time one of the little ones comes running up the entrance way with a white "rifle". At first I think it is a "prod stick," and I am surprised stopping dead in my tracks then watch it morph into a thin wooden white rifle that resembles what high school kids carry in their marching bands. He is looking at me and I am looking at him; we are both holding our weapons ready to whack and shoot but I know that he has won this game and I lower my yardstick.

I awake and open my eyes that immediately go to the area above the closet door, and sense activity in the room; I can smell the little one. On the ceiling is an enormous rectangle that seems to have writing on it. I can see what might be a picture and different colors reminding me of the front page of a newspaper. The whole thing is blurry and faint, and I am unable to read it or clearly see what is on it.

I head for the bathroom, and am aware that the huge rectangle is falling down off of the ceiling as if being peeled from it. It is following me into the bathroom, and I am thinking that they must really want me to see what is on it. I see streaks of white moving around the bedroom everywhere. I am sitting in the bathroom watching the bathroom door because there is a lot of activity on the other side. I can see little white people scurrying around; I think it is little white people but they aren't clear enough to see their whole body at one time.

Suddenly the rectangle with the writing and picture appears at the bathroom door carried by two little greys, one on each side of the bottom, and even though it is now the size of the doorway it is still blurry and unclear. Somehow I know that it is a hologram, but the two little ones are straining to carry it as if it were a heavy billboard. From the doorway where they had paused, they carry it into the bathroom turning the billboard sideways so that the picture and writing is facing me as I sit. It reaches from the floor almost to the ceiling and is about five feet wide.

My first thought is surprise that they would bring it into the bathroom. I think that they really must want me to read it if they brought it in here but I couldn't because it was still distorted having been enlarged so much. I then think this is hilarious, and I threw my head back and started laughing. It struck me funny that they would turn the damn thing sideways and haul it into the bathroom where I was sitting so that I could see it and even though it was inches from my face, I still couldn't see it clearly. The "newspaper" instantly disappeared but I could still get glimpses of them moving on the other side of the bathroom door. I was still laughing as I headed back to the bed.

When I crawled back into bed I knew they were still there and they were not finished. That old nasty feeling of creepy fear would surge through me, but I fought it with all I had and each time I was able to calm myself down before I finally fell asleep. My thoughts are always the same---"Don't let them see that you are afraid" and yet I am well aware that they know as they read my mind like a book. Why do they allow me to think that I am winning this battle? Is it part of a learning thing?

Were my family and I taken last night, or was it just me? Was this one of the "role" playing situations where they set up a situation throwing me into it to see how I will react and what I will do? I have had many of these but not one like this. Just maybe I got loose on the ship with some sort of a weapon in my hand and I walloped the daylights out of unsuspecting beings. That is what I think happened.

Chapter 34

Sunday, 16 November 2008, these creatures must get bored like us earthlings for they seem to present a subject then move on to something else. Now it seems as though I am to see more things in the sky.

Driving home from work yesterday evening around 6:45 PM, it was dark and I could only see two stars in the sky due to the lights from town. I'm sailing down the road at the speed limit, and to my left the one star seems to have a light shining straight down from it to an area behind some houses. I saw only a couple of seconds of it before trees and houses blocked out the view. My impulse was to slam on the brakes and back up as there were no cars behind me but there was a sharp curve in the road and it was dark. From then on my head was swiveling to the left but I did not see it again although I could see the two stars. I began to wonder if they really were UFOs, especially the one that had the light shining down from it. It could also have been a reflection off of the windshield but I don't think so because I had seen it through the side window.

Friday, 5 December 2008, it's been awhile since I have made an entry into the Journal. Actually not much spectacular has happened although there have been a few things, and I will hit the highlights.

My son and granddaughter came for Thanksgiving and I admit to being somewhat hesitant not knowing what the aliens would do as both have been in my dreams with the aliens. Every morning upon inquiry I was assured that they slept well and had no strange dreams. My granddaughter denies even dreaming, however, I had one very short dream with her in it.

My granddaughter and I are walking together holding hands, and we are in a hurry to get some place. I know where we are and it is vast. I turn to her and say, "Oh, I hope that I haven't lost my necklace, I mustn't lose it," and reach up to my neck to feel for the pearls finding them. I then pop out of my body and see myself feeling for the pearls while holding my grand-daughter's hand. We are dressed in white, and I can also see the gold chain that I wear but didn't feel. We are excited. I remember nothing more.

The second event occurred when my sister and her husband arrived in December. They will be visiting with me for six weeks then will leave on a business trip in Florida.

Friday, 12 December 2008, I woke about 6 AM, it was still dark out, and I began to see designs floating in the air and had the impression that four little beings were floating out of the bedroom window. I will have to wait until my sister wakes up and find out if she had any dreams last night. Staggering into the kitchen with eyes not yet focused for greeting a new day she mumbled that although she dreams every night she hadn't dreamt about the beings last night.

Sunday, 14 December 2008 1:00 AM, my sister and I went to our rooms to go to bed, and read around 8:30PM leaving her husband sitting in the living room watching TV. I read for a while then turned out the light and fell asleep. I am dreaming.

I am in a house looking for someone or something. Someone is with me, maybe family, but I don't know which family member but it is okay, I've been in this house before. We look through the house then head back towards the front and meet a relative of the friend who owns the place. He tells me to go downstairs into a room, and I will find what I am looking for, so I head downstairs thinking that whoever is with me is coming too but when I get to the room I find I am alone.

I am looking at a Mayan shaman somehow I know who he is. He is very real, and is aware that I am looking at him. He has shape-shifted until I am tired of it and say, "Show yourself, I am not afraid." He is tall, dark skinned, brown eyed, hook nose, large ears, black straight hair cut below the ears, long robe which is a tan or light brown and wears a headdress of multiple colored feathers sitting like a halo on top of his head. He is regal.

I am awake and hear the squeak of the closet door opening. I feel the hair on my face stand up and have that crazy familiar feeling of being charged with electricity. I feel no fear, and I know that they are here but I don't know for sure what is going to happen. I feel myself being quickly moved onto my back then floated into the closet, and rising up into the air. There are two of them one on each side holding my arms. I grab the one on my left and throw him away and down from me, and he grabs onto my ankles. The one on my right is still guiding me and I can feel the weight of the one hanging onto my ankles as we continue to rise in the air. I grab the one holding my right arm and throw him down and away from me and he floats off. The next thing I know

I am back in my bed yelling "NO, NO, NO!" as I hear the closet door squeak again.

I lie there for a minute catching my breath then turn on the bedroom light and see one of my cats emerge from the closet. The door was closed when I went to bed but now it is open, and neither of the cats have the talent of opening doors. The time is 11:50 PM.

I can see light through the space at the bottom of the bedroom door, and that my brother-in-law is just now turning off the living room lights. After he left the room I went into the kitchen and peeked through the window blind. A neighbor is starting up his red pick-up, and I can hear another car moving in the street but do not see the beings or a ship. In the past they have always come in the middle of the night when no one is up. The next day my brother-in-law said he had not heard or seen anything.

I am surprised at my behavior; in the past I've looked forward to their visits. Last night I had felt no fear or anger, I just did not want to go with them and threw them off of me, and what is surprising is that they let me. There was no doubt in my mind that it was them with that funny feeling of my hair standing up on my face, the feeling of electricity running through my body and the floating sensation. I realized that when the hair stood up on my face that I have telepathically said to them in the past not to be afraid that I would not hurt them but I had no intention of saying it this time. I did not want to go with them.

So what has happened to make me feel this way? I was somewhat shaken after this experience because I am not one who purposefully endangers another living creature. I wonder what has happened to make me not give a crap about them throwing them off of me while we are floating upward. I hadn't considered what would happen to them when I threw them off or what would happen to me without them holding on to me, yet I was safely back in my bed.

I have looked forward to their coming and learning about them but since the last episode where I ran around smacking them with all of my strength I feel a definite apathy towards them. It could very well be that I was taken last night and awoke while being returned letting me think that I had escaped being taken. Hmmm, the more I think about it I betcha that is what happened.

Monday, 15 December 2008, my poor black long legged beautiful Jezebel is very sick. I took her to the vets and had to leave her for them to do blood work and evaluate her condition. I hated to leave her; she runs and hides when the doorbell rings how on earth will she tolerate left in a strange place with strange people in a cage being poked and prodded? She will be terrified! I silently cry for her and reluctantly hand her over to girls in the office, and go to work.

The doctor called me at work telling me she was gravely ill, and I had to decide whether or not to put her through treatment for possible leukemia or an autoimmune disease. When I returned to the office they brought her out to me with an IV in her little arm. I had heard her cry like a small frightened child either in pain or fear when she was lifted from her cage and my heart broke for her. I couldn't put her through the torture of needles and blood transfusions, and trips back and forth for treatment. He put her to sleep while I hovered over her sobbing, and whispering in her ear how much I loved her. It was awful, heartbreaking. My brother-in-law buried Jezebel under my bedroom window, and that night I could hear a cat meowing by my bedroom window. Later I could hear the cat meow in the bedroom and as I write this book, I can tell you that she is still here as I have seen her many times in the house.

Wednesday, 31 December 2008, since they have changed their style of visits and activities, I have yet to figure out what their new scenario is, and I have felt somewhat abandoned. There is a chance that many would say that I should feel grateful but I have not as the beings are fascinating even though I do not understand them. To be in touch with a living being from another world who is not malevolent is a gift. It is the fault of neither that I don't know what to do with this gift.

I become aware that I am dreaming and there is a tug of war within me to get up and go to the bathroom. A participant in my dream is urging me to get up and go while I am resisting but eventually I snap completely awake, and go into the bathroom. I no sooner get into the bathroom than I become aware of writing beginning to form in front of me. At the same time I am also aware of a familiar feeling of not what we earthlings call love but of a deep fondness and acceptance; I know which group is here.

I am unable to read the white English letters forming on the white background and the poster like picture moves to my right so that it has the background of the white bathroom door and the writing seems clearer. Three pictures are presented but I am unable to discern detail and therefore unable to read the English letters forming words. The pictures are about two by three feet.

The first one has writing on it, and a pair of arms with the palms of the hands pressed together as if in prayer. The hands stop me cold and I no longer try to read the words as I am trying to count the fingers on the hands because they are long and narrow and seemingly unlike human hands yet like human hands.

The picture changes to the second one but my mind is still focused on the hands, and I do not remember what is on the second picture.

The third picture has a raised square on it divided into four distinct areas and I think I see "H" and "E" written four times but again I am not sure. I had the impression that whatever was written could be read in any direction and felt it was very clever yet when I tried to distinguish the letters I could not do so.

As I made my way back to bed I was disappointed because once again I could not make out the detail and therefore was unable to read the writing gaining the message within. I lay there for quite awhile thinking about the pictures shown and began to see the face of a dark gray male with large lumpy jowls. The eyes were white on an expressionless face then it disappeared. Was this the face of the artist, certainly not the one I had seen before because he was black? I thought perhaps it was because the style was different from the others. These had not been cartoons but more like the huge poster the little ones had carried into the bathroom the night I thought I had played while whacking the daylights out of them.

It is the long narrow arms and hands that continue to linger in my mind. What did the writing say yet I felt that I had understood what was written on the last one. Did my subconscious understand it and that was the intent? Today I know no more than I did yesterday.

Chapter 35

Friday, 2 January 2009, my brother-in-law had installed a motion detector light at my bedroom window that turned on about 1 AM and was so bright that I could see its light shinning around the blackout drapes. Did they set it off not knowing it was there or was it a night creature? I looked out of the window seeing nothing that shouldn't be there. It was 3:10 AM when I crawled back into bed.

The very strong smell of a grey permeated the room, but was different from the little one and his friend yet similar and just as repellant. I told him not to be afraid that I wouldn't hurt him, and the smell grew stronger but I still could not see him. I asked him where the little one was and was told that he was busy in another area and would be back another time. I said that I was having trouble sleeping. Instantly a pattern of the cartoon man; the head, large nose, neck and shoulders appeared cleverly made entirely of different sized triangles then abruptly changing color into a startling vivid blue and then to burnt orange. It was the artist, it was his character.

The blue became the outline of the triangle shapes with the burnt orange in the middle forming the facial features, a beautiful color combination. The pattern then seemed to take a shape reminding me of a snake, and began to swirl forming a whirlpool that was spectacular, but instead of drawing me down into it, it began to make me nauseous and I cried out, "I'm going to vomit!" It stopped immediately. I was surprised because I do not remember becoming nauseous before. I turned onto my back and looked about the room seeing orbs, white and red balls and white cloud-like swirls becoming very hot and throwing the blankets off of me. A few minutes later I became cold and said, "I am cold" and the cold went away. The smell faded in and out as if it approached the bed then backed off.

I got out of bed and went into the living room and sat in the dark where I also saw orbs, white and red balls and white cloud-like swirls, and thought that with all of this activity I should be taking pictures but was too tired to get up and get the camera. It was 5:10 AM when I saw a light glide across the back area of the house at the speed as if someone were walking but the light did not bob up and down as if carried. It was about a twelve-inch diameter ball casually floating across the back porch area. I sat there watching the white balls appear and then reappear somewhere else like tiny twinkling stars then went back to bed and slept.

Friday, 9 January 2009, I am undecided if I waste time thinking about them. They occupy a great deal of my thoughts when not dealing with human issues. The cruel trick would be to find out that they are not who I think they are, that I am a subject of a human military study yet I am convinced that no human has the capabilities these beings reveal.

Friday, 16 January 2009, I went in for surgery yesterday to have excess skin on the upper eyelids that hang down blocking your peripheral vision when driving removed, a Blepharoplasty. When I looked in the mirror I had a view of Frankenstein's sister. Even though I slept like a rock the night before then had the deep sleep during surgery, I conked out mid-afternoon then was unable to sleep last night, up and down all night.

Last night they were here not to take me but to look at me. I felt the hair stand up on my face as if a hand had brushed very lightly across it twice, and the sensation of fear charged through me that I had to work at to calm myself down. I saw faces of surprise and alarm in front of me as if the beings were shocked to find my face looking so swollen and bruised. I finally fell into a "twilight sleep" after 5 AM becoming aware that I am playing a black and white number game, two on one, three on two, etc. It made no sense as I randomly placed numbers on numbers, and didn't care. I opened my eyes and could see a little white ball hanging above my head slightly to the right as well as the "game board", and wondered what happened to the colors they always use. When I closed my eyes it was as if someone flipped a switch, the game board was now in colors.

Saturday, 24 January 2009, I became aware of a very strong odor in the room as I was being shown a familiar design by the artist.

The picture began in detail of a design seen countless times only I was not being shown the entire picture but the center of the design close-up. Still remaining close-up it fanned outward to my left onto an outer circle with a design between the center of the circle and the picture. The picture then turned so that I was looking at the design as if looking at a picture on the wall while standing to its left against the wall. The entire design is complicated and beautiful. Every time I see it I think of the "Tree of Life", could that be what it is or is it what we would call an alien design?

Even though I was given the opportunity to study the circle

in detail I could never draw it. In the past the artist's visits can come on their own or preceding a visit from the group. I am aware that he has taken the place of the little one. Although I have smelled the little one faintly on occasion, he has not come back since my rampage on the ship. I hope he is alright, and I am told that he is. I got up and was then unable to sleep. This is becoming such a habit now, and it is not as it was before when I welcomed their visits. There are nights when things begin to happen, and I am out of the bed in a flash. I still want to be awake when they come but now I am trying to forestall their visits, and I know that I cannot do that. Things have changed but I don't know in what way. I want to know more about them.

Friday, 30 January 2009, I was lying in bed on my right side with Buster curled up behind my knees. The lights were off and I was unsuccessfully attempting to go to sleep; I opened my eyes and looked around. I saw a faint flash in the living room and debated whether or not to get up and investigate but surely hated to leave my comfortable warm bed, so I watched the bedroom door. Within thirty seconds a thin black being ran into my bedroom and stopped by my bed. I could see the outline of the being's back, and the elbow of the right arm bent towards his back in a running position, and there was a slight shuffling noise on the carpet when he stopped. The being was approximately five feet tall and did not seem to have rounded shoulders like the tall greys, standing straight as it ran. No other colors, just black.

After I gained control of my surprise and rid myself of the sensation of fear, I raised myself up on my right elbow. "Wow," I said, "Who are you? You know that I see you." There was no answer or detected movement. I looked around the room and saw no other beings but did see several small white balls, one by my right eye and one sitting on my chest. When I sat up one of them was bouncing around from chest to arm then back to chest and from chest to hand and stopped. The black being was gone.

For two days the strong desire to draw some of the recently seen faces forced me to pull out pad and charcoal pencil. It has occurred to me that the drawing of the orange man seen the other night done with triangles resembled a cartoon figure I cannot place. I tried to draw him without much success. I drew the artist when he peered over the table at me but the eyes are not right. They were not big and slanted like the grey's eyes but more like ours only slightly larger. They reflected shyness and intelligence. I was given a picture of something that I can draw that looks like a tail with white on the underside and covered with orange bubbles on the other three sides. The bubbles seemed to float off in clouds that drifted away.

Monday, 16 February 2009, I received a call from my sister while she was in Florida asking me "what do you think about these hypotheses?"

There is a large group of scientists from many disciplines who attend Trekkie Conventions, seminars, etc. because personal experiences can be relayed in a hypothetical manner and remain anonymous. The scientists discuss the experience in a group forum and no one has to say "I've been taken". There is no proof for them as there is no proof for any of us.

What if a scientist verified that they are alive, that there are good and bad ones just like there are humans, that they have been visiting us for thousands of years?

What if you learned that there really are miracles but they are actually the result of being able to enter, not a dimension per say or even another level, but another "phase", and return healed or saved from death.

What would you say if you learned that most people who are injured while being taken is a result of something they did themselves during the taking most likely out of fear and that it was not intended by the beings?

What would you say if you learned that I could remember it all if I changed the way I ask them to be allowed to remember?

What would you say to all of these things? What better forum could you have if you wanted to remain anonymous? Where else could hypotheses centered on the beings be exchanged within a scientific group, and not be laughed out of the building with reputations ruined?

Friday, 20 February 2009, as I was getting ready for bed last night, the little one and I talked which we have not done in months. He broke into my thoughts, and of course, when this happens regardless of the voice, the thought that I am crazy as a loon goes through my mind. I read, went to sleep and woke up tired. When I opened my eyes it was 7:30 AM, Buster was very restless walking around the bed, sniffing my face and nightclothes. He even began smelling and licking my lips, which I cannot recall him ever doing, and

I wondered what on earth was wrong with him.

As I prepared to shower I noted dark blue bruises on my upper arms, both sides with my left showing what could be three finger marks. The marks are as if someone stood in front of me and grasped my arms tightly. I could place the fingers of my right hand over them easily except that they are too close together, as if the fingers are thinner than mine. I studied my face in the mirror, I look tired.

Chapter 36

Wednesday 25 February 2009
Permission given by my buddy to include this email received on February 17th:

I wish I could put into words what I feel about this "alien" thing...in words that make sense and be understandable. But the words elude me. Sometimes I am given answers and have no clue where the words come from, so maybe they do put words in my head...a double-sided answer. Do they or don't they? I know I have come a long way from the thoughts I had about them in the early '90's when this all opened up to me.

I think then I saw it as happening but at the same time it wasn't real. Like a dream you could turn off and on but I wasn't necessarily the one with the remote. As long as I didn't have to face it I could always put it in a category that didn't really exist in our world. It's real, it happens, but it didn't. It's just so hard to explain something you can't see / feel / touch or have any tangible contact with in the clear light of day. They can cause our minds to play tricks on us, they shape-shift to suit whatever idea they are trying to get across. We still don't know what the idea is or what they are trying to tell us. WHY can't they just TELL us in our plain old hardheaded English?

Is our everyday world just make-believe? We can see it...feel it...it is tangible to us in our mind, but is it REAL?

Sometimes I find myself "yearning" to be free of this body

and to travel the stars, is that a normal thought? Nut doctors would say I had a lot of loose screws. In reality I have no desire to leave this life and our earthly world, yet I want to know what is beyond it. Am I two people or do I just have conflicting thoughts?

Years ago during one of my "episodes" when a bright light landed a craft in the yard of what I was left to believe was my sons little house at the time (This craft) unloaded a group of people who looked human and were so happy to be "home". Some of them came into the house and were sitting here and there. As I looked at them and watched I knew they weren't really human, only pretending. I didn't know what it meant. I don't recall the entire "dream" but I went to the door, as the craft was ready to leave. I went out. This craft was not real big; it was round shaped, stood on 3 or 4 "legs" as the craft itself did not sit on the ground. It had a landing platform that the "people" came down on. At the top of the landing platform was a doorway and going up the ramp was a Being...I feel he was my "Instructor". He was tall, dressed in a silver or white shiny type body suit. I can't recall his features; I just felt he was someone I knew.

He asked me my name, I think I told him, but don't remember if it was actually my name. He turned and went on up the ramp to the door...when he reached the doorway he stopped, turned, looked at me and said, "You have another name." I have tried and tried to understand what that means...and to know my "other" name. It has been nearly 20 years and I haven't been enlightened.

Was he trying to tell me I was not "of this world"...only putting in time in this human form?

During another episode...and I think I told you of it. I was taken aboard a craft that was being "driven" or run by the insect being Mantis or the ones who look something like "walking sticks"... just stick figures with ant like heads. While I saw this figure he totally ignored me and went about his business. The "Being" who was showing me around I think was the same one from the craft that landed and let the people off, again, I could not get a clear thought of his features, only that he was tall and dressed in a shiny body suit. By tall, maybe 5' 8 or 9", a whole lot taller than my almost 5 foot. He was taking me through the ship and brought me to a room full of little black boxes that fit in the wall from floor to ceiling and all around, there were hundreds of them. He told me this is where they stored the souls for transportation to the next realm of existence. The souls could choose to go through a "resting" period or they could choose to enter another life form. It was totally their decision, but they had a time to sort of "regroup" before making that decision. I never questioned as to whether these souls were always kept on board the craft or taken somewhere else until they were ready to make their decision. I wish I had.

Before this particular episode, least I think it was before, I was having a lot of problem accepting the fact that I could be of use or help in any situation given my body's inability to move fast, I am physically unable to do a lot of things.

It was then and I am sure it was my "Instructor" then... I knew I was again in a "learning / class type" episode, where I was in the company of various Beings and we were being taught what our "jobs" were.

I was taken to a house, a yellow two-story house that sat on the edge of a bluff over-looking the ocean. I have always thought it was northern California or Oregon. It was storming and the house began to slide down the bluff and fill with mud. The mud was oozing through the windows and doors. Inside were two little kids, a boy and a girl, about 4 and 5 years old. I found myself inside this house just as the mud was covering the children. I knew they were going to suffocate. I took each by a hand and lifted them out of the house and while I could see their physical bodies I also knew they weren't in them. I took their "souls" by the hand at the moment of death. I don't recall what happened after that. I was just left with the thought that this was my job, to escort the souls of those whose physical bodies die tragically and unexpectedly; to calm them and take them to the next point. I wasn't given the next point, so maybe it was those little black boxes on board the craft.

It helps to clarify the Trinity...the Father / the Son / the Holy Spirit...all different, all the same. We all have the desire to live on. (End)

And my reply on February 24th:
You have had so many sightings! I can only talk about what is going on in my mind and you know where that can lead a person----to the crazy farm.

My sister met an interesting person while in Florida and learned some information that I have already passed on to you. Is this a coincidence? No, and that made me very suspicious. Answer: "Officially they don't exist as there is no proof."

A friend of my sisters suggested reading *Survivors of Atlantis: Their Impact on World Culture* by Frank Joseph. The author is so bent on convincing you that Atlantis existed as well as survivors that it is turning me off but I trudge on. It does make sense but I'm not necessarily a believer. I can't see how the Atlantians tie in with the beings yet it is possible. There is still so much to learn.

Based on the four cataclysms that occurred which destroyed the Atlantian's world, the book may very much tie in to them, the visitors. Is it coincidence that they have massive ships? Is it coincidence that they have collected DNA, human and maybe otherwise? Then you hit me with your story of remembrance when you were shown the boxes of souls waiting for their next stop. It all sort of came together of what the future could be if the earth is due for more cataclysms in the near future which it seems TV programs are brimming with it.

Is the reason we connect our God to the heavens because this is where the visitors' ships are seen? Is it possible that people throughout history have witnessed soul's rising up and collected by the visitors in their little black boxes? This is unsettling to me. Is our existence, body, soul and mind, dependent or controlled by beings from space or another level? Are they what our God looks like, terrifying because there is nothing on earth that looks like them that we can relate to? Are we an experiment or are we them?

Many creatures I've seen seem to have animal parts but are on a mental level above me. Think of the lizards, the praying mantis, snakes, etc. similar to life on earth but with knowledge that is superior to our own. Were we all sent down here as an experiment? Is everything on earth the descendents of "Noah's" ship, and we humans evolved to a higher level than the other species and as a result we, in our superior status, are destroying the rest of life as if they have no value? There is this thought that I have had for years then there is this new thought which involves cataclysm. Are they connected? It could be that the earth is facing a destruction that will wipe out everything that we know today and then start over. One could easily become an agnostic if thought about too much. Is the great "coming" actually ships beaming souls up to store in black boxes until the earth or some other planet is ready for new transplants. I remember visiting other places, was I choosing where to live in my next life or was I just being shown other places? Is this the bases for psychics who say we have lived many lives? I've been told I am an old spirit who has lived nine lives, could this be true?

Whew! I feel better getting these thoughts down as I work my way through this confusion, it boils down to the same old thing, trust versus suspicion. Have they taken advantage of our belief in an omnipotent God who is not seen but is everywhere? They, the beings, come at night while we are asleep, find ourselves separated from other humans even though, in some cases, there are many around but no one remembers the event. Do we get them confused with our belief in God? Think about it, did he show you the spirit inside the box? No, I bet he led you around filling your mind with all kinds of thoughts, but allowed you to remember only the boxes because they fit in with what else you have been taught---the taking of souls from dying bodies. You were being assured that they were safe.

Yes, I look forward to the beings coming. I want to know more about them, not necessarily scientific information because although interested my mind skips the surface of science. I want to know about them as living beings, their families and connections, the place where their home is, have they lived their entire lives on a ship, what they eat and so on.

I'm not afraid of them but fear over the past several months has crept in, and I have to fight it, fight it, fight it. What has changed to cause the fear? They are no better than us, just more advanced. Yes, they could wipe me out with a wink, but then so could a car accident, a heart attack, or a stroke. I think they like the fear, like to watch how we react, watch us crawl within ourselves crying for "Mama". I won't do it, damn their sneaky minds! I'll work with them but they will never own my soul, my mind, my body or me. God alone will do that, and they will not insert themselves in my belief of God. I'm tired of their games.

Well, there you have it. I have so many other thoughts but they elude me at this point. I go through these periods of frustration and discontent because I have no control whatever, I am a puppet on strings that I can't see or feel therefore I am unable to sever them. (End)

Wednesday, 3 March 2009, last Sunday and Monday I had the faint smell of sweaty socks, socks warmed by shoes, not strong and unpleasant but the odor was not mine. Monday I not only smelled the socks but whiffs of frying bacon as well. My neighbors were not home so the odor was not wafting from their kitchen. Tuesday I smelled the frying bacon but not the socks. The sock odor was more prevalent at the couch where I set while the bacon smell was throughout the house. I wonder if odors can waft through portals. I wonder what is on the other side; people who fry bacon?

When I went to bed last night, I fell asleep without a problem becoming aware during the night of being very hot and restless throwing the covers off. I opened my eyes and looked around. Suddenly there was one of the little balls on my right eye, and it turned on as if a switch had been flicked. It was not at either side of the eye but seemed to be lying on the cornea. It became brighter and started to swiftly move across the eye from one side to the other as if on the eye, and I followed its movements with my eye. The last time the ball moved and stopped, it became fainter but I could still see it then it shot over by the curtains changing into a cloudy orb, about three inches in diameter and disappeared. I looked at the clock; it was 3:20 AM. I turned over and wondered if they set on my eyeballs when I sleep, and if this was a way to monitor what level of sleep I am in.

Thursday, 25 February 2009, the little one's voice said to me regarding our different worlds: "Your world is real to you and my world is real to me but my world is not real to you nor is your world real to me. They don't exist, there is nothing there. Because they don't exist there are no barriers."

Is he referring to other dimensions, other planets and plains of existence? Is this what happens to people having OOBE who simply pass into where ever they wish to go? What is reality? Is it something we have been taught from birth and reinforced throughout our lives? If I pass into another world is it all phantasms because I don't believe it exists, or does it exist only when I am there? Is this what shamans, sorcerers and medicine men have learned? Is there nothing to stop any of us from passing into other worlds except ourselves and our beliefs as to what is reality? We can go anywhere; there are no barriers!

The little one doesn't say they don't exist it is their world that doesn't exist to me or mine to him. But somewhere during our interactions his world does become real to me, in their ships, in my bedroom when I am touched, and when we fly through the air. Have our worlds overlapped under their control or has he told me this knowing I will dwell on it because it makes sense?

Was he speaking about another dimension, outer space or both, or does it even matter? If there are no barriers then we can cross back and forth without encumbrance into worlds that do not exist but once there would they exist, yes of course they would. I would think they would have to otherwise how would you know that you are there? But what assurance do I have of returning to the one that I know exists, my world? Trust? Trust in what, myself? Yes, how else would you get there except through yourself also your vehicle to return?

Saturday, 28 February 2009, it rained a lot yesterday. The dark cloudy sky was familiar to me having been raised in the Midwest, and if snow had fallen it would have been no surprise except it was too warm and it's still too warm this morning. I have three days off together and had decided since I had no plans to go any-where yesterday, it was a free day. I stopped at the local hardware store and bought the items needed to remove wallpaper then treated myself to a 350 pedicure, manicure and eyebrows, painfully waxed, then spent the rest of the day reading a book. As evening approached I found myself becoming restless and didn't go to bed until 1:30 after skimming the Internet for new UFO stuff and sending my buddy a note.

It was a restless twilight sleep where I am neither awake nor asleep, one of tossing and turning. Having made the decision to get up I opened my eyes seeing lots of little white balls flying around and landing on me. I felt excitement in the air and welcomed them as I headed for the bathroom. I looked at the clock and saw that it was nearly 3:30 AM.

I don't know if events are planned by them to occur in the bathroom or if it is coincidence, I don't believe in coincidence, but why the bathroom? In our world it is a necessary and somewhat humbling process, and we are pretty much incapacitated at that moment, captive.

In a sitting position I see to my right something very quickly coming at me. I see the eyes first but they are not the eyes of a grey but are puffy eyes more like a human. I look harder at them as a small shape takes on form out of a swirling wispy white mass. The being is about four feet tall; his face is only inches from mine. I see that there is the same swirling wispy white mass several feet behind him in the doorway, and as it takes on form it is much taller, about 5 ½ to 6 feet tall. His eyes are the same puffy eyes and he seems to have on a white robe. My first thought was of Merlin, the magician written in fables.

I said, "Oh, I am so happy to see you!" With those spoken

words, the tall one's expression turns to surprise then to alarm, and I knew he was frightened. Instantly, colored outlines of flowers and other shapes appeared mesmerizingly drifting downward to the floor as the tall being disappeared.

I didn't want them to leave and felt I better do something to let them know that I would not harm them, I said, "I will not harm you. You are welcomed here."

I lay in the bed with my back towards the bathroom door with my eyes closed waiting to see what else was going to happen. Suddenly colored abstract visions filled my eyes and brain then began swirling downward into a vortex. The last time this had happened, it had made me nauseous because it went too fast, but this time it went slower. I realized that I was being put to sleep, gave into it and I don't remember a thing after that.

Thoughts, first, I take them on their terms as there is no other way to learn more about them and I am so curious to learn more. Second, I have read and been told that weather effects their coming but the heavy rain that one night had not keep them away, they come when they want. Third, the little one has told me they can come through the floor as easily as the roof. Fourth, I have seen the display of colored dancing outline of little shapes before at the side of my bed when I thought that I had seen eyes or a figure and called the shapes daisies. Fifth, my last thought as I swirled down into the vortex was wondering if the tall being was the one who always accompanies me standing on my left.

Chapter 37

Sunday, 1 March 2009. This evening I was cleaning up a mess after finishing a laborious chore of scraping wallpaper, and began hauling stuff to the trash. On the second trip I looked for Buster because he has a habit of slipping out if the door doesn't shut immediately. I found him lying on the couch watching what I was doing but when I came in from the third trip he was not there. I looked for him calling his name and realized that he could have sneaked out the door on the last trip. The night was cold and damp with water dripping off of the roofs from the melting snow. I was worried that he would either get run over by a car or catch a cold from being out in this unpleasant weather. I called for him, left the front porch light on, and began a systematic search of the house but could not find him. I called again and this time I heard a soulful reply finding him locked on the back porch. How in heavens name did he get there? That I cannot answer as the porch had been locked up earlier, and he had been lying on the couch the last time I went out the front door.

Tuesday, 3 March 2009, I came home from work yesterday evening with muscles aching and tired from scraping wallpaper, cleaning and moving furniture over the weekend. I couldn't wait to get into my comfortable nightclothes. I finished the email to my buddy and relaxed, but found as the evening wore on the relaxing part was not going to happen, ending up playing computer games until 3:30 AM then I went to bed.

The room lit up with a white bright cold light that faded away and I knew they were here. I looked towards the living room that was pitch black, then a flash occurred and everything turned a deep dark red that seeped in bathing everything in the bedroom. Little twinkling balls danced about the room zooming in towards me then out. I rolled over and tried to go to sleep.

My body began quivering, an unnatural feeling which prompted me to get out of bed to play more computer games until 5 AM. Come on, I wanted to yell, do something, get on with it! I went back to bed ignoring everything and was annoyed. The little one's voice was in my head saying they were very excited as I was going to get the first run through of me doing the job I'd been trained for. He told me that his name was Bugoha or maybe it was Bugaho, which ever, I told him I was really bad on names that I would probably not remember it, and he replied to just call him the "little one".

This name has to be a joke---bug-a-ho, get real, is he a bug? The voice didn't sound right but close. He said that I would remember everything and would then understand more. Personally, I think they were just playing games and needed a laugh, as upon waking this morning I remember nothing, however, the closet door is open. From childhood a closet door is never left open in the room where I sleep, after all, who knows what lurks inside?

Tuesday, 10 March 2009, I fell asleep easily after reading. I am dreaming.

I am living in the state where I had lived for many years before moving south, and visiting with close friends at their house when I discover that I have forgotten to bring something we need and must drive back home to get it. It is dark but they live only a few minutes away so I jump into the car and drive home. The land is flat almost barren so unlike where I lived but as dreams go, I wasn't troubled by this difference.

I turn right at the corner knowing that I should have turned left to go home, but do it anyway because this is the way I am supposed to go.

There is a car in front of me driving too slowly and I want to pass it but I know that there is a stoplight ahead. There is a stretch of road before the light where I feel I will have enough time to pass it before reaching the light. I pull out to pass then decide it's going to be too close to the stoplight as it seems like the light is closer than I had thought. I am unable to pull back behind the slow car because another one has pulled up into the place I had vacated but it slowed down and let me in. We stop for the red light, three cars in a row, the only ones at the crossroads. I see the driver in front is out of his car looking up at the sky as well as the driver behind me. I get out of my car too, and looking up at the sky I ask, "At what are you looking?" The driver of the front car says, "I am looking at a space ship in the sky. It is the mother ship." I look at the sky and am awestruck as I watch an enormous bullet shaped ship very high up descending rapidly as it advances in our direction. There is something on the bottom of it and I'm not sure if it is rust, but it isn't the ship that I feel it should be. The man in front gets back into his car and the woman in the car behind me, a tall grey haired lady, also gets back into her car. I suddenly find all three of our cars in a roofed shelter attached to a house that sits back from the road at the corner of the light.

I walk out of the shelter and look at the stoplight to see if it has turned green, and see that the light is no longer working.

I announce that it must be a space ship because the power is no longer working then I see both of their cars on the road each turning around and heading back the way we had come. I realize the tall grey haired woman is not a human woman, and I had known they were coming. It is at this point that I realize I am dreaming and extremely hot.

I am awake, and throw the covers off then look around the bedroom in the dark because I know they are here. I can see twinkling white balls and a beautiful blue eye a safe distance away. My body feels funny as it does when they come for me, my heart is pumping, and it is difficult to breath. With difficulty, I said out loud, "I know you are here. I won't hurt you." A laughing voice which sounds like the little one replies, "Oh yes, we are here." It was at this point that my sister's cat, Percy, starts yowling in the living room sounding frightened while Buster lay beside me not moving or making a noise.

I yell to Percy that it is all right, that it's okay and then concentrated on calming my body down and gaining some control. I wasn't sure if I was frightened or if this was the reaction prior to being taken or brought back, but I was not going to let them frighten me. I calm myself down, and Percy yowls again. I turn on the light and go out to him with Buster right behind me, finding poor Percy frantically pacing the floor. I look out of the sliding glass door and see that there is a full moon. I talk and pet both cats then we go back to bed.

I wonder who these beings are and if it was the same group, if so they did not know there was a new cat in the house. Percy had hidden in my bedroom when my sister went to put him in their car before they left for Florida. She was heartbroken but she will be back next year, and by then he will be ready to go home, he's probably ready now.

I straighten up the askew bed linen and lay there feeling that I am being watched. I become so hot that I think I will catch on fire and throw everything but the sheet off of me. The last time I look at the clock it is 3:30 AM, and I remember nothing more.

Tuesday, 24 March 2009, it has been very quiet around here, perhaps it is because my little home reeks of paint odor but it is finally neat and clean. My sister called to tell me of her dream.

She has wanted her husband to recognize that there are beings from another world and when they came for her last Monday, March 16th, she talked a being into allowing her husband to see the craft. She describes the craft as being very large, round and looking as if a short portion of the bottom of a canning jar was on the bottom and the top of the ship with white lights shining around the middle. She was aware that her husband was standing beside her, and that his comment was if he had not seen it he wouldn't believe it, then it was gone.

Two small beings that she believes were little greys were dressed in blue and wearing helmets. She was told that they were dressed for protection because they were going to play. Then I was brought in to the large room, and she said that we began to play with the abandon of small carefree children. We played tag, hide and seek, and all kinds of games we had played as children. She said that our two cousins were brought in both semiconscious seemingly unaware of where they were and did not join in the games. She said the beings and us communicated through thought and had a wonderful time, and that she was very aware that they were laughing and enjoying the fun as much as we were.

She described the protective suits as the head and body portions were triangular shaped with the arms and legs extending through the body triangle. We were talking by cell phone, and she was in an area where she kept breaking up, so we had to end the conversation. Unfortunately she does not write down her experiences, so much detail is lost in a short period of time.

I did wake up Tuesday morning, March 16th tired but I attributed it to the paint odor and stress of my home being in complete chaos, perhaps, more happened that night than I remember. This was her dream.

She said that she was told that the little boxes that held souls did hold souls as well as the mind. The mind had the freedom to roam but the souls were kept in the boxes for protection until the time was right to move on. She said that I shouldn't worry about the souls in the boxes but I can't help wanting further explanation, because if this is true, then once again I have to ask what is the being's relationship to The Creator? Could it be possible that they have learned to capture the mass of energy, our soul, as it leaves the body? Are they soul-snatchers?

Wednesday, 25 March 2009, I was instantly awakened by the newly installed security system going off with a three-beep alert followed by a bright flash. I lay there in bed intently awake listening, noting that it was still dark out, and debating if I should press the buttons for the police, one more sound and the buttons will be pressed. I looked toward the bedroom window and a large blue flash appeared on the curtains. I then looked at the clock and saw that it was after 7 AM and was still dark outside because it was raining.

Did they set the alarm off because they didn't know it was there? Did they do it as a joke or did it go off by its self? Because of the flashes I believe they were letting me know they knew it was there.

Saturday, 4 April 2009, I lay in the bed facing the bedroom window, and my eyes are drawn towards the corner of the room where suddenly designs appear coming from a central point. First they are as white as the room is black, and I wonder why there is no color then a color design appears and as it floats out, another one, then another one, and I am caught up with the beauty, originality and simplicity of each design wondering if the artist created these then I am gone.

I am with a young man who is telling me and another man about how he must sacrifice his ship that he does not want to do this but has no choice.

The other man and I are standing outside of what looks like a R.V. that has a tree on the other side towards the rear. We are scanning the star-studded sky when the man next to me says he should be along soon. We both see the massive ship coming from our right moving and descending as if in slow motion. As it crosses the sky above us we see it is a golden bullet shaped ship with a white-hot nose as if heated by a blacksmiths forge. I strain to see if I can see the pilot wishing I could tell him how brave he is. We watch the gold ship led by the white hot nose descend towards our left disappearing then feel the ground shake as we hear and see the huge explosion. Flames can be seen rising in the black sky shutting out the bright stars, and I let out my breath not realizing that I had been holding it. It is over and I feel sadness within me, he is a loss.

I think to myself, it has begun and there is no turning back, the time is now. The man and I climb into the R.V.

Chapter 38

Wednesday, 8 April 2009, I slept well until 3 AM when I suddenly woke due to the motion light shining around the bedroom curtain. The room was so well lit that I could see the detail of everything in it. Percy was yowling as he paced up and down the living room while Buster lay curled up in my arm with his head facing mine. Suddenly there is a flash of light coming from the window that streaked across about five feet above the bed headed toward the dresser mirror. It was nearly two feet long and looked like a lit glass rod, and when Buster jumped and turned his head then I knew that I had not imagined it. With Percy yelling in the background I laid there a few minutes and nothing more happened. I got up, reassured Percy and peeked out of the bedroom window which was now dark as the motion light had turned off, then looked out through the vertical blinds onto the porch. There was an almost full moon that threw off a great deal of light. I went back to bed and slept.

Saturday, 18 April 2009, last night before I went to bed I locked up the house and set the security system and one minute later the last beep sounded. This morning when I got up the security system was off.

Saturday, 25 April 2009, there is a new being who comes, day or night, and the only way I know is by its awful smell. I don't know how to describe the smell other than if it weren't watered down it would burn the nostrils, and when I smell it I think of acid. I can't imagine being in a room with a group smelling like this, your lungs would catch on fire. Last night before going to bed the smell was wafting through the house. I am dreaming.

My sister and I are side by side in the back seat of a vehicle. It is dark but there is enough light from the instrument panel on the dashboard that we can see within the vehicle. My youngest son is driving, and there is someone in the passenger seat. It is a surprisingly smooth ride traveling on the dirt road.

We pull onto a railroad track crossing and the vehicle stops; no one seems concerned that we are sitting on the railroad tracks. I see a white light shinning down the tracks traveling fast towards us, and I began to freak out. I say to my sister, "I need to get this car off of the tracks or we will be killed!" and jump out of the back seat, tear open the front door and command my son to move over as fast as his body can move. He jumps out of the car and I realize he is only eight or nine years old but it didn't seem unusual to me. I am unable to get in the car fast enough to move the vehicle and the white light is almost upon us. I get out and stand by the vehicle watching the light now only a short distance from us thinking we will just all go together, knowing that this is the right thing to do; it is inevitable that we all go together.

I awake in the bed the time is nearly 3:30 AM. I feel myself drifting off again and I am thinking this is good, and if I can just let myself drift I will be led to where I need to go. I am drifting into a place where I know that something is going to be revealed that gives me knowledge and understanding. Suddenly Percy is yowling again and I can hear his yowls coming from different areas of the house as he must be frantically pacing the place. I am waking up when I hear a sound almost like the *Dog Whisperer* going "chitt" but not quite. It sounded like their mechanical tone, and poor little Percy didn't make another sound.

When I woke my mouth felt as if it had been glued shut and was dry as if lined with cotton. There was a tasteless texture to whatever had been placed in my mouth that dissolved as I kept opening and closing it.

I know that I was taken last night. The ride was in one of their vehicles driven by a grey, and we must have had a rendezvous with another ship because of the light coming down what I thought were railroad tracks. The passenger is the same as the one with me when I am with them, always someone that is there but remains unseen, unidentified, someone I feel safe with, and over time I have become convinced that it is one of the old ones, a guide.

Buster has not seemed to get upset with their visits while Percy becomes extremely agitated. I have seen him set in the living room facing the sliding glass door and growl several times in the late evenings. Each time that I know they are here it is within seconds that he becomes restless and vocal.

My evening patterns have changed since I found the smoked cigarettes in a little pile outside the back door. Someone had been standing in one spot smoking one cigarette after another outside the back porch area. I do not feel safe leaving the sliding glass door open in the late evenings allowing Buster and Percy to go in and out to the screened in porch like I have been doing. I feel as if I need to be able to see beyond the little patio when the door is left open. I resent having to adjust my life to this interference but I don't know what this nut would do to my little cats or to me.

Monday, 4 May 2009, I have been cleaning house and going

through drawers and closets, filling bags for the Paralyzed Veterans of America and setting things aside that I want to keep. Amazing how much useless stuff I've collected over the years, stuff I just liked but did not need. At 5:00 I was winding down taking a break out on the back porch, relaxing, sipping coffee and enjoying my addiction to nicotine. I noticed that in the corner of the left side of the door, the screen looked way too wavy and decided I needed to check it out. On examination it was clear that the wood strip covering the screen edges had been pulled away. Well, it's been there since 2000, so just from age alone it was possible to have worked loose.

The wood showed no scraping or signs that it had been tampered with, looking as if the narrow wood batten had popped off of the finishing nail heads going up the side of the 2x4 to the center and across the bottom. I gently lifted the wood and noted that there were no finishing nails! What? If the wood had popped off of the nails then the nails should still be in the 2x4 but there were none and none among the rocks on the ground! Paralyzing chills and anger flashed through me.

I retrieved nails and a hammer, stretched the screen tight and hammered them into the wood, up and down both sides and across the bottom and middle then did the same on the other side of the door. I was aggravated; this didn't happen without help, the nails did not extricate themselves on their own and then disappear. I called the police who listened patiently, but could do nothing; a crime had not been committed.

Saturday, 9 May 2009, the last time I looked at the clock it was 3 AM. I opened my eyes and looked up seeing a colorful picture covering the entire ceiling. In front of the picture was an elaborately designed flat black lattice allowing portions of the picture behind it to be seen. The combination was striking.

I knew only the artist would go to the trouble of presenting me this lovely piece, and as I acknowledged his gift the piece began to slide slowly to my right then disappear. It was 4:30 AM. Buster was beside me while Percy was in the living room roaming and howling. In the middle of his second howl there was a guttural sounding noise that sounded like "hush" and Percy stopped mid yowl, and that was my last conscious awareness.

Sunday, 17 May 2009, I worked 1-6 PM yesterday, came home, ate, went to bed about 8:30 and finished the book I was reading then started another until I became sleepy. I could hear the rain on the roof and finding it relaxing, I turned off the bedside lamp, and settled in laying on my right side. A light began glowing from the left eye area then instead of the usual white ball there was a bold red ball of considerable size. Suddenly the light stopped, the red ball disappeared, and it was dark followed by the flash of a blue rectangle. In front of the rectangle was a large white circle, and in front of the circle was a red ball, bip, bip, bip one after the other with each one slightly smaller than the one behind it. There was enough time for me to note this combination had never happened before and I was gone, I remember nothing. I awoke at some point during the night soaked in sweat but do not remember the time or if anything happened.

I've given thought to the times I have awoken with my mouth glued shut by a tasteless substance, and have decided that the consistency is like mashed potatoes as it dissolves.

Also noted for the past several weeks but not recorded before is a green light that has been appearing on the dashboard of my car. It is in the area of the turn indicator lights that are also green. When it flashes it draws my attention as the turn indicator should not be on when I am driving down the road without intention to turn a corner. They have invaded every aspect of my life, home, work and everything in between.

Monday, 18 May 2009, last night I awoke at 1:25 AM seeing spindly white cobweb shapes swirling around the bathroom door. They seemed like they were beginning to form shapes then about four incomplete rows of triangles appeared. In the middle of each triangle was an emblem followed by the swirls. I looked harder and could see a little grey's face standing backed against the bedroom wall with his head facing me, probably about five feet away. I nodded my head and smiled to acknowledge him and he faded away. I don't think he is one of the ones who usually come, but I'm not sure, as there was no odor. I then looked closely amongst the cobweb stuff swirling in the doorway to see if the tall one was there. The swirling cobweb stuff turned into a sheet of haze blocking my view into the bathroom yet did not cover the entire doorway. It was as if someone with a wide brush full of paint had zigzagged paint across the doorway not covering all of it but enough to obscure the main view. I got up, walked through the haze which disappeared then went back to bed.

I remember nothing else.

Friday, 29 May 2009, Thursday I had a dental appointment to replace two small porcelain fillings that had fallen out on the upper left side. I hadn't noticed they had fallen out until the teeth were cleaned last week. My mind raced to the event several weeks ago when I woke up unable to open my mouth wondering if the suction had pulled the fillings out. Maybe there is no connection whatsoever but since they have come, everything seems to be of importance.

Last night before I went to bed I sat the security alarm. This morning when I got up it was off.

Monday, 6 July 2009, my sister and I were on a coveted genealogy trek when the following occurred in Allentown, PA. It was 3:30 AM when I looked at the clock after having the dream.

I am sitting in the front seat of a large car with a large windshield my ex-husband is in the driver's seat. We are driving on a country road paved with gravel and have come to a curve which has an elevated railroad crossing. There are two railroad crossing warning signals facing us, one on each side of the road instead of only one on the right side, both have their arms up indicating that it is safe to cross. As we approach the mound to cross over the railroad track the arms drop, the red lights start flashing, the warning bells begin clanging, and we stop.

The bells have set off an alarm within me, and I am suddenly terrified, absolutely terrified. The fear is overwhelming. I jump up from my seat, and stand behind it looking through the windshield at the flashing railroad crossing signs. The car is no longer a car but a craft with two high back seats and a large curved window in the front above the dashboard. The man with me is not my ex-husband but a male who leisurely gets up from his chair and stands behind it facing me. He has what looks like a smirk on his face. I am popping in and out of my body so that I can see the entire event while experiencing it at the same time. It is the bells that have upset me and they continue to loudly clang.

I am back in my body, hyperventilating with my lips open and my jaw clenched shut breathing through my teeth. I pop out again and see the wide-eyed helpless and terrified expression on my face. I am back in my body again and realize that I am suffocating, unable to draw in enough air through my teeth making no effort to breathe through my nose. I face him mentally asking, "Why are you doing this?" I see his face clearly he is smiling, enjoying my discomfort and fear. I do not know who he is. He is brown with humanoid features but he is not human. I wake up.

Thursday, 13 August 2009, I woke up at 2:20 AM having had a violent dream.

My child and I are in a two-story house, our home. It is dark. There is confusion about many things that I seem to have no control over, and nothing is going right yet everything is orderly. It is time to go to bed and I take my child to his bed. I'm not sure who the child is, I thought perhaps a small grey but later I realized it could have been my grandchild because I heard his voice.

I am in the process of checking the doors and windows to

make sure they are locked. One door is already disabled and although locked, I'm unable to set the alarm for it. I check the window in my child's room and realize that it has been tampered with. I can clearly see the metal strip that has been stapled to the bottom of the inside window is bent and dented as though someone was trying to remove it, my vision had zoomed in on the metal strip as a microscope would on a glass slide. I become alarmed.

Suddenly I am struck with paralyzing fear that ran through my gut making my hair stand on end. I know from where it comes and escape only to meet up with it again and again as I struggle to move down the hall. I know my husband is upstairs in our bedroom, and I am desperately trying to make my way to the stairs. I call out to him for help but my voice isn't working.

Suddenly I am upstairs in the round bedroom that has a round bed and open tieback draperies on a fake window, things are not right. I see my husband standing with his arms crossed as if waiting rather than rushing to help me. I am relieved to see him and puzzled by his actions.

Suddenly I am back downstairs in the hallway being pushed and shoved when I am picked up by an unseen force and thrown against the wall. My back hits the wall, and I slide down landing in a sitting position with my legs stretched out in front of me. The awful fear is coming in waves. I cannot see who is throwing me around like a rag doll. I crawl to the stairs still trying to yell for my husband and am able to call out once. I realize that this has to be a dream and decide to finish it out as I have not been hurt only frightened, badly frightened.

I continue to crawl up the stairs and yell for my husband to help me. Abruptly I am floated up the stairwell. The bedroom door is yanked open and I see a tall grey streak from the room and run down the stairs, this is not my husband. I am back on the stairs looking up at my husband with relief. He is yelling, "What is wrong with you! Why don't you shape up and stop this nonsense!" We are now standing in the upstairs bedroom. I am no longer frightened, I am very angry because this is a dream interfered with, and it has been violent.

The being comes into focus and I get a good look at him. He is tall with a light tan body, a triangular shaped head with two long thin ears that stand up on each side below the triangular point of his head then folding down like dog-ears, and wide open eyes. He does not look at all threatening, and I sense that he is unsure about what to do. We are standing face to face and I begin to unleash my verbal anger on him for this display of violence, and his slowness to come to my aid.

I am awake lying on my left side looking at the wall where the bedroom window is. The room is in complete darkness but I can faintly see two beings standing by the bed. I am mentally yelling, pointing my finger at them saying "How dare you do this to me" and yada, yada, yada all the while shaking my finger at them. There is movement in their area and a fading in and out which I cannot see clearly mostly sensing. I wonder if the triangular head seen on the being in the bedroom was protection as the little greys had worn when we played in my sister's dream,

In the distance I can hear my grandson's voice calling for

"Nana". Having said all that needed saying, I got up and went into the bathroom. I crawled back into bed and mentally sent myself to my grandson to hold and comfort him, to rock and sing nursery rhymes, to let him know that he is loved and safe. I fell asleep.

Tuesday, 24 March 2009. I have finished reading *Hunt for the Skinwalker* by Colm A. Kelleher, Ph.D., and George Knapp and found the first part scary.

Tuesday, 25 August 2009, I lay in bed with my eyes closed waiting to drift off to sleep. As I relaxed and let my mind wonder a ragged looking wolf-like face appeared with a snout that had a flattened nose like a pig. The face did not fade in and out like so many do, and the eyes were wild looking, fearsome. I told it to go away, and as it faded out the smell of wet dog lingered in the room. I said to God, "Please don't let it be hungry. Please don't let it be hungry." Both cats were on the bed with me and neither seemed to react to the odor. I wondered if it was just in my mind rather than in the room; the image used by the beings because I had just finished reading *Hunt for the Skinwalker*? I am uncertain what I am dealing with. The first beings that came repeatedly let me understand that they were scientists studying me, but the beings that are following seem to be of a different nature, prone to violence. I think they are of the same group but have no certainty of this. They seem to be neither good nor evil, they are just there, intruding into my mind when the lights go out and I try to sleep. Whatever the beings are and wherever the beings are from, they need to move on and leave me in peace. I am not sure where this is heading.

Chapter 39

On Monday night, 31 of August 2009, something was here. I had closed my eyes and almost immediately there were two instant white flashes followed by a red blotch in front of my face. I opened my eyes and there was a black rectangle with white English letters formed of white dots within my vision. I asked why they couldn't make the letters clearer rather than have me struggling and guessing what was written. The first line was an "m", the second line an "mm", the third was "mu" and the fourth was a very clear "6". Is this a code of some sort? I fell asleep.

This morning I'm watching the History Channel and they spoke of the land of "Mu" which was Atlantis.

The beings love to do stuff like this knowing I will dwell on it, running it over and over in my mind until I form some conclusion, discard it or shelve it in storage until they decide it is time to reveal a meaning, and that they do not do. I miss the first group that was here as they let me remember and knowingly participate in activities even though they were staged. Have they trained me so well it is no longer necessary? Have they gained so great a control over me that they no longer need to reveal themselves so clearly? Tonight is a full moon.

Friday, 4 September 2009, I've been sick with a sinus infection that has knocked me off of my feet.

Thursday, 10 September 2009, it isn't that I hate or love the aliens although there are several that I am fond of. I feel towards them as I would a human and that means there are virtually few humans I would trust with my most valued possession, my life. Yet these buggers have that control without my consent. However, if I get the chance to meet with them in a my full blown conscious mind, I would jump at it as I want to know more about them but this is not the way their plan works.

Every night before I go to bed I mull over the possibility that "they" may come. Sometimes I feel that they will not, sometimes I know they will, and other nights I just don't give a damn. The moon is no longer full but it is still very bright and the sky was clear last night, so I suspected there might be a visit. A lot of their ability to remain undetected is to not be predictable. When I have this strong feeling that they may come, I am unable to sleep. This is not new and I go with many unnecessary sleepless nights. I finally dozed off around 2:30 AM. I am dreaming.

I am in an unfamiliar house but one I am familiar with such as dreams go. My sister is working at a table in one of the rooms and I am busy in the kitchen. I look out of a window in the front room and see a long cylindrical silver vehicle in the front pulling up to the curb and stop.

I go back to the room where my sister is working and say to her, "You have company. Someone is here to see you." She responds, "I'm not going out with them, you go". I laugh and say "Not me. They are here for you!"

I look out of the window again, the vehicle is still there. I flee to the kitchen passing my sister who now calmly sets at the table watching me. I head towards the back door where I can see trees and an old wooden shed through the door window. I open the door to run out and stop dead in my tracks. I instantly feel terrified and I don't understand why. The smell is strong. I immediately know what is happening and am instantly awake.

I begin deep breathing to relax as I know my body was responding to whatever force they use to take you and bring you back. As I breathed deeply, I could feel my body relax and the feeling subsided, the odor became faint. I was very much awake and was disappointed that they had stopped. I wanted to know what happened.

The smell had been heavy and unpleasant yet one I am familiar with. I recognized the odor of the one who "drops" in off and on. Facing the bedroom window I could see white wispy swirls, and at one time I thought I had seen the face of a grey and something else. There is no conscious thought or decision making once they have made up their mind. I closed my eyes and saw white English letters on a black background. I am always dismayed when none of them form words making sense however, there was one symbol that I grasped. It was a figure with a right angle bottom with three straight lines starting from each end and at the corner of the right angle. The lines ended at a single point at the top forming three triangles. That is the last thing I remember. An hour later I awoke catty-cornered on top of the bed.

I have drawn the symbol as described above many times unable to duplicate what I saw.

Friday, 18 September 2009, it has been four years since I found the space suit in the doorway.

Yesterday was rather disappointing as I had set it aside to work on genealogy and finding nothing of interest to speed me along in that area, I ended up finishing a book by an author I enjoy.

My sister called and we had a lengthy discussion about the beings and how they have affected our lives. We question whether or not we are a part of them, and if so how? We feel our relationship with them is different than what we hear others saying about their experiences. As the day crept into evening I thought I could almost smell one of the little ones but the odor never completed. Somewhere in the back of my mind I had felt they would come last night and I wasn't disappointed, they or one of them did.

It was 3:30 AM the last time I looked at the clock. When I closed my eyes a bright light appeared in the room then faded and the full body of the "artist" appeared. He is black as night except for his white eyes. I began to see red scribble coming in waves, not letters or words but designs, scribble designs which meant nothing to me but were interesting to look at. I turned onto my other side and wondered if changing directions would make a difference as to what I saw. I've wondered many times if I create this within myself depending on which side I lay on, nothing changed. I tossed and turned nearly falling asleep several times but my brain would not shut down, and something new would pop up to think about. Eventually I turned onto my stomach and instantly I could smell one of them so strongly that I knew they were by the bed on the side by the window. I fell asleep.

I had gone to bed around 2 AM. I can't imagine lying in the

bed not sleeping for an hour and a half without getting up. If I haven't fallen asleep within thirty minutes, I get up. I really do not know if I remained in the bed or if I was taken. I could have dozed but my thought processes did not seem to have been interrupted. At one time I had felt a sharp pain in my left jaw that persisted, and I remember admonishing them for allowing humans or any life form to feel pain in their presence as they have the ability to disallow it. I also admonished them for frightening people when it was unnecessary, as it wasn't going to strengthen a positive relationship with humans if that is what they want.

Sunday, 27 September 2009, I am dreaming.

I am on a bus sitting in the first row on the right hand side. In the middle of the bus behind me are three people. I am unaware that there is anyone else in the bus except for the driver who I do not see but assume there is one. There are windows on both sides and through them I can see clouds and blue sky.

I look over my left shoulder at the three people behind me. Two of them are sitting on bus seats with the third sitting on a chair in the aisle beside them. The two in the seats are the tall and short greys with the tall grey setting by the window. I look closely at the person sitting in the aisle that is looking at the grey next to him and talking then turns towards me. He leans back into his chair, folds his arms across his chest, places his left leg over his right knee and gives me a smug look, and I wonder what he has said to them. I realize that the man is my former husband divorced five years ago. I turn around in my seat, pop out of myself and see the entire bus and occupants except for the driver.

I remember nothing more.

Tuesday, 6 October 2009, I set the security alarm last night before going to bed; it was off when I got up. What the hell do I do at night?

I finished watching the well-presented documentary, *I Know What I Saw,* this morning then cut up cheese for a party we're having at work today. I sat down to eat before leaving and realized that I had this feeling of waiting. I'm waiting. What the hell am I waiting for and why? I am biding my time for them, the beings. What is going to happen? What if they, after all of their studying of earth people, appear in the form of Jesus or another spiritual leader? It would be far less frightening then their own forms and would ensure some people listening to them. What if, what if and I am waiting.

Friday, 23 October 2009, 2AM. It has been my misfortune of late to not be able to sleep at night. I may doze off but then wake to pace the floor multiple times before sleep becomes final then awake late in the morning. I understand that "old" people require less continuous hours of sleep but that is bull pucky. Unable to sleep and bored watching TV, I grabbed the camera and began taking random pictures.

This picture was rather exciting because they were here without a hint of presence.

It looks like a tall figure was caught off guard throwing its hands up in the air. Was it a reaction to the camera flash?

The strange head is on the right side at the top of the old hutch. Both are in the same picture.

Chapter 40

Friday, 23 October 2009, another sleepless night and I found myself up and down, reading, watching TV, and back in bed until sleep finally overtook me.

I am aware of the feeling of being taken, of the moment of confusion that occurs when I become aware of their presence, and my body's reaction to their "force field", if that is what it is. My first instinct is to fight, and that is what I do until I realize it is the little ones who are here. We are sailing through the house and stop at my insistence. They put me down and we hold a discussion. I apologize for my reactions, and promise that I will not harm them and will cooperate. We take off flying upwards with me holding their arms above the wrists.

I am in the country house where our children were raised with someone I don't know. We go outside and climb into the car sitting in the driveway. I am in the driver's seat and need to push the seat back and raise the steering wheel making the comment that whoever had last driven this car was really small and we laugh at the joke. We are talking and in a good mood. I am looking forward to wherever we are going. I am unable to remember what happened except there are people and activity around me.

Back in my bed I reposition myself and feel the familiar sensation of their presence, I relax and this time I go willingly with them through the front door. As we pass through the living room I see there are many of them all over my home examining everything, they are curious. As I cross over the front door threshold there is a human male waiting for me who grabs me and plants a long hard kiss on my lips. I pull back in surprise and look at this human who is smiling and obviously pleased to see me. He is young, a little taller than me, stocky, blond, blue eyes, and pink cheeks. I don't know who he is but I suspect that he is someone who I have been doing genealogy on and think it is my father's grandfather. I am comfortable with him. He pulls me back into the house to the china cabinet, and points at a piece of china telling me that he and my great-great-grandmother were given this as a wedding gift. The greys run over to look at what he is pointing. We hold hands as we walk back through the front door and look towards the street where there is a great deal of activity suggesting to me, a block party, and we go amongst the group to check things out.

Again I am in my bed and to my surprise the sensation of being taken overwhelms me again. I am surprised that this is happening three times in one night but as before I go willingly with them wondering what lies in store this time. I pop out of my body and see my back. I am looking out of the bedroom window in a house we had rented when our youngest was born. I am sad, longing for something but I don't know what.

It was in this house that I had heard a knock at the front door, opened it and it is blown wide open, and even with my full weight against the door, I had difficulty closing it. That night I began seeing eyes on the bedroom walls when the light was turned off and had the strange feeling that something was watching. The eyes were the shape of the grey's eyes but at the time I didn't know about the greys. My husband denied seeing them but my four year old daughter did.

Back in my bed I fervently try to remember everything that has happened during the three visits so that I can write it down in the journal but as I bring each event into my mind it begins to blur together with details lost except for what is written. What really happened?

They have a sense of humor and are inventive working around our "simple" thoughts, feelings and activities. Could it be that they "entertained" my mind while something entirely different was actually happening? Yes, I'm sure of it. I've become a cynic.

Sunday, 25 October 2009, last night when I had gotten up to go to the bathroom a picture popped up under the window. I could see that it was a cartoon and recognized the style and figures as the artist's work. I was unable to read the words as it was too far away and gave up trying. On the way back to bed I expressed dismay that I could not read the words and asked why he presented his work many times under conditions where I am unable to see it properly. After I was settled in bed, I told the artist that if he planned on re-showing his art please make sure that I can see it. Instantly a page appeared with writing on it. I commented that it was too far away. It moved closer, than closer, and I could see the figures were possibly Hebrew, and was pleased that I could actually see them when it moved closer and closer again, until it was on the tip of my nose, and too close to make out detail then it vanished. I started laughing. Good one, Artist!

Thursday, 29 October 2009, at 4:57 this morning I awoke

with something in the room with me and quite close. A white bar or rectangle appeared in front of my eyes. On the bar were four symbols outlined in black with granular brown on the inside. I remember only one symbol, a circle. I could see them easily, and I wondered what language they were and what they meant. Suddenly my body began to deep breath and I wondered what was going to happen next as I didn't have that awful feeling that I get when being taken yet it was almost there but not complete. Then it was gone and I went back to sleep.

Monday, 23 November 2009, when I was at the kitchen sink fixing my morning coffee there was a rectangular flash on the left chest area of my pajamas and I admit to finding that amusing because they had a very close up view of what I was doing. While showering I thought over the idea that I have invited them to live with me, to observe what daily earth life is opposed to their manufacturing situations to observe my reactions. I remember telling them a "staged" setting will never reveal a real life situation response. They do not bother me, they observe and they always let me know they are here.

Tuesday, 1 December 2009, what was once open and obvious has now become secretive. The flashes are even shorter, the balls are smaller, the contacts subtle, and would be completely overlooked by anyone with me. Is this change a "safety" move to protect them or one to make it less obvious to me? The question begging an answer is why are they here every day of my life anyway? I know the answer... I want to know more about them.

Monday, 7 December 2009, early morning, I am dreaming.

I am in a metal house. There is no furniture as we humans know furniture and even though I do not see any my mind places quick images of furniture at different spots that I know are not real. There is a meeting, an important meeting where a serious discussion is held and at the end, I was not happy with the outcome but I cannot say why. I am left with the impression the humans there are my friends from the past yet they don't seem "right" but I can't say in what way.

That night when I flopped into the bed for long sought after sleep, I could feel the tingly sensation on my entire right leg that one gets just before you get zapped. It occurred three times and I knew that they were in the room. Then the smell came, a strong moldy smell that reminded me of a musty basement, not at all like the other beings that have come in the past. I told him, "Go away and send the others I don't know you." He replied, "They are elsewhere. I have been assigned to you, and I don't have time for this crap." "Crap"? In my head I yell, "LEAVE! SEND THE OTHERS!" and with this, his smell disappears. I began to see the lacey picture the artist has shown me often, and settled in to see what creation he had designed for tonight. It changed into scratchy lines that formed multiple designs which were not unpleasant to look at. The lines begin to move and gently swirl, the smell is back, and I remember nothing else.

Friday, 11 December 2009, sometime during the night I became aware of the odor of the little one which persisted but never became overwhelming. We spoke briefly mostly me confirming that it was him. I opened my eyes and there was black on gray writing on the wall, print large enough to read. I didn't read it instead rolling over onto my right side where the print also appeared. I made no effort to read it closing my eyes where the print also appeared. I didn't really care what it said and made no effort to study it, shutting it out of my mind. That is the last I remember. Wednesday, 30 December 2009, this evening about 9:30, I began taking pictures because the cats were acting strange and knew that something was going on. My sister and her husband were spending the holidays with me and while he went into their bedroom to read, she sat in the wingback chair working on her marvelous beading.

"Oh," she said my ears are ringing so loudly!" "Tell them to lower the sound," I replied, and she said that they did. She said, "I have such heaviness about my head. Do you feel it?" "No," I answered as I aimed the camera at her pressing the button but the flash did not go off the first time. We downloaded the shot and examined it finding the Christmas tree bulb shaped object with a red ring around it pointing at her about two feet from her head. We went through all of the pictures I had taken and found this object in many of them.

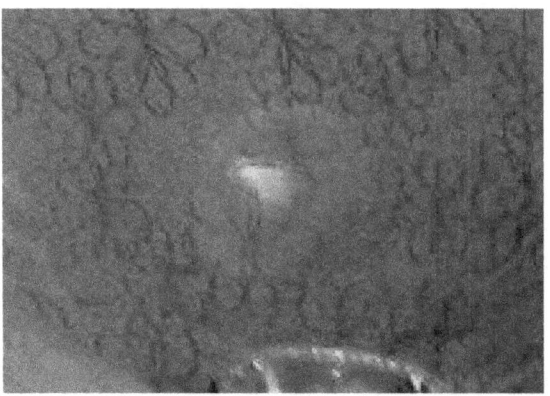

Wednesday, 7 January 2010, I had a dream which started out being the usual nonsensical dream when it abruptly stopped. I became aware of a variety of "chicken scratches" which immediately went away leaving a snowy white screen. A square with rounded edges appeared with about five or six different colored unknown symbols followed by three more squares with different symbols. The squares rested long enough for me to read if I had known the language. I must have fallen asleep following the fourth square as I remember nothing more.

Monday, 11 January 2010, my sister and her husband left last Saturday morning and Percy willingly left with his mommy. The beings really disturbed him, and he began peeing on the carpets while Buster sprayed the walls in retaliation, something he had never done before. I was running around with carpet cleaner and rags in one hand and air freshener in the other. It didn't matter how many cat pans I sat out or where they were placed, the old boys did what they wanted when I wasn't looking. Two old dominant feline males in the same house can be a headache. Neither my sister nor I recalled anything much happening with the beings while they were here other than seeing some flashing, black and white balls and weird dreams that just seemed to be the usual human weird dreams.

While Percy was visiting I had taken random pictures, one is of him on my bed with a softball sized orb above him. Another picture was taken within the same minute showing his head turned to face the object that had suddenly appeared at the side of the bed. Percy was aware of it but I wasn't.

The object enlarged appears to be the faint head of a being without the famous slanted eyes of a grey.

Friday, 5 February 2010, yesterday I went to have my taxes done. The accountant looked at the Social Security income statement that showed a minus sign at the total. This meant that although I had been receiving monthly payments and monies were removed to pay Parts B & D, I would have to repay all of it. We were both stunned.

He set me up at a telephone to call S.S. to straighten out this discrepancy. After going through the long drawn out punching of buttons and unrelated messages, I finally connected with a living human being. I began to explain what the statement said number by number that she said, having my record pulled up, she could follow. We got to the last number and there was NO minus sign. I was flummoxed, called the accountant over, handed him the paper, gave my permission to discuss my personal account, and he could no longer see the minus sign either. We hung up embarrassed and throughout the remaining tax preparation he would look at the paper to check that there was still no minus sign. He had no idea what was going on but I had my suspicions. Later when I got into the car I threw back my head and laughed at their joke.

Tuesday, 9 February 2010, I was told by a voice that they were coming last night, and as usual I really didn't believe it. I read, turned off the lights, saw many little white balls and that was it. I couldn't sleep, up and down, and the last time back to bed the top of one head bent forward was shown to me. The head rose exposing the face, and for a brief second I saw it before it began shape-shifting. The feeling in my gut said that I knew it and it was the one in control tonight. I fell asleep. I am dreaming.

I am with my oldest son and for whatever reason we must attend a meeting in a place where I am reluctant to go. I think he said it something about Boy Scouts but I'm not sure.

With his encouragement we arrive at a concrete looking building where inside are multiple floors with many small rustic rooms, wooden floors, wooden banisters, wooden chairs and tables, etc. We accomplish whatever it is we are to do then we are told we have to leave immediately, and to lock up before we go. We walk around checking to make sure that no one is left in the building. He has the key in his hand, and as we are about to go out the door he sees four adorable little children with big brown eyes. I can't imagine where they have come from and am slightly annoyed because we have to leave immediately and cannot leave them here. We search but are unable to find their parents. I can't understand why any parent would leave their small children unattended. We are told we have to vacate the building now! The pressure is on.

We are up in another part of the building, and my son has found a sort of wagon which we can place the children in that will carry them out of the building. I place the children in the wagon and try to put a makeshift seat belt on the smallest one. The seat belt looks as though it is made of rubber bands and will not latch together. I give up fumbling with it instead wrapping a blanket around them, and we are ready to go. Before pulling it, I turn to look at the children and see that the sides of the wagon have collapsed and they are sprawled in a little pile asleep by the wagon on the floor. I sigh and am once again annoyed due to this unforeseen obstacle because we must leave immediately. I go about placing the children back into the wagon, carefully locking the sides, front, and back, so that no one gets pinched while closing them, and so they will not fall out. Again I wrap them in the blanket and see that the children are having a wonderful time, little smirks on their faces while I am becoming so frustrated that I want to scream. We have to leave. The wagon collapses again. This time I plop the children back into the wagon, and was on the verge of some pointed finger shaking when I realize these were assorted sized little greys and it was a dream interfered with. Damn! Now I am awake and can hear my deep breathing but I want to fool them so that I can remember what is going on. They are here!

Somehow or other, the little ones are back in the wagon and we are hastily proceeding to the door. We go down the steps with the wagon full of little ones and through a room which is crowded with many people who seem to be working. We go down another flight of steps and exit the door that my son turns and locks. We stand there and I know that it is over. I am amazed that I was able to hold my temper.

Instantly there is a light olive green sheet of paper with rust colored writing on it. It is writing not printing, and pretty with this color combination. There are many paragraphs with what I presume to be a large title across the middle at a slant. The letters are English but make absolutely no sense, and I wonder if subconsciously I can read this and know what it means. I look at it then turn my head; I don't want to know what it says. I am pissed. I am lying on my left side in the bed and I begin dissing them about all of the subterfuge, disturbance of sleep, and punching all of my buttons in an attempt to anger me to see just how far I will go before I start to implode or explode, pushing me to do something that I would normally not do. They are not finished and are not going to release me. My eyes are open now and there is no pretense of sleep. I see the wispy swirls which form into the outline of a skinny grey face with big eyes. The face floats back and forth each time coming closer to my eyes, and I yell at him, "No! You are NOT going to do that to me!" and jump out of the bed.

There is an instant flash above the closet door then one to my right on the way to the bathroom that I am aware they are sending me, and this also makes me angry because I am a puppet; I'm not even allowed to decide when I pee.

I go back to bed; it is 4:30 AM. I cannot sleep, tossing and turning, trying to relax, trying to gain some control. I can smell the little one or his friend, and I am uncomfortable because my body feels as if it is on the verge of being taken yet does not complete. They are punishing me and the feeling is relentless. I cannot stand it anymore. I get out of bed and go into the living room, walk around, turn down the heat because I am sweating, and go back to bed.

They still are not finished. The chicken scratches begin then morph into writing, then into the olive and rust colored paper; I know they are bound and determined that I am to read it. I don't want to cooperate with them not because I don't like them but because it is their method of obtaining research and control that I don't like. I am a naughty child, and they will get what they want but I don't have to make it easy for them. At some point I look at the clock again, it is 5:30 AM, and I am surprised at how much time has passed. I remember nothing more and am exhausted when I awake and have the post visit hang-over.

The feeling that I had all evening and this morning is "It Has Begun" and I am receiving instructions. I also feel that I am being judged on my behavior by those who said not to judge others, who resented being judged themselves.

Chapter 41

Saturday, 13 February 2010, 12:01AM, I went to bed early about 7:30 PM, read, turned off the light, and closed my eyes. The glasses appeared, darkened, and a greenish rectangle on its end appeared. It is as if I am in a completely darkened room seeing a lit doorway in the distance. I find myself closer to the doorway and am able to see a shimmering within it the other side is a lime green. There seems to be a huge bare tree standing in the middle with a few black dots toward the top of the tree. Suddenly a swarm of black dots fly and land all around each other covering the top of the tree as if a living mass. I fall asleep.

I am being taken for questioning by a woman who is about my height, small boned, and pleasant. We are in a little room sitting on chairs with a small table between us, and I find myself bouncing in and out, being myself and the observer.

She asks me a few questions then asks me what is wrong. I decide there is no reason to not tell her the truth and explain to her that I am depressed, and suffer this periodically but find that I can work my way through it. She listens, nods her head seemingly satisfied with my answer.

We are walking around throughout the multilayered complex, and I tell her about my job, she replies that they are looking for help in this area and that I would be good there. She ushers me into the room with her "boss" who is addressing a group of people. She walks up to the one at the lectern, and signals for me to stand next to her where we face the man speaking, and when he is finished we leave.

I am uncomfortable with this, remembering my mother telling me that when she was in nursing school, patients would be brought into the lecture room and discussed as if they weren't there. Was I discussed?

We walk down stairs, around corners, and I spy a small break area when I exclaim that there are ashtrays! She said that we can smoke and she will get us coffee. I follow her to the end of the short hall to help with the coffee and see an enclosed patio to our right surrounded by grass, trees, and a tall wooden fence. We walk out onto the cement flagged patio and I tell her how lovely it is here when a young child runs through the doors yelling, "Mommy, Mommy!" I ask her if this is her child and she says, "Yes, it is." She bends down on one knee on the patio floor and seems to be tangled up in tree branches and leaves. I remove a small tree branch that is stuck to her sweater by what looks like cobwebs. She is freed and gets up and now I also find myself bent on one knee on the patio floor. I see a medium sized white dog with big eyes sitting on the grass near a corner of the patio watching us. I shake the branch at the dog hoping that he will want to play but he does not move, and I say that he doesn't seem to want to play and wake up.

I go to swallow and find that my tongue is glued to the roof of my mouth and is so dry that it takes a few tries to moisten and release it. There are lights coming from the bedroom window and don't seem to be natural because there are two lights shining through onto the wall which is the side the motion detector is on, while the other only has one light shining through. When the motion detector is on, the entire area around the curtain is lit up. I get up to check and see that it has snowed and is melting.

Prior to this dream I had a conversation with a coworker about depression. I also had a conversation with the old one about the visit from the mean being the other night when I was pushed and thrown. He said that they were aware and that measures would be taken to prevent it happening again. The most telling that connects this episode to the beings is my mouth is glued shut, and the little white dog with big eyes sitting on the patio is probably a disguised grey looking exactly like my sister's dog.

I fell back asleep when a second dream began. My ex-husband picks me up to go somewhere together but I don't know where, and I am surprised but at the same time I'm not surprised. The table and chairs where we sit are like the old wrought iron sets found in soda shops when I was growing up. Across the small round wooden topped table is sitting a man dressed in a brown suit with a white shirt and red tie. The wall behind the man is beige with nothing on it.

He is a mean looking man with dark wrinkled skin, and I think he might be from another country. He and my ex-husband are having a lot of off and on eye contact as if seeking approval and support from each other. Warnings were given from the man to me that if I didn't submit to whatever it is they want litigation or a lawsuit may result. I look hard at him and realize he is the mean man I had seen several nights ago and know this is a sham. When the man was finished with the threats, I said that I needed to go to the bathroom and left the table. I knew where it was and entered through the door.

On the floor was a tall cylindrical aluminum looking contraption with a curved nozzle sticking out of the top.

I flicked the proper switch on the top and the bottom portion of the cylinder spun out that was the seat of the commode, at the same time the curved nozzle swung around over my head as I sat down and began spraying me with a liquid. I reached around shutting it off and was instantly awake needing to go to the bathroom.

Was this another bathroom dream or was the need to go to the bathroom an interruption to a dream interfered with left unfinished? I never looked at who I thought was my ex-husband just assumed that it was him.

There was a third dream preceded with "chicken scratches" often seen, but I remember nothing about it feeling it was a regular dream.

Thursday, 18 February 2010, I am on the couch holding Buster in my arms, he is snuggled in contentedly purring. My left hand is towards the left side of his head and in it is the TV remote control. Suddenly there is a flash of a blue rectangle on the TV screen and we both jump, he is not a happy camper anymore but remains to be petted.

When I went to bed and turned off the bedside light a room appeared on my closed eyelids and suddenly I am in it. I don't remember much about the room except there is a tall grey to my right slightly bent over a high table working on something with his back towards me and the center of the room. Occasionally he stands upright looking at something eye level then bends forward again. The light seems to be general yet the room is not well lit. My focus is on the being in front of me who is short with very dark brown features, brown eyes, a face without a redeeming feature, with long tight curls hanging off of his head and shoulders looking directly at me. I cannot see the rest of his body clearly and his face is partially covered with the long curled hair. Suddenly the curls part and his face can be seen; he smiles at me, turns to his right and leaves the room. The picture is gone and I am in my bed.

I am about to suffer from a nervous breakdown, and need to get away from all of this having no idea where to run. I seek beauty, peace and God's reassuring presence.

Thursday, 25 February 2010, I turned the light off about 1:30 AM, pulled the covers up and scrunched down in the bed. As I settled in I thought about trying to find a position where I wouldn't wake up with my hair a mess. Instantly, before the thought was totally finished in my head, a mustard colored screen appeared with white pencil-like cartoon heads and shoulders of females with different hair lengths all messed up! There must have been four different ways a person can wake up with messy hair. The cartoons were "drawn" on the side of the paper so that I would have to turn the paper or my head to clearly see them. As I turned my head the paper turned so that it would never appear straight on. I laughed, it was the artist, and I was waiting for the pictures to come up to my nose but they didn't, instead they faded out and I fell asleep soon after.

Saturday, 6 March 2010, I was unable to fall asleep due to the "musty" odor of one of them which seemed to stand rather close to the bed. It seemed to come closer when I would start to doze off and would instantly awaken due to the smothering odor. I asked him if I could wash his clothes but received no reply.   Suddenly I was watching a snowstorm. There was one dark bare tree in the distance and the falling snowflakes were huge and mesmerizing. I loved it. The wind picked up and the snow became thick and slanted sideways, so dense that the tree in the background could barely be seen. The wind blowing the snow sideways increased in speed and fury becoming trance-like. Suddenly it ended shooting off to my right and I felt my brain sliding sideways with it becoming instantly awake. I wanted the snowstorm to return as I found it relaxing but realized it was one of their hypnotizing gimmicks that hadn't worked. It was a long wakeful night.

Tuesday, 9 March 2010, I read, fell asleep and was instantly awake, opened my eyes and rolled onto my back. There was a rectangular white flash seen from the corner of my right eye on the wall above the lamp near the bathroom door. Writing appeared on the ceiling and a small white dot was in the area of the now dark rectangle. The writing was an assortment of letters spelling nothing then faded leaving me annoyed and frustrated. I got up to go into the bathroom, and as I passed the rectangle I shook my finger at it announcing that if they were going to spend the time sending writing then send something I can read! I closed the bathroom door when I came out. I crawled back into bed, tossed and turned unable to fall back to sleep then got up and snapped pictures in the bedroom and living room. Sometimes the flash went off sometimes it didn't then I went back to bed and slept.

Monday, 15 March 2010, I came home from work, made coffee and instead of doing the usual routine, I went into the closet to change shoes and put on my pajamas. I opened the closet door and entered without turning on the light looking down to avoid stepping on shoes carelessly thrown on the floor coming to a sudden halt. On the floor was an orb the size of a basketball which disappeared instantly, I completed my task, and avoided stepping on the spot where I had seen the ball.

Monday, 29 March 2010, I turned off the light last night around 11 PM. I wasn't tired and didn't think I would fall asleep; I awoke at 1 AM, hot. I sat up on the side of the bed facing the bathroom door and saw a quick glimpse of a white ball. The ball darkened then lit again as it hit the center of my chest, darkened and hit my left upper arm, darkened and hit my right upper arm then landed on my right shoulder with a dim glow that faded out. I was happy to see the ball as it is the one that interacts with me and greeted it warmly. I looked towards the bathroom door which seemed to be filled with a dim design of white balls which floated moving slowly. It was very relaxing; I thanked the ball for the pleasure of sharing the design. I was totally charged and unable to fall back to sleep.

During our communication he told me that he travels all over and visits many interesting places and people. I asked him if he was talking about our world and he said yes, he was. He denied being in the military but is part of a group that protects the ship if necessary, so in a way he is military although it is not his main function. He says he likes his job. I asked how often he ate and he told me he eats about once every twenty-four hours.

Tuesday, 6 April 2010, I have been extremely tired since last Thursday. I had some work done at the house that required me cleaning up then I did some outside chores. I don't recuperate as quickly as I once did when younger.

I am still trudging through the fascinating book that never ends, *The Secret Teachings of All Ages*, by Manly P. Hall. There is no way anyone can absorb all of the information given in one read through beckoning to be studied. I try to get through at least one chapter a night but often fall asleep before. Last night I didn't even attempt it, I just turned off the light and fell asleep. Just before I fell asleep there was a bright flash in the room above my bed and I become aware of a terrible smell next to me. At first I thought it is one I am familiar with but the smell is slightly different and more powerful. A rectangle with a silver-like colored back ground with a shade of tan letters, or maybe it was the other way around, appeared. The letters are English which did not spell anything but were grouped as if words, one word on top of another with the ends sticking out so that I could see there were multiple words, none that I could read. I yelled for the little one asking him where he was, telling him that I didn't want to go with a being that I didn't know, and was told the little one was busy elsewhere and couldn't come. I thought to myself that if I was in a room full of beings that smell like this I would suffocate and the being backed off.

I got up walked around then went back to bed with my mind clear of everything and fell back to sleep. Sometime after that I feel I am suffocating and become panicky, than I relax and am unaware of anything else. This morning I have small bruises on the inside of both upper arms.

Wednesday, 7 April 2010, I woke up early this morning while it was still dark outside feeling drugged. When I looked towards the bathroom door I could see thin hazy white sketch marks everywhere about the door forming nothing in particular, and I knew they were here. I entered the bathroom and looked intently at the door seeing the vague shapes of a short one entering into the bathroom stopping about a foot away from me, and a tall one who remained in the doorway. I could see the little one's eyes, and spoke to him then looked up at the tall one in the doorway, and spoke to him, he vanished but did not leave falling colored petals behind as he had in the past. The little one remained in place and I told him I needed to pass through the doorway.

I went back to bed and slept some more. I'm glad they are back. I had talked with the old one last night before falling asleep asking him if he was my guide. He replied, yes he was, and I thanked him for always being there with me. He told me that when things "change" that my family would be safe and we would be together, that I would be a healer therefore an ambassador. When he no longer wanted to talk my mind floated off into nothingness, and I am unable to maintain a thought.

Friday, 16 April 2010, I read more of *The Secret Teachings of All Ages*, turned out the light, and the room seemed to come alive.

A shading of blue appeared throughout the room very similar to the shading on the basement wall the night "Casper" flew up the steps (3 October1980). The glasses are snapped onto my face blocking my view. I could feel being touched, and could see many shadowy faces peering closely at me. I fell asleep waking up at 1:20 AM with a strong urge to visit the bathroom.

There is writing all over the bathroom composed of English letters, print and cursive. Some appeared to be phrases while others one word. Some were underlined and embellished as in a fancy script while others were plain. All were different colors and sizes gently moving in, out, and around. If the script was meant to be read, I was unable to do so as the artistic grouping and colors held my attention to the point that I was enjoying the total picture rather than targeting separate aspects. I was pleased with what I was shown and thanked the artist for this special treat, as soon as I had vocalized this thought the amazing spectacle disappeared and the bathroom became as it was when I entered, dark. A small shadow, with its head at the level of my head while seated ran in front of me and through the bathroom door. I went back to bed and slept.

Saturday, 17 April 2010, last night I took pictures of the bedroom and found a green head, this morning I reviewed it under magnification. The being appears to be a medium green with humanoid features with a sort of "frill" around his neck, and slightly bent backwards green spikes growing from his head. The nose lies flat just below the eyes and the mouth seems to be quite large.

I went to bed on the verge of controlled hysteria eventually justifying this being showing himself so that I wouldn't run or die of fear when he does. He could have harmed me but he didn't, and he doesn't want me running away when he does appear. I have asked repeatedly for them to show themselves, and when one does in whatever manner he / she decides, I must be willing to accept for that which

I have asked.

This morning while showering we talked. He is not a grey. He eats by his mouth, has flatulence like humans, and the green spikes from his head are sensors. He does not bath in water but in "termite solution". He says the closet is the portal, and he does not like the perfumes we douse ourselves with, soap, fabric softener, etc., finding it offensive. He must have been done speaking as my mind drifted off to human thoughts of why do we perfume everything? When I came out of the closet with the clothes I am wearing today, I nearly stepped on a blue orb about an inch and a half in diameter lying just outside of the closet door.

Chapter 42

Sunday, 18 April 2010, I learned about the Scientific Paranormal Investigative Research Information and Technology (S.P.I.R.I.T.) **www.spinvestigations.org** when I was looking for information on portals. David M. Rountree had written a paper on them, **www.perception9.com/david-rountree-paranormal-science/research-experiments-equipment.php?article=Portals-Vortices-and-Wormholes-Part-1** . I emailed him, and he was kind enough to answer some questions I had about portals. I researched his web site and was impressed by how his group investigates the paranormal using scientific methods. I told him about the beings and my experiences. It was him I turned to sending a copy of a picture with the Christmas tree bulb asking for his opinion.

My buddy met with part of her old UFO group tonight. I am interested to hear how the meeting went.

Sunday, 25 April 2010, I am dreaming.

I am in a home that I think is my home, there are children present; I am busy organizing, and being a mom. There is a young girl, around 12, maybe younger. She has blond curly hair, her presence feels comfortable and she is of great help. I become aware that I have to go to the bathroom, and take off towards it whereupon she decides that she must come with me. I enter the bathroom and find the toilet bowl and seat slid under the top that looks like metal. I had never seen one like it but at the time I didn't care. I pulled the bowl-seat portion out, sat and woke up.

I opened my eyes and there was writing everywhere, white English letters on a dull grey background coupled together not spelling anything that I was familiar with. The "words" were of different sizes and moved gently around, over to the side, and under each other. I knew they were here and was pleased. I went into the bathroom and watched the words fill the bathroom, on the walls and hanging in space. I said, "Hi, I know you are here," the words vanished.

Climbing back into bed and seeing nothing, I closed my eyes and began to fall asleep when the odor of the little one became strong. Not opening my eyes I thought, "I can smell you, little one. I'm glad you are here. Where have you been?" The returned voice was not that of the little one. I asked him why his smell was the same but his voice is different, and the smell faded away. "I have many voices," he replied. I asked him where he has been replying that he has been busy at many places. I then asked him if he had come to get me, replying, yes that we were going to the ship. I said okay, and fell asleep. It was 1:20 am.

Wednesday, 28 April 2010, I have been corresponding with David Rountree, who has a calming influence which I sorely need. Per his recommendation I sent the camera to the manufacturer to be checked to see if it is working properly. I sent it with the card and five pictures last Wednesday and was notified today that it is being shipped back. It was in and out of their shop in one day being returned by UPS ground, so it probably won't be here until next Monday. I have my fingers crossed that it is functioning properly.

I finished the fiction book *Haunted Mesa* by Louis L' Amour last night at 1:30 am. I don't think I enjoyed it as much as I would have if I didn't think I had a portal in my own home. I am dreaming.

I am with my boss from work. We are with a child who comes into our shop frequently, and has a lot of behavior problems resulting in few friends. My boss is trying to get the child to want to play with others rather than bossing them around. I don't know where we are, some place that is not familiar, and I need to go to the bathroom as always in these dreams. I am delighted to find the bathroom which has a regular earth toilet when my boss tells me the child has to use it. The little girl sits on the commode that has risen into the air allowing the child's face to be even with my bosses who happens to be tall. She is quietly reasoning with the child causing a look of doubt on the child's face. Meanwhile, I am thinking that I still have to go to the bathroom and am told to use the other one in another room. I enter the room and find that the toilet looks like a shampoo chair in a beauty shop, and think that this is a totally weird setup. I am awake.

I open my eyes and there is white writing on a grey background all over the room. It is floating and moving around and I head for the bathroom that also has floating letters in it. I find there is no urgency in this matter and thanked them for waking me. The writing disappeared and the clock read 5:20 AM as I crawled back into bed. My sister says that they have been known to wake her up too when she has to go to the bathroom.

Friday, 30 April 2010, I turned off the light and snuggled into my comfortable bed. The room deepened in darkness then quickly lightened, and I had an immediate feeling of dizziness. A white light flashed twice by the right side of my head, I opened my eyes and it flashed twice again. I read the article by David about portals, so I am watching closely what is happening in my home.

Saturday, 1 May 2010, I suddenly awake aware that something is in the room with me and spot a slightly glowing lime green rectangular shaped object with rounded edges about ten by twelve inches and maybe three to four inches thick hovering on the ceiling above the dresser. I decide that it is a miniature ship and wonder what beings are in it. I am wishing that I had a broom handle because I would jam it into the ship destroying it. Suddenly three objects fly from the side of the craft in an arc until they are hovering over the bed in front of me. I am now sitting up in the bed with my back against the headboard.

There are two men and one woman, human shaped, and covered from head to toe in brightly colored form fitting outfits. The male in front center is wearing blue, the female to his right wears yellow, and the male is to his left is wearing red. Only the eyes, nose, mouth and hands are exposed. I am not slow to act and yell, "Leave!" and begin calling on the Archangel Michael to bring his sword and chase these beings from my home because they do not belong here. The male in the middle extends his arm and points at me, as if I will not forget you or I will get you, an intimidating gesture. All three fly back into the green ship on the ceiling and the ship disappears.

I sat in the bed quivering, stroking Buster with mindless

effort thinking I would like to give the idiot who inscribed earth and where it is on the voyager a piece of my mind, a large piece. I am also thinking the beings must have a huge network sharing information, and I'm on the list. I thanked Archangel Michael and fell asleep.

Sunday, 2 May 2010, I fell asleep early and become aware that I am dreaming about a woman and a family. I am an observer trying to help her.

Everything is going well when suddenly, sitting in front of her computer, the woman becomes terrified. I go in front of the monitor to look at her and see that her face looks so sad. She has her elbows on her desk holding her hands and leaning slightly forward. She looks more like a cartoon character rather than a real person and I'm not sure which one she is. She is in her thirties with long curly black hair and looks stricken. I don't understand why she has become so frightened.

I am awakened by a slight tingling of my right leg and find I am on my back. Suddenly there is a bright white flash of a square in front of my face with red areas in it. Immediately there are other flashes around it and I know they are here. It is 11:30 pm and I remember nothing else yet I know there is more.

Wednesday, 5 May 2010, my handy little camera is not working properly and cannot be fixed. I notified David about the camera results and decide to take his advice, keep the old one and buy a new one. I bought an HP CB350 that should be here by Monday at the earliest.

Last night, well, last night I'm not sure what the heck

happened. I went to bed drained of energy, didn't read, turned out the light and fell asleep. At 12:30, I was awakened by an abrupt short guttural noise coming from the other side of the bed. I laid there deciding that I must have been dreaming when it repeated. There were no odors, little balls or other noise, I got up.

I sat up for awhile then went back to bed. I became aware of a light in the room and thought I was looking through my eyelids when I realized that the eyelid next to the pillow was slightly open. Lying on my left side I was facing the outer corner of the bedroom where a golden object sat cattycornered on the bedside table emitting a bright light. The light was not the bright white cold light seen before instead it emitted an almost golden glow that was bright in the dark room. The object looked to be at least the size of a square foot shaped like a throw pillow with a three inch panel running around the sides giving it depth. I could see what looked to be engraving on the square; one long slanted line, perhaps an inch wide, from the left bottom corner towards the upper right corner, ending a few inches from the top and bottom, plus a few other shapes. The engraving was deep enough to cause shadows within the object but they were not deep enough to make the shapes clear. I lost consciousness.

Saturday, 8 May 2010, the new camera is smaller with a better quality picture. I can download pictures into the program or delete them from the camera and that's pretty much the basics of my ability.

I held the old camera up with the new one, as Dave suggested, and snapped pictures. Only the old camera showed the Christmas tree bulb in six out of ten pictures. There we are, the old camera does not work properly. About 12:30 last night I took random shots and picked up some orbs, nice ones with one on my pillow. I sent the better ones to Dave for input as I need some guidance.

I went to bed around 1 AM, read, turned off the light, and fell asleep waking up hot. I don't remember what time it was when I turned the air down a notch, and went back to bed laying on my left side in a curled up position. Little white dots appeared then developed into the shape of a square, like a tiny square room. The dotted walls of the room began to shimmer and a rectangle outlined in white appeared sitting on my arm facing me. I moved my head slightly and the rectangle blinked out then came on again when I stilled. The little room, pitch black with the shimmering dots and the stark white rectangle, was rather pretty and I decided this had to be a hologram as I could think of no other explanation when the whole thing disappeared. I remember nothing more.

Tuesday, 11 May 2010, I got up this morning more tired than when I went to bed. The new little cat, Kitty, was into the cupcakes, and when finished there, she hauled the banana bread across the living room floor. Funny little cat, I can't seem to fill her up, and she is looking for something she wants or needs to eat but can't tell me what. I have done this myself, a bite of this, a bite of that until the right bite and the body is satisfied.

Buster was depressed after Percy left and was not himself. He had gone from three buddies losing them one by one until only he was left then Percy came and now he has gone home. I went to the animal shelter and picked out the only spayed female they had. She is white with one green and one yellow eye, is a year old, feisty, torments him, and he comes running to me like a child. She wants to play and he wants no part of her. It takes time for cats to get settled. Personality wise she is not the best choice but given time she will settle down then we can have some peace and Buster will not be alone.

David suggests that I continue using the old camera along with the new one to verify something is there such as orbs. So yesterday evening I shot a total of 89 pictures between both cameras. The old camera did not always work, so the shots are not one for one but will try to match them up based on time. By 1:00 AM I was ready for bed.

At five this morning I open my eyes and instead of seeing writing I am looking at math equations one after the other. I said to them, "I'm awake, you can turn it off now", and the picture of equations turned disappeared and I fell back into a restless sleep until nine this morning. Are they telling me they know about David who is working on his PhD in Physics? Yes, I think that is exactly right.

Thursday, 13 May 2010, I don't know what time I turned off the light last night but suspect it was around 12-12:30 AM. I have started a new book, *Flight of the Seventh Moon* by Lynn V. Andrews which holds my attention. I woke up at 3 AM, went into the bathroom, and closed the door when I came out because there was a little grey in the bathroom. I fell back to sleep.

I am dreaming.

I am in another country, I think somewhere in the Middle East with people who are dark skinned and speak English. I am one of them and we are poor. We are very busy with so much work to do and as we work we talk about different things. As usual my dreams include the bathroom and I tell them I must visit the bathroom. I am on the commode in a room that is too large to be a bathroom. On the floor is what looks like old fashioned brown linoleum found in old institutions. I lean over a bit to examine the floor when it turns black, and I see white balls scatter around from my direction outward filling me with a sensation of fear. I know my sister is in a room close by, and I yell out, "Sis, do you want to sleep with me tonight?" but there is no answer. I wake up.

I am on my right side looking into the bathroom where moonlight is shinning in through the bathroom window. I watch a lime green object carefully maneuver sideways through the closed bathroom window and hover in the bathroom. The color is the same as the little green "face" I found in a recent picture also the color of the green ship seen on the ceiling on May 1st. The object looks hazy and appears to be round then as it hovers, it turns facing me. It looks to be a concave five sided polygon, reminding me of a satellite dish, with some sort of a stem in the back. It vanishes, and I can hear various parts of the attic creak then stop. I lie there waiting to see what else will happen but nothing does. I look at the clock it is 4:48 AM, and I ask myself how did the bathroom door become open?

Saturday, 15 May 2010, I went to bed very early last night, around 8:30 and read more of *Flight of the Seventh Moon*. The woman is searching to learn about her womanliness

with the help of a Cree Indian medicine women in Manitoba, Canada. Very interesting to learn there is male and female in all of us and that there needs to be a balance between the two. I've always known that there were both in me and use to wonder if I had been born in the wrong body, a female body, yet I am comfortable in this body. I like it. As I read the book I am put in mind of *The Secret Teaching of All Ages* by Manly P. Hall, that many similarities among the ancient views have been lost through misunderstanding and fear. I turned out the light and fell asleep.
I am dreaming.

I am with my two boys and ex-husband. We are in a large house with many rooms that seem to run in every direction with no pattern of forethought. The house is cluttered, stuff everywhere, and I must clean it up, which I do and it is an awesome task. The four of us begin to load up a truck with boxes. The boys are helpful but are moving too slow to suit me, and my husband seems to want to be a director rather than a worker. I am becoming frustrated. Finally the last box is placed in the rear and my oldest son and husband jump in the truck leaving me to close the rear gate. I close the gate but it doesn't latch. I close it again, and again, and again but it still doesn't latch each time slamming it harder and harder. The engine starts and the truck begins to move slowly forward, and I watch the boxes shift from the movement of the truck. I realize that everything is going to shift out the back of the truck onto the ground, I yell out loud in my human voice, "I can't close the back!" I am awake.

In the dark I am never sure if my eyes are open or closed but often it doesn't matter as I can see in front of open eyes what I see with eyes closed but this time I had my left eye open in a slit. The audible words had no sooner left my lips when a white object flashed on the headboard. It was a white square disk with a hole in the middle with three lines at each rounded corner reminding me of an old type speaker. Then all sorts of lights began popping around my head, red, white and yellow, as well as little balls zooming around. Colored swirling lines danced in front of my eyes that I closed immediately because I didn't want them to know I was awake. I wanted to see what was going to happen. I tried to control my breathing and keep relaxed. A white ball landed on my eye and everything changed. The white disk vanished, the lights stopped flashing and the colored swirls stopped. They knew that I was awake, so I changed positions and faced the bathroom door. A denser black, blacker then the surrounding black, head and shoulders was popping up in front of my face, and after the third popup I swatted at it. A white ball zoomed into my eye and the room became quiet.

I decided that their command post had to be sitting on the bureau at the foot of my bed where observation would be easy. I was thinking about how many crazy dreams I have had wondering through a maze of a house, usually with my three children when they were little, trying to find a way out that was always a basement window. How the houses are always old, isolated and rather creepy, never modern, and that this had been very much like them only now I was packing up and apparently moving. I realized this dream was another dream "interfered with" testing my frustration level, and it had been hit as I was about to burst with it. I became hot and sweaty and knew that they wanted me to throw the blankets off but I was not going to do that, so I lay there uncomfortable, dripping with sweat, knowing I would eventually cool off or pass out from heat stroke. The air conditioner turned on but it didn't seem like the room became cooler. I was not throwing the covers off and that was my last conscious thought.

Chapter 43

Sunday, 16 May 2010, I went into work yesterday in a strange mood, and as always, the children that come into the store ground me, each is special and beautiful. We weren't very busy, so I had time to think about what occurred the night before. Although it wasn't that much different from other nights I found this to be more unsettling. The underlying factor is that I think they are trying to push me to where I will lose control of my temper, and although I have come close, it has not yet happened.

I suspected that the disk with rounded corners sent to the headboard of the bed was probably a device to pick up any words spoken aloud during sleep. My ex-husband occasionally talked in his sleep but I found that I was never able to understand what was said. I suspect that they were trying to pick up my mumbled words to try to understand what I was saying. There would be no point in designing and directing dreams if they were unable to read my dream thoughts and telepathically pick up my dream words, but last night I had spoken aloud and this must have been a surprise to them. If I spoke aloud in my sleep routinely, the device would have already been on the headboard, perhaps it is but this is the first time I saw it.

A friend in Florida, Sheila Benjamin, sent an email telling me she had contact with a Reiki Master, Jo Mooy at www.starsoundings.com who is very familiar with what my sister and I are going through and had many questions. She wants us to talk. I tried to get hold of my sister last night but she had her phone turned off later telling me that her husband does not want her to talk about aliens anymore.

Monday, 17 May 2010, I went to bed late as I was having difficulty just going to bed due to the experiences of the past few days. I had seen a few flashing lights and what looked like a little grey run in front of me. I turned out the light, lay on my back petting Buster, the glasses appeared on my face, and I could see what looked like a boxed in white light in the upper left rim. I moved my eyes, it vanished then reappeared and this time from my peripheral vision, I saw movement in it. I said in my head, "I can see you," and it vanished reappearing in front and slightly above the glasses. I could see what looked like a blue outfit directly in the front of the lighted space, and believed it was checking out the "glasses" they had put on my face. When I laughed and again said in my head, "I can see you", it vanished. There were misty swirls in the room and I eventually fell asleep. It rained last night.

Thursday, 20 May 2010, when I opened the back door this morning to let the cats out onto the porch the dowel was not wedged in and the sliding glass door was unlocked. I know that I locked it and tried it before inserting the wedge.

I stood in front of the mirror while combing my hair, getting ready to go to work, and said to the beings, "I am of this earth. My parents are of this earth. The earth is my home. I live here and only here. I am not one of you. If earth is destroyed, I chose to die with it. This is my life. You are interfering in it and in the things that I want to do. Leave me in peace."

July, 2010, I am dreaming.

I am with an older man, a human man, wearing a long white

robe, who has a fleshy face with large thick rubbery lips. I do not like this man. He is talking, trying to convince me of something of what I do not know. I am popping in and out of my body, and see that we are standing in the middle of a vast space, I think of a park. He places his left arm across my shoulders continuing to reason with me. Instantly I am back in my body, grab his arm, and throw him over my hip judo style, and think thank you, Daddy, for your lessons. It takes me two tries but over he goes landing squarely on his buttocks in a sitting position holding his right forearm to his forehead. "Good," I thought, "you piece of shit." Suddenly the greys appear from places unseen, I had seen a few but not this many, to help him up. They guide him to what looks to me like a white park bench. He is sitting in a slumped position with both elbows draped across the back of the bench preventing him from sliding off of the seat. I have popped out of my body again and see him in this position, and see myself standing with my legs apart with my hands on my hips ready for action. I have had enough. I wake up.

Thursday, 12 August 2010, I have not been making entries in the journal as I have in the past five years. The beings do not deserve the importance that I have given them and are no longer welcome; I want them to leave permanently. I stood in the bathroom looking at myself in the mirror and said to the beings, "I release you from any promises you have made to me and now you must release me from any I have made to you."

I have had the opportunity to speak with the lovely Reiki ladies, Jo and her partner, Patricia, over the phone. They were supportive, understanding my dilemma, and knowledgeable about the beings. They encouraged smudging to remove negativity from my home and the use of the protective bubble of Light. We are guided where we need to be. I was guided to them as I was to David.

That night after I fall asleep I am suddenly awake and aware of a malicious being standing by the bedside. I'm not sure which one it is. I feel it is a young adult grey that is resentful of my noncompliance, and believe it affects him and his leadership in some way. He stands by the bed waiting. I am well aware that he intends to do me harm, and I will under no circumstances acknowledge his presence. I do not move, mentally focusing on wrapping and rewrapping my entire body, limb by limb, inch by inch, with the Light.

I begin with a plea to God for protection then call upon The Archangel Michael to bring his great and powerful sword, and upon Lord Melchizedek to come to my aid. I tell them to hurry, they are needed. I then call upon my ancestors to give aid, if need be, and continue wrapping my body with the Light.

I feel the being now standing at the end of the bed where my feet lay, one upon the other, as I am laying on my stomach. I lay motionless continuing to wrap with the power of the Light now solely concentrating on my legs and feet. It is as if time is standing still. Nothing else exists except the being standing at my feet, me lying on the bed and the powers of God that I have called upon for protection. I wait. I wait for him to make a move. Suddenly I feel the being grab hold of my left foot, the one on top, and give it a cruel twist. Instantly I have a vision of him being thrown, head first, back down, through the bedroom door into the living room and vanish.

The room is quiet. It is finished. I take a deep breath that I hadn't realized I had been holding, open my eyes, and curl into a ball. I give gratitude for protection to the Power of God, The Creator of everything, to the Archangel Michael, to Lord Melchizedek, and to my ancestors. I have a vision of an unknown small white animal with large black round eyes reminding me of a white baby seal with four legs. It curls up in a lying position, so that it faces me emanating love, nothing but love that comforts and relaxes me until I fall asleep. I know that I have witnessed something very special and it wasn't the greys. It was the power of God's love.

I want them gone!

At 2 AM last night a white ball was present in my eyes followed by the face of the grey with whom I had a tussle for power followed by severe foot cramps. I got out of bed and drank grapefruit juice then went back to bed. Nothing else occurred except a progressive tingling of my feet and legs which eventually stopped after much wrapping with the Light.

Last night was a new moon. I smudged this morning.

Sunday, 12 September 2010, I am dreaming.

I am in a cement house in a country setting. There is green grass, trees, fenced in horses, and old men, not ancient men with long beards, but old men with pot bellies and bald heads. My cousin and sister are there.

My cousin is finished talking with the men and leaves. My sister says she needs to speak with them. I wait in the cement house until she is finished. I hear water dripping and investigate the source. The structure is poorly constructed with gaps between the joints of the poured cement surfaces but I am unable to locate the source of the water sound. I look through the window and see my sister with the two men sitting in lawn chairs at the side of the house and decide to go outside through the front door.

There is a huge black mare standing on the dirt road, it appears that she has gotten out of the fenced in area. I head to the side of the house to tell the men that there is a horse loose. A large colt comes dashing towards me as I am running to the side of the house, everyone is now aware of the loose horses. The colt knocks me down and I quickly stand up fully aware of what sharp hoofs are capable of doing, and remain still. I don't want the mare to think that I am in anyway threatening to her colt because she is headed directly towards me then stops when she sees her colt take off unharmed.

My sister has left and as the two men walk toward me I hear them discussing her. I hear them talking about her health issues and they seem doubtful. To my left there is the sound of an engine, a loud sound as if it is not functioning properly, then after the initial sound it sputters twice, catches, and nothing more of it can be heard. I am awake lying on my stomach with my head facing to my right. The sound is behind me on the side of the bed where the bathroom door is. I open my eyes and see the room is dark. I am aware that it is the beings coming for me, and I am going to fight them.

I feel paralyzed but know that if I struggle, I can resist them as I have done it before. I begin by raising my head then my upper body using my arms and start yelling. The voice coming out of my body is not my voice. It sounds strange, distorted and is one I have heard before coming from me once when the little one was present, a mechanical voice following an uncomfortable manipulation of something in my throat. It is a struggle raising myself up from the bed, and it is a struggle to keep on yelling, calling on God telling Him that I need Him now. I have raised myself until my arms are straight arms, my head up, and my voice little by little becoming my voice. Everything stops; the room clears and is silent. I look at the clock it is 7:49 AM.

Sunday, 12 September 2010, I stewed all day over the beings, swinging from anger to frustration, to not giving a damn about any of it by the end of the day. This was a three day weekend for me and had been wonderfully productive and relaxing. I enjoyed the rest of the day.

Sunday night I read then turned off the light about 1AM and instantly there was a bright white light shining under the left side of my head. As I lay there thinking what now, I could see part of what looked like a white rectangle on the wall above the bed and there appeared to be movement in it. I looked up and all of it disappeared but as soon as I looked down, it reappeared with the movement continuing. I lay there with the white light aimed at the left side of my head to see what was going to happen. I had had enough, and like the flexible person of my youth, I leapt upon my knees in the middle of the headboard, pointed my finger at where I had seen the rectangle and yelled, "I ban you from my home, my presence, and from the face of the earth!" and with that I turned on the light, and flounced into the living room.

At 3 AM I went back to bed and no sooner had the light been turned off, the bright white light was shining at my head. I lay there for awhile thinking what the hell can I do? I was not frightened nor did I feel threatened, and I had come to terms that it is up to me to stop them.

I am racking my brain for a solution then remember an old TV program about a schizophrenic who thought aliens were messing with his brain so he wore aluminum foil on his head. Why not, I thought, anything is better than nothing. I jumped out of bed, ran to the kitchen, ripped off a strip of heavy duty aluminum foil, folded it in half, plastered it against the left side of my head, and went back to bed lying on my left side. I held the foil firmly so they couldn't get between it and my head. The light became larger and more intense and I waited for it to burn my hand but all I felt was a slight increase in warmth.

The little white balls began dancing around my face. I could see movement in the room, and the outline of faces peering at me. I could see through my closed left eyelid that the white light was now larger and more intense, so I folded the foil into fourths then reapplied it to my head. More movement in the room occurred, and now I can see through my eyelid, the foil, my hand, and the pillow to the light. I can also see that there is an orange rectangle surrounded by a thick black line with four thick black lines running from side to side on it pointed at my head. I lay there looking at it then noticed that on the foil there seemed to be waves. It reminded me of dropping a pebble into water and watching the resulting ripples. It appeared as if the waves came towards my head then moved outward.

My next course of action was to let them get going and then move, always keeping the left side of my head towards the pillow. I didn't want to present a position that would give them the advantage to get next to my skin. It was about this time when I began to smell the musty smell of the one I had asked if I could wash his clothes. This went on until 5AM when they left, and I fell into a much needed deep sleep.

Later that day I had to laugh. It is human versus alien, one "simple" human with aluminum foil on her head versus a shipload of technically advanced aliens.

Thursday, 16 September 2010, Dave suggests I call in ghost hunters who will do an EMF survey of the house as part of their hunt. What a blessing that would be if that is all it is.

Chapter 44

Friday, 17 September 2010, today is the 5 year anniversary of their arrival.

This morning at 4:49, I sat up on the side of the bed and saw a misty white object about ten inches in diameter disintegrate on the bedside table. At the same time a white ball a few feet away from me zoomed towards me hitting me in the stomach area then sliding up to stop on my chest. What I felt was happiness in seeing me again. There has been only one white ball which leads me into the bathroom and sets on my hand when asked, and this is it.

I contacted a ghost hunter group in my state and set up a hunt to be held within the next four weeks. Halloween is nearing and apparently this is their busiest time of the year. I am to keep a diary and assured them that would not be a problem.

Saturday, 18 Sept 2010, I turned out the light and there were multiple small white balls then a larger white light above my head. I ignored them and fell asleep.

Saturday, 18 September 2010, I can hardly wait for the ghost hunt; the beings will not be expecting this.

Last night after the light was turned off I lay on my right side and the little balls danced around my eyes. I began to see faces, than began twilight dreaming of nothing specific but enough to hold my attention. I became aware of a light beaming down on the exposed left side of my face. Every time I opened my eyes it disappeared, but it was strong enough that I could see it through my closed eyelids. I grabbed the foil and plastered it to the left side of my face holding it tightly so the light could not get through. A little ball tried several times to maneuver between the foil and my face. At one point I tried to smash it but it zipped out after a narrow escape. I fell asleep and slept well.

Wednesday, 22 September 2010, there were things flying around the bedroom last night I've never seen before. It started off with a blood red ball directly in front of my face then changed into what looked like fire without flames. Shape-shifting blood red faces appeared within the center of the blood red fire, each face more terrible then the one before it. I began to feel uncomfortable, something didn't seem right, and I felt a pang of fear, it stopped instantly. After it disappeared it was followed with a vision of multiple stacked black blocks with a cluster of blood red flowers in each block and a yellow line below each cluster. It was strikingly beautiful. I knew they were trying to intimidate me.

I lay in the dark watching the dark. I saw orbs dipping and zooming, a bluish "shooting marble" sized orb doing a zigzag dance up and down and all around, ghostly faces came in close then backed off and other things I couldn't quite make out. Something fairly large streaked across the room from the bedroom door onto the wall at the side of the head of the bed. The room was alive, too alive; I got up.

Saturday, 25 September 2010, I am dreaming about Nannie Maude although I never see her, only an empty unmade bed. My sister, who is not my sister, is with me talking about them. We are in the Nannies' house. I look around everything appears correct but it is not. I become aware this is their dream and not my own, not even a dream interfered with; the entire dream is of their creation. My sister says that the stories Nannies told me about Abraham Lincoln are not events they remember but ones they were told and passed on to me. That was not an epiphany, I knew that. I open my eyes and everywhere in the room there is gray script on a slightly lighter gray background, impossible to read. It is 4:59 AM.

Sunday, 26 September 2010, I smudged yesterday morning. Before going to bed, I took pictures capturing several orbs but not on both cameras in the same shot. The old camera is unreliable to snap on command and the time is difficult to match up with the new camera.

I turned off the light at 1:30 AM and snuggled in on my right side. The light appeared immediately at the corner of the left eye looking like a rectangle with an object in it. Each time I closed my eyes it would reappear, and each time I popped them open I got a glimpse of it as it disappeared. Closing my eyes again the light reappeared. I reached over onto the bedside table, felt around for the aluminum foil and smacked it onto the left side of my head holding it in place. The light became brighter and then brighter as it was trying to penetrate the foil. I moved my hand and left the foil lying on its' own. Meanwhile, Buster could not get settled and was moving back and forth on either side of my head. This movement didn't disturb the light, it continued to shine. The light hit a high intensity then turned off. I wondered if the light had reflected off of the foil somehow affecting the carrier of the light finding pleasure in the thought. It turned back on but not at the same intensity.

Then a tiny little ball flew under the foil followed by another, the room became dark, and I fell asleep.

Monday, 27 September 2010, last night when the light was turned off, and I had settled on my back, I began encasing my body, the bed, and my home in every protection I could think of, a bright light shown down on my face. I pulled the covers up over my head and thought I would suffocate, so I had to lower them back onto the bed. The tiny white ball had flown under the blankets several times probably to see what I was doing. Mental pictures began to form in my head and as each one formed I mentally destroyed it than sent it down into the earth never to return. New faces began to appear, and I did the same with them until there was nothing left but darkness.

I looked around and saw formless clusters of white wispy things, and a large one which hovered over me far too long. A face came towards me causing my chest to reflexively constrict. I didn't have a good feeling about this one. I refused to look in its eyes looking instead all about its' head avoiding the eyes. It left as well as the feeling. I fell asleep.

Wednesday, September 29, 2010, I settled down for the night with Buster next to me. Kitty lay at the bottom of the bed. A picture popped into my head, and I mentally broke it up sending it into the earth. The second picture sent had a black sky with little clusters of clouds present along with other interesting looking things but I refused to look at it saying, "Move on". The picture become as debris gently sliding downward and I realized the motion in itself was becoming hypnotic. I attempted to change the direction of the flow upward finding that it was endless. I fell asleep.

I want them to leave. I no longer welcome them and will try to make their visits as unpleasant as possible. David suggested that I get an electromagnetic ultrasonic pest repeller and a black light to see if they would interfere with the beings activities. Let's see how they react to these, I can hardly wait.

Thursday, 30 September 2010, I will do whatever it takes to disrupt them causing confusion. Desperation can lead to being creative and David is very helpful in this area. Last night I brought the vacuum sweeper into the bedroom and hooked up the hand attachment. I stood naked in the room with the light turned off with the attachment in my hand. The blinking white balls were flitting around watching, this is not my usual routine. I flipped the switch to the vacuum sweeper and began to vacuum my body starting at my feet working upward, and if a ball got too close my plan was to suck it into the machine. As I vacuumed I envisioned myself wrapped in the Light of protection and balls sucked up into the machine by the thousands.

When I turned the machine off there were many more little blinking white balls hovering in the room, and knew they were trying to figure out what I was doing. I put on my pajamas then headed to put the vacuum back into the closet then to the kitchen to turn off the stove light.

When I opened the bedroom door and entered the living room there was a large orb in front of the china cabinet where I had to walk. As I neared the china cabinet the orb suddenly covered my right eye. Backlit by the stove light I could see into the orb. There was a black ellipse shaped object thickly covered with hair-like projections within it.

When I brushed it away with my hand, it had a soft, plushy feel. Then I frantically began brushing it away because I thought it was trying to attach itself to my face then I realized, in horror that it was trying to get into my eye. I called upon The Archangel Michael to come with his sword and it was gone.

There were balls flying around, one faint white flash, and a faint red splotch followed by the vision of a very angry heavy set man then of another angry creature. The man was one of the two men who met with my cousin, my sister, and me in the dream on September 12th. I think he is a leader, and looked similar to the ugly face in the blood red ball I had seen but I can't say for sure it was him.

I put the vacuum away, turned off the stove light, went to bed, and there was darkness like it should be when you close your eyes. After awhile a few incomplete images appeared, and I decided to do nothing that would open the door acknowledging contact. I began to feel a mental heaviness that was strange yet familiar then suddenly a full picture burst forth and sat there. It was a picture of the orb with the hairy creature. The bottom of the orb was open dripping a clear liquid like water, and the hairy creature, now looking wet, descending in slow motion within the liquid downward through the bottom of the picture then the picture vanished. It looked dead and I hoped it was. The balls were flying around but did not land on me nor did the awful bright light shine on the left side of my head. I slept like a rock.

Tuesday, October 5, 2010, last night none of us slept, me because of the black light and the cats because of me. I had no idea a black light would put out so much light. Tonight I have plugged in the pest repeller and will see what will happen with both the light and the repeller on at the same time.

I lay in bed reading and could feel pressure on my forehead, as if something was trying to penetrate it. I smacked it with the open book I was reading, it didn't come back. I removed the lamp shade, screwed in the black light, turned it on, and crawled into bed. I turned onto my left side put the aluminum foil shield on my face and the ball appeared. I tossed and turned for a solid half hour, got up, retrieved only the new camera from the desk as the old one no longer functions, and took pictures that revealed nothing. I went back to bed tossed and turned some more, got up again returning to bed at 4 AM, their latest starting hour of mischief. I placed the foil shield back on the left side of my face rolled onto that side and tried to sleep.

As I relaxed the shield became less firmly fixed on my head allowing the lit rectangle to appear between the foil and my head. I could see there was more than one compartment in the lit rectangle. I grabbed the water mister, also a suggestion from David, that I had put in the bed earlier in the evening, and gave the rectangle a squirt, it disappeared then came back. This time I took careful aim and squirted it again, and watched in satisfaction as it slid down to the bottom of the foil. Gotcha! The ball came rushing in and I squirted it too, both disappeared.

I began receiving visions of mean angry looking faces and a picture of the now alive hairy creature. At 6 AM, the blacklight was turned off, and I hit the bed not giving a damn who or what came because if it bothered me it would be dead; I was tired.

They don't like water; I wonder what else they don't like.

Thursday, 7 October 2010, they are beginning to penetrate the foil. I could see about a three inch circular area of tiny pinprick sized holes through which I could see their light.

I had placed a gardenia perfume in the mister last night, and have had to change all of the linen and wash the blankets and comforter this morning. Fortunately I had placed an old shower curtain under the mattress pad to protect the mattress. It is powerful stuff when sprayed all over the bed. I had thought about using vinegar but have tossed that idea out after using the perfume, alcohol might work and then there is Lysol or maybe air freshener. I want to annoy them but not harm myself or the babes in the process.

Friday, 8 October 2010, I smudged today. My ears started ringing as the day wore on and I saw one faint ball when I closed my eyes and that was it, nothing more! I take a spray bottle of water to bed with me now to spray them if they annoy me.

Saturday, 9 October 2010, as far as I can tell there is usually only one white ball here at night although early this morning when I turned off the black light there were at least 6 clustered within a three foot space above the dresser too far away to hit them with the spray.

Last night the water bottle was left on the bedside table

because the night before the lid came unscrewed and the bed soaked. I have been using the black light and repeller and can't tell if they have any effect at all on the beings because they are still here. I think the repeller and black light effect me more than them as they are not sleep conducive for me, especially the black light. One interesting thing did happen last night.

The light came from above the right eye rather than from below the left eye. I grabbed the foil now fortified with two large pliable refrigerator magnets, also a suggestion from David that it was unable to penetrate. I saw a ball on my right eye several times, waited for a slower take off then sprayed it with a travel sized container of hair spray, missed, then sprayed it again when it came back. The light went back on above the eye; I shot it again and must have hit it as it went out. Seconds later I felt cold little pin pricks on my right forearm. If it was droplets from the hair spray I should have felt them as I sprayed but this was a little too long after, plus my arm hadn't been in the area where I sprayed. It then went for my feet. Little did it know I was prepared for that too, so he caused no harm other than a strange sensation in my feet and legs. It stopped and came back to my face where I shot it again with hair spray then it left. My arm began to itch so I got up to see why. There were little raised red pin point areas over the lower arm. Did it rinse itself off by using a chemical contained within the ball that dropped onto my arm irritating the skin? I think yes, it did. I washed the arm well, the itching stopped, and today there is nothing there.

Buster has finally gotten the gardenia smell off of him and now he smells like hair spray, the poor guy. Kitty sleeps on the bed in the guest bedroom or on top of the kitchen cabinet in the corner by the outside wall.

Monday, 11 October 2010, last night I left the pest repeller in the socket blinking its green and red lights and turned off everything else. The ball came up to my eyes and blinked faintly. I put the foil over the right side of my head and waited for it to check it out, that it did. I laid there waiting for a good shot with baby oil in a small aerosol bottle. It became bolder and bolder zipping around and then I shot it! It would disappear and reappear and get shot again sometimes a few inches from my face. We did this for about thirty minutes with seemingly no effect from the baby oil. I'm as slick as a greased pig, and it is still flying around blinking as usual. At one point a bright flash of light went off startling me, the white rectangle was back but skittish. It didn't stay in one spot near my head but for a second, so I couldn't get a shot at it. I slept.

Tonight, I am not turning on the black light and am unplugging the pest repeller. I am not going to bed armed with a spray. I am not sleeping with magnets wrapped with foil on my head. If the light shines down on my head or the little rectangle or the balls appear, I will visualize them being stomped on, splattered like a bug on the front bumper of a car going sixty miles an hour, blood and guts everywhere. Yes, that appeals to my violent nature that they have been trying to unleash.

Chapter 45

Tuesday, 10 October 2010, the stomping was not successful. The balls would flash in front of my eyes, open or closed, and I would visualize stomping them with heavy boots but was unsuccessful. I then mentally created and tried smacking them with a wooden spoon, then throwing globs of mud but neither was effective. Frustrated, I found "Gotcha" by accident. It is my game, a new one, created and developed by me. They are the target and I get to shoot them with nothing more than focused visual contact mentally saying, "Gotcha". Let the games begin.

A ball shot in front of my eyes, I beamed in on it and said, "Gotcha" and the ball was mine. Another one took its place, and I "Gotcha" it too. I grabbed them placing them in a vacuum container that I envisioned. The game was on playing a deadly game of tag. The balls were not all the same size, flying in and out, dodging the "Gotcha", and when one was tagged more took its place. This game went on night after night for weeks, and I was filling up newly created containers with balls. I created a hidden room with a shelf where the containers were stored placing the gardenia perfume in it as one of the containers. The number of blinking balls coming nightly dwindled, then one night when I went to find the room with the containers, it was gone, and I suspected they had found it. Now, I just "Gotcha" them and do not store them anywhere. I could never get a good beam on the rectangle it was always just out of my line of direct vision.

Suddenly I am aware that there is a being standing by the side of my bed. I find that I am unable to breathe in or out;

there is no air to breathe! I am in a vacuum just like the vacuum I placed the "gotcha" beings in! If this lasted I knew I would die just as they had probably died. I understood the message. He came back one other night with this repeated message. They knew what I had done, and it must have been effective why else would he have let me know what it feels like to be in a vacuum? He was showing me his power, of what he could do to me. I am not afraid of him.

Monday, 8 November 2010, I am dreaming.

I find myself in the country house where our children were raised. My favorite rooms were the living room and dining room, and they look the same as when I lived there. I enter the living room through the front door that we never used, and there is my ex-husband's new wife sitting on my couch. I see that my plants have survived even though I know that they have all died but I am happy to see them alive and thriving.

I ask, "What are you doing here? We sold this house." She responds, "I live here now, it is my house. My husband and I now live here." I feel a sudden wave of jealousy that she is living in my house. It was so strong that I was startled at the intensity as I had thought I was ambivalent towards him and therefore her. She wanted to argue and attempted to engage in accusations but I didn't respond walking around the room looking at my things.

Suddenly the paneled living room walls became outlandishly wallpapered, something cheap and flashy. I asked her if she had removed the paneling putting up drywall, she answered yes, she had. I felt a sudden surge of anger as the country charm of the room had been destroyed.

I notice the window has been changed and walk into the dining room and find that window has also been changed. I ask, "Did you change the windows?" She replies, "Yes". I walk over to the dining room window and look out into the backyard where our children had played, and I am filled with pleasant contented memories. The yard looks the same as it always has. I look closely at the window that seems to have been made of thick glass or thick clear plastic, and I am surprised for the need of this thickness. The view outside is not distorted even though the windows are extremely thick, perhaps eight to ten inches thick, and the edge of the window wraps all the way around the edge of the wall. I pop out of my body and can see that the edge of the window also wraps around the wall on the outside of the house. This is not my old home. I pop back into my body, turn to her and say, "This is your house, do as you please. I no longer care." I walk away. I awake in my bed and see a white ball blink not far from my face.

The dream was staged and because I pop in and out of my body, I believe we were on a ship. They wanted my intensity and they got a short shot of it but that was all. I must be at a certain level of awareness in order to produce an intense emotion that is their goal and which, I think, allows me to remember what happens.

On a weekend in the middle of November, 2010, the Ghost Hunters arrive.

The ghost hunter group came four times over a period of months. On the first visit they felt there was activity in the guest room but on the remaining visits they found the strongest consistent activity in my bedroom. EVPs were done and several different male voices could be heard and replied to questions asked with one of the group clearly asking who was talking to them. The leader said he understood the EVPs, although I could not, eventually saying that something really hated me with my immediate thought going to the being who twisted my foot. At one point the leader of the ghost hunter group asked for whoever it was to show themselves, and I felt as if something was about to happen. The room began to feel dense, heavy, thick, intense then the feeling passed. He had snapped a picture at that moment showing a tall legless concave image in front of me as I sat on the side of the bed. On this, their last visit I had not had a good feeling about what was happening, something felt wrong, very wrong. The hatred the leader felt could have been directed toward anyone in the room but the picture showed an unclear image standing in front of me. The leader asked to return. Unfortunately he developed life threatening health issues, and I believe the group has now fragmented along with it, the results of their findings. That morning I smudged when the sun came up.

The ghost hunter group had been told briefly about my experience with the beings, I had not mislead them. I also knew that if the beings wanted to show themselves they could and did not need an invitation. The voices on the EVPs sounded as if we had interrupted a conversation, and I wondered if somehow we had through the portal. I had not felt evil during any of the ghost hunter searches but I knew that whatever they had contacted during the last visit I did not want it in my home. There will be no further ghost hunts.

I purchased a KII EMF meter and found my home to be within normal range verified by David.

Tuesday, 15 November 2010; early this morning I became aware that I was playing games, computer games, and there is a bug in one of the slots where a number should be. When I realized that I was aware I knew that I could control what was happening in this dream. I looked at the game board, spotted the bug, and beat it into a pulp with my fists destroying it. The game disappeared and I slept.

This morning I smudged.

Wednesday, 17 November 2010, the only thing I remember happening last night was just after I turned off the light a light shown down onto my left eye. I covered myself with protection and was able to block it out. A couple of white balls darted into my eyes but I grabbed them and put them in the envisioned vacuum container. I slept well.

Tuesday, 14 December 2010, my sister and her husband are here along with Percy, and it is wonderful to be with her again. They will be leaving for Florida in February and hopefully I will get to go with her. My sister walked into her bedroom and closed the door. Suddenly I'm attacked from the back by something unseen striking my head causing such dizziness that I fell from the chair followed by a wave of nausea so strong that I began retching. I wrapped myself in the Light, picked up *The Book of Jasher* my sister had brought to me, and started reading. The words brought comfort and relief.

Both my sister and I were periodically attacked in this

manner, and left feeling as if our brains had been sucked dry. After research on the internet, I believe that it was what is called an "energy vampire" rather than an action by the beings which had been my initial belief. Then I began having a mental vision of the top and back of my head covered by the large mouth of an unknown entity sucking on it. I began visualizing my brain and head wrapped in protection followed by a covering of something sour. I could make the covering as thick as desired. The attacks continued becoming more infrequent then stopped.

My oldest son has given me the Hebrew translated to English Tanakh for Christmas, and I am looking forward to reading it.

Monday, 10 January 2011, it is snowing and the freshly covered ground, houses and trees are pristine beautiful, a winter wonderland filling me with pleasant childhood memories, and memories of my own children playing in the snow. I stood out front taking pictures.

This picture was taken Jan. 1, 2011 at 12:19 AM in front of the house. When the picture was cropped it looks as if a translucent being is sitting on top of the car with his left hand resting on his knee. His head and eyes can be seen.

At the end of February, 2011, my sister and I drove to the Big Cypress Shootout Seminole War Reenactment in Florida. I found dried yellow corn thrown around in the showers rousing my curiosity. I learned that corn is sacred to Native Americans and thrown to scare away negativity then planted in the spring. In this case, corn was thrown in the shower because water is a conduit of negativity. I had Indian corn that had hung on my front door during the Thanksgiving Holiday. When I got home I hung it where the moon and sun could shine on it for several days, removed the kernels from the cob, and had a new weapon to use against the beings.

On the way home we stopped in Albany, Georgia to admire one of our most endangered native animals, the magnificent and beautiful Red Wolves that once freely roamed the southeast. Starting with fourteen captured animals, a breeding program was introduced to repopulate the land.

Sunday, 22 May 2011, my sister, called to tell me about a dream she had the night before. It seems that both of us had a dream, and though it wasn't about Big Cypress the settings were there. Her dream concerned family members and mine concerned an individual who answered a question followed by a mass of yellow symbols. Neither one of us could remember anything more.

Monday, 23 May 2011, during the evening while I read in the living room, I kept seeing out of the corner of my eye a reddish rectangle which seemed to be hanging in the top of the doorway to my bedroom. The third time I narrowed my eyes to get a better look but it disappeared, and I didn't see it again.

When I turned out the light a brilliant circle of purple appeared and faces began appearing, many faces that were not human or grey or of anything I have seen before. Some were round with only one big eye on it with scant tufts of black hair covering the forehead. A light had appeared at the side of my left eye then went out. A protuberance extended out from the middle of the purple circle surrounded by a concave back. It was a beautiful color, and I wanted to stare at it resisting because there is danger in staring at their art, you get sucked in. I continued to cover myself with protection and when I finished, the purple object and faces disappeared. I fell asleep. Is this another new group?

I am awake again but didn't look at the clock, they are back. There is a black lattice design, and I think of the artist who uses this design. When it is completed, there are eye catching little bright lights in the open areas of the lattice. Not wanting to be sucked in I opened my eyes and find the same design spread out across the ceiling. I focus my mind on other things, refusing to look at it or think about it, and it goes away.

It seems that the general protection I use doesn't stop or even slow them down; mentally I have to resist them. I tightened my personal protection and envisioned zapping the balls with a beam of light. I became aware of the rectangular light to the left side of my face but so far back that it was out of my direct line of vision. I zapped in that direction and it moved to the right side but still I couldn't get a beam on it. I suspected they were trying to see what my range of fire was. Rather than destroy I wanted to annoy, and began envisioning throwing black polyurethane to coat the balls permanently blocking their vision but never got a good shot at the lit rectangle.

I began seeing some really weird faces and other things, and suspected they were holograms sent from the light next to my face. When there was one bright white design and at the same time I could see an extremely bright curved line in the light I knew I was right and not to waste energy on the holograms but to get to the sender. Meanwhile the hologram changed to faces resembling humans with huge liquid eyes that I have seen before but not often. I envisioned hurling blobs of black polyurethane at the light which then went out, and I fell asleep.

Wednesday, 25 May 2011, for the past few nights the cats have difficulty settling down, Buster, in particular that is so unlike him. He won't sleep on the side of the bed he has for years, jumps up and runs to the other side as if he's spooked, it's probably Kitty stalking him; I suspected something was different but didn't know what.

I don't know if they can read my mind. I don't think they can otherwise I wouldn't be able to surprise them. Their focus seems to be my eyes which must tell them at what level my consciousness is, I think by pupil dilation or constriction. So the question is can I control that?

Chapter 46

Friday, 27 May 2011, I smudged yesterday and burned sweetgrass making my little home smell clean and feel good. I took the first dose of Chantix and smoked. I had trouble falling asleep, and was up and down several times before dozing off.

I am dreaming.

I am in a structure of some sort with many hallways. I'm responsible for something which I don't know what, and am trying to locate the people I need to see for what I don't know. I am being sent all over the place looking for them, and as I move down the hallways I see pieces of wood, saws, hammers, and nails scattered on the floor.

I find that everyone I speak with talks so that their words are muffled, and the last person I talk with turns their head as they talk, and can't be understood at all. I head back to where I started perplexed that I can't understand anyone finding this hall floor also covered with building equipment. I hurry down the hall and become aware of the acrid odor of one of the beings and am immediately awake. There are yellow symbols all over the room. "I'm getting the 'cold shoulder," I thought. I got out of bed, began taking pictures then went back to bed, and lay half awake smelling the being off and on finally falling into a restless sleep.

I got up to go into the bathroom and could see the outlines of shelves or boxes in different colors and sizes begin to take shape across the bathroom wall and on into the bedroom above my bed. There were items sitting in the boxes that I couldn't completely identify unless they were things I was familiar with like books. My eye was caught by what looked like a white frog sitting on the top of a box just outside the bathroom door. The frog jumped down onto the floor, and I began seeing other things moving around. I shrugged my shoulders and went back to bed, I didn't care. I had thought I heard Buster climbing up the pet stairs but couldn't feel him on the bed and was concerned because Kitty had been chasing him earlier. I leaned over the side of the bed to see if he was sitting on the floor coming face to face with a white tube shaped thing which immediately backed away as I backed away in the other direction. Buster jumped up on the bed, and we both went back to sleep.

Saturday, 28 May 2011, I am dreaming.

 We are in a vehicle, it could be a car, and I do not know who the driver is although I can see him, I don't really look at him. I feel comfortable, safe. We are on the way to the bathroom as not only do I have to go but I have a lot of discomfort down in that area and I don't know why.

We are on a street which I think is a brick street. I only look out of the driver's side window not out of my window, and can see large houses sitting back from the road. I think of haunted houses, one after another, all grey with no lights shining through the windows. There are no trees, no bushes, no plants, it is desolate. We stop at a sand pit, and I gingerly crawl down a short distance and do as the cats do. The man stands at the top of the pit with his hands on his hips watching me. I have the feeling that he would like me to slide down into the pit disappearing into its depths. I wake up with the same discomfort as I had in the dream and have it this morning but it disappeared after I was up for awhile. I think I was taken last night and something done to me.

I continue to read the Tanakh. I have always wanted to read the Old Testament in Hebrew, to see what was written before changes were made. Not being able to read or speak Hebrew, a translation has satisfied me.

On one of the *Ancient Alien* TV programs, *The 12th Planet* by Zecharia Sitchin was mentioned. The local library had the book, checked it out, read it and was weighed down by the heavy message of his translation of the Sumerian tablets. If there is truth behind the Sumerian tablets and the translation is accurate, it would change everything I have been raised to believe. I wanted my sister to read it to give me her opinion.

August, 2011 over the years I wished that I had a video camera in a ceiling corner of the bedroom to capture the beings and other activity that has been going on. I contacted David at S.P.I.R.I.T. to get a recommendation for one that would be affordable; his suggestion was a low light camera. I was on a mission. I wanted to catch those daggone suckers in the act, a glimpse, anything that would give me tangible proof that they live. David provided guidance on programs to download, the cable to purchase, and I was in business.

I screwed in the black light, hooked up the camera and was disappointed with the findings. I began moving the camera into different positions but even then the pictures were too dark. I found the camera functioned best in daylight with the window shade drawn and bathroom door shut and was dumbfounded by the first video taken. The wall was alive with undulating movement at times extending out over the bed showing light shifting and things like bubbles moving around, the same things that I had seen during the nights. I had found the portal and was told by David that what I am seeing is energy. Apparently the beings do not enter or exit through it.

September, 2011, it has been six years since the space suit was seen in the doorway.

Wednesday, 16 November 2011, my sister has arrived along with an increase in activity. I had told her about feeling like something was living with me which occupied the guest room. I had been keeping the door shut to cut down on the heating bill then one morning when I smudged in that room, the smudge bowl was suddenly tipped so that all of the burning ashes fell out onto the carpet. I was frantic to get the spray bottle to put out the burning ashes but while doing this the soles of my shoes became wet from the wet carpet. I thoroughly smudged the room then headed for the front entrance hall. As I rounded the corner the wet soles of my shoes slipped on the wooden floor causing an awkward and painful twist of the left ankle. I finished smudging the house, nothing was going to stop me until it was completed, nothing, not after the smudge bowl was tipped. Later that day, after a visit to my physician and an x-ray, I learned that I had sustained a hairline fracture of the left leg.

Thursday, 17 November 2011, this morning my sister tells me about meeting the thing in the room after she turned off the light. She said after she crawled into bed and lay on her back, a black mass-like thing "fell" on her letting out a noisy-like breath and was gone. She felt it was telling her it wasn't pleased she was in the room but felt that it had left. She also said the beings were there during the night showing her lots of blue--the beings blue is an intense color of blue. I've been seeing things running around, and poor little Kitty is spooked big time.

Friday, November 18, 2011, last night the beings were creating vividly colored dreams then amidst the colors, there was an instant when their blue color became a liquid and poured over the other colors. It was so quick, looking so natural, the blue acting like a liquid, something I had not seen before, and knew that in that second I was paralyzed, and they were in the room. I fought and was able to open a corner of my mouth drawing in air and yelling which released me from it.

I ran and crawled in bed with my sister thinking about what happened. I realized that I should have grabbed the camera and run outside to snap pictures above and around the house.

Wednesday, 23 November 2011, my sister and I drove down to Mississippi to visit family over the Thanksgiving Holiday. Our first night there, before going to bed I went outside to have a cigarette and thought I saw a UFO. I invited my sister to sit on the front steps of the house with me, and she spotted it too. It was a dark clear calm night, stars were visible there that are hidden by street lights where I live.

We watched the craft as it slowly maneuvered its way in our direction. Periodically I could see what looked liked light beams shooting down to the ground like search lights as if searching for something. It was impossible for me to determine how high up it was in the dark. My sister said she could see red on the top of it, and although I didn't see the red, it looked as if it was a very large cigar shaped ship. We sat there watching as it slowly maneuvered closer and lower until it began shooting beams in our direction. I saw the beam coming as if a pebble had been thrown into a pond making ripples, the ripples coming directly at me. I went into the house while my sister continued to watch it. Were they tracking us? I was uncomfortable with this thought.

We shared a room with a double bed and attached bathroom. Both of us snore and if I can get to sleep before she does, I'm fine otherwise I'm awake for most of the night. We both read, turned out the light, and she fell instantly asleep leaving me to study the shadows in the room. Eventually I took my pillow, located a blanket in the closet, folded it in half then crawled between the fold on the floor at the foot of the bed.

I had just found a comfortable position when a white beam of light shown down from the ceiling inches from my face. At the bottom of the beam a one inch square shaped rod about a foot long spread out from each side of the beam on top of the carpet. A grey rectangle about the size of my 3 ½ x 2 ½ inch camera materialized at the side of the beam on or slightly above the rod, paused and disappeared followed by the disappearance of the rod then the beam. "Beam me down, Scotty." Son of a bitch, I thought, and crawled into bed with my sister covered us both with protection and finally slept. We left to come home on the 26th.

Friday, 9 December 2011, last night I was aware my body lay

on the bed and that my senses were more acute. I am looking at the artist's lattice work with little flashing lights behind it, the lights have been there before but the flashing was new.

I am dreaming.
There are two little kids digging in the dirt outside my front door, and my deceased daughter is sitting on a wooden chest by the fireplace talking to me. I go out to check on the children and usher them inside sending them upstairs to be with their family. When I turn around my daughter is not my daughter but an angry looking thin woman who is giving me hell about some advice I had given her, advice, what advice, what is she talking about? I ignore her and become aware something is wrong. I am lying on my stomach and cannot move I am paralyzed; they are here.

I fight, willing myself to move, to resist them. It takes what seems like a long time before, even though air is moving through my throat, I can advance from a frail shallow breath to a scream effective enough to wake up my sister in the guest room. The smell was that of the stinky one that left when she came into my room. It was 6:42 AM.

On another night soon after I am again dreaming. I am sitting at a table with my ex-husband and he is giving me hell about something. I can hear nothing nor am I picking up any thoughts other than anger. Eventually he communicates to me that he wants me to reconsider my decision, and I tell him it will never change, never. He becomes really angry, gets up, and as he walks away from me I can see that he is wearing a long, thin, colorful robe that flaps behind him with each step he takes. He is not my ex-husband. He is the man

I had thrown over my shoulder.

Thursday, 26 January 2012, I am pregnant and with my parents. I have popped out of my body and see my legs spread giving birth. A woman picks up the baby, and I watch myself get up to go into the bathroom where the placenta is delivered. I watch myself walking unsteadily back to bed as if in a stupor then pop back into my body. A woman comes to help me walk and asks me if I would like to see the baby, I reply that I would.

My mother walks over to me carrying the small baby wrapped in a white blanket with a corner pulled over the baby's face. She pulls the corner back revealing something bloody. It isn't a baby's head! It is a uterine fundus with the fallopian tubes and ovaries attached hanging out at the sides of the fundus like two crazily distorted ears with small pom-poms attached at the ends. I am baffled, how can this be? Then I realize I am dreaming that it is not my dream but that of the aliens. I am immediately awake.

My eyes snap open and I look directly into the bathroom. Filling the entire bathroom is a square containing a fainting couch with white fluffy pillows spread over it. Sitting in the middle of the pillows like a sultan in a movie, is a man with short legs and a plump torso wearing a red outfit. He has eyes slightly larger than human eyes and a misshapen head in that the cranial portion is elongated and angled backward from the high forehead. I know that he has a hump on his back and has difficulty walking. His mouth is wide open exposing his teeth with his head thrown backwards in laughter as he slaps his hand against his right thigh. He is enjoying this moment to the max. The joke is on me, and I am ready to kill.

I shot out of bed like a launched ballistic missile digging corn out of the container next to the bed throwing handfuls at the being in the bathroom willing the kernels to penetrate his body like bullets from a machine gun. One handful lands on him and his couch, and he looks surprised; another handful is thrown at him, and I can hear it bouncing off of the bathroom walls; the third handful hits and bounces off of the closed bathroom door. I had closed it before going to bed. When I opened the door there was corn in the bathroom and on the bedroom floor.

If they wanted to unleash my anger, they succeeded. Was there meaning behind this, yes, there was. I knew the man on the fainting couch, he was the one on the same type of couch seen years before at a festive "party" on board one of their ships, and I believe he is the son of the man I threw over my shoulder. He was laughing because they had what they wanted, the fruit of my womb. I could leave them but they had a part of me, the babies I had unwittingly carried for them over the years, the laugh was on me. Or is this what they want me to think?

Chapter 47

Wednesday, 29 February 2012, my sister and I drove back to Mississippi to visit our family; we are of that age now when you never know if this trip will be the last. We went out to dinner, visited then went to bed exhausted. I immediately fell into a deep sleep, this time we had separate bedrooms. Waking up hot and sweaty, I saw balls in the room, and was receiving images that stopped when I looked directly at the lit balls that immediately became dark. I fell back into a restless sleep then suddenly awakened again looking at the fire alarm light above the bedroom door. My eyes shifted slightly to the left where I saw a dark gray rectangle approximately one foot wide by ten inches long, sliding across the ceiling towards the window stopping about a foot from the outside wall. I watched it as it launched thin white lined sketchy star-like designs down closer and closer to me. I had brought Indian corn and having some in my hand, I threw it at the rectangle which then disappeared. I fell back into a restless sleep.

I awake again to find the object back on the ceiling in the same spot sending another design at me. This time the design is like a whirlpool, one following the other, each with black centers coming faster and deeper, and I realize that if I continue to watch them I will be sucked in. I had already used all of the corn I had brought, so I roll over and began wrapping myself with the Light until they stopped, and I fall asleep again. Suddenly I am awakened by a bright light in the room coming from a large white rectangle covering half of the ceiling directly above me. There was so much light from it that every object in the room was easily seen. Towards the bottom of the rectangle was a brown round object moving within that I took to be the head of a being bent over the panel. I thrust out my left arm pointing at the being and see his head rise to look at me, the light went out. I fell back asleep and was not disturbed further that night.

Do they have territories?

Thursday night I slept and Friday night was another restless night. I was very uneasy there, feeling as though something "bad" was about to happen. I wanted to get away as soon as possible to go home. We left that morning.

Kitty has bitten my sister rather badly. She had bitten me occasionally but never as badly as she had my sister. I returned her to the shelter explaining what had happened. She was put down, and we were notified that she was negative for rabies. When I take an animal into my home I am committed to it. I felt as though I had let her down and was deeply saddened. My sister's arm healed and we were relieved because she is a diabetic. My sister returned to her home and family the following week. Once again it is Buster and me.

Friday, 13 March 2012, I sleep with corn in the bed now and have the spray bottle filled with water on the bedside table within easy reach. I count the kernels each night before I go to bed and each morning when I get up returning them to the basket by the bed unless I throw some, then I pick them up from the floor placing them in a separate basket in a different room to be planted.

Around 1:30 AM, I was suddenly awakened watching an object floating into the room about a foot from the upper outside corner of the bedroom wall. It was outlined in white light with a clear interior and shaped similar to a flower with five petals or a five leafed clover with dangling appendages reminding me of a jellyfish. Immediately, I threw corn at it, and knew that I had hit it because it seemed to lose its balance plunging downward at an angle, then regained itself and continued on towards the opposite wall disappearing. It was from the portal.

Unable to go back to sleep I lay on my back with Buster curled up under my arm gently snoring, looking at the small flashing lights, the shifts of darkness, the streaks of light, and the general mottled appearance of the entire room. If this was indeed a portal, I marveled at the idea that it was in my home, my bedroom and that "whatever" could enter through it into my life, our world. Not a comfortable thought. I had been told that only energy entered through the portal but this energy had an unexpected shape.

Earlier I had been reading *The art of dreaming* by Carlos Castaneda, and wondered how Don Juan would have dealt with the beings, and that it would make for an interesting story. I closed my eyes and tried to fall asleep and remain aware that I was falling asleep but was not successful. I've tried this before but wake up unaware that I've fallen asleep. It sounded easy. I have read all of Carlos Castaneda's books searching for answers, always searching.

The little white light balls and the bluish white rectangle appeared followed by whatever images they want to send to my mind, and although I had applied protection earlier, I reapplied it from the top of my head to the bottom of my feet. Out of the corner of my eye I saw a straight shaft of white light pass from the ceiling towards the floor in front of the closet door. I wasn't sure if the bluish white rectangle was leaving because I had blocked him, or if they had sent something else as back up.

The faint odor of the stinky one began to waft about causing me to become extremely alert as this one is up to no good. The odor would disappear when I looked about the room then return when I closed my eyes. I tightly grasped the corn in my right hand, waiting for the odor to come closer, planning to throw it so hard at the being that it would penetrate him like bullets from an oozie. The last time I looked at the clock it was 5:30 AM.

Wednesday, 21 March 2012, the rectangle was persistently shining a bright light into my left eye last night. If I turned onto the other side it merely floated above my head. I turned from side to side several times ending up on the left side again. I reached under my head to adjust the pillow accidently pulling a clump of hair across the left eye as the hand came out. I have long hair now. The light reappeared but was unable to penetrate the hair barrier. Little white balls were flying around also trying to get through the hair fibers. Since that night of discovery, there have been several occasions when the light has become intensely bright trying to penetrate the hair barrier but if I slip a few corn kernels between the outside of my closed eyelid and the hair it stops them. I have a new weapon, my hair, and use it every night as needed.

Tuesday, 8 May 2012, I am dreaming.

I live in a small room in a tall building. A friend drops by to pick me up but a woman with her child had dropped by earlier and have not left. I knew I had an appointment but had forgotten. I am trying to help the woman with the child find what it is she needs, searching through my room finally finding it in what looks like the laundry room. I grab it without looking at it and hand it to her, she replies with a nod of her head and leaves.

My friend is hurrying me along, and I tell her that I need to go to the bathroom before we leave. She says there is no time that we have to leave now, than hurries through the doorway. I also leave finding myself at the bottom of a very long wide white staircase. I look up and she is already at the top turned around urging me to hurry. I run up a third of the way then remember that I have forgotten the object I am supposed to bring, turning around I ran back to my apartment. I am fumbling with the key to unlock the door when a woman wearing a smile suddenly opens it and asks me if everything is okay. I tell her that I forgot something I was supposed to bring. She thrusts forth something the length of a curling iron with a tapering luminescent rectangular affair, almost like a triangle, on the tip of what would be the heating portion of the iron. She turns it off at the switch, hands it to me telling me to keep this one as she has another. I take it from her and head for the stairs running up them to meet my friend who is impatiently waiting at the top.

We enter into a room with chairs pushed up to tables that could be either a large dining room or a small restaurant. We must enter into another room through a small trap door in the wall that my friend is holding up signaling me to hurry and crawl through. I am on my hands and knees but I'm not willing to go through the small hole remembering how the window had changed size when I attempted to rescue the kittens (Wednesday, 22 November 2006), when suddenly I am pushed from behind through the hole.

My friend and I are to meet with a group of men and women in a round room with a large window, but first we must go see so and so just a little ways off. She knocks on the door and a young woman answers. When the woman opens the door an awful stench flows out. I make a comment about the need to clean her house and she says, "Yes, I do clean, just ignore it. You will be gone soon. This will only take a few seconds." The stench is really powerful. The woman comes back and hands my friend something that I cannot see, and we leave returning to the men and woman in the round room, and sit at the large table with them. I wonder if we have come to eat, I'm not really sure why we are here. When we finish, my friend and I get up, go outside onto a small rounded white balcony with a white banister, and while looking around we discuss the view.

I smell something burning and see smoke coming from my purse that I am surprised to find hanging from my left shoulder. There is the rod sticking out of it. I pull it out and see the tapering luminescent rectangle / triangle is turned on. I turn it off returning it to the purse, and find that it has burned holes through both sides. Someone yells we have to leave now, and we hurry down a hallway.

My friend has put me in front of her and we are briskly entering into a narrow hallway that can go straight up a short staircase to a door or turn right. She says turn right, I do, and a few steps later the narrow hall turns left.

I suddenly stop because in front of me is the trap door. I cautiously push it open and see through the small square hole people sitting at tables eating, and they all turn to look at me.

My friend says, "You have to go through it," and I know that I will be unable to squeeze my generous body through this small square opening especially if they make it smaller, then I will be trapped in it. She is too close behind me, keeping me confined in this small space, blocking the only exit. I feel the panic rising within me and know there is no way I am crawling through that opening. I yell, "Go back the other way!" and she replies, "We can't!" "We have too! I know someone else who went through the other way because they couldn't have come this way." I shove her out of my way to get to the stairs because this is the way I am going, and she can come if she wants.

I wake up laughing. It is 2:42 AM. I roll over and pet Buster then get out of bed. As I pass the clock it now says 2:40 AM. I must have looked at it wrong.

Sunday, 3 June 2012, I am becoming more creative as time goes on. They use mental power to control me, to send messages, faces, scenes, and artwork to subdue me into seeing what they want me to see while doing something else entirely. I am learning to use mental power back at them in my own "simple" way, and so far it seems effective at least here on earth.

Last night, I finished the book I was reading, turned off the light and pounded the pillow into shape nestling into a comfortable position on my left side. The lit rectangle immediately lit up by my left eye, and I reached over pulling a thick clump of hair over that eye forcing the rectangle to become brighter trying to penetrate the hair barrier. I mentally set out my paints and chose black and a thick bristled brush. I painted black over the lit rectangle as it changed into many different designs than I painted English letters on the rectangle, "Go away. Do not come back. You are not wanted here. Leave and never come back."

The white lit rectangle then changed to black, so that the black paint could not be seen. I looked at my paints, found a fluorescent green, and began painting over the black, "Leave and never come back." Instantly a red face appeared with raised bumps on his face, no ears and big angry green eyes. Instantly another face appeared over it, then another face appeared over that one. I began painting over them all with fluorescent green, they disappeared and I fell asleep.

Thursday, 21 June 2012, I have reread *The 12th Planet* by Zecharia Sitchin. As with many children of my generation we were taken to Sunday school and church every Sunday where we learned to control our childish impulse of a constantly moving body and noisy investigation of the hymnals that sat temptingly within reach. It was during a forced moment following the parental look that clearly stated, "Don't move or you will be sorry later," that I heard the pastor read a passage from the Bible about the "gods." As he droned on my inquisitive mind stopped and grasped thought of the gods; if there is only one God then who were they, the gods? The Bible speaks of them as well as the Tanakh. Many have given me answers over the years as to who are the gods but none have been satisfactory until *The 12th Planet,* for a potential answer that makes sense to me.

Sitchin's translation provides the answer why we all descend from the same female but not the same male leading me back to the beings. Were we created by them?

If the humans I have seen on their ships are the gods they, not the greys or any of the others that I have seen, match the description of the Nefilim who intermarried with the daughters of man according to Sitchin, the Bible and the Tanakh. I ask why would the Nefilim be associating with a variety of beings where all seem to be working together for an unknown purpose? I resist believing the Nefilim as the creator of man then worshipped as gods when they are as imperfect as we are per Sitchin's translation. Impossible! I want to believe in a perfect God. He states, if the gods did create man then who created the gods? I need to read the book again and closely compare it to the Tanakh regarding references to the gods and their physical presence on earth.

If the beings who have interfered in my life for the past six years are associated with the gods who created us, then they have no need to study our emotions, because our emotions are the same as theirs, we are compatible. I was raised with the belief that if it doesn't feel right then it isn't and I won't abandon that wisdom now. To me they are what they said they are, scientists here to study us and are not gods and never will be to me.

Monday, 2 July 2012, my hairbrush has been missing for the past five days, and I have looked everywhere for it. The hairbrush is replaced in the same drawer after every use and this morning I have found it, easily seen lying on the floor by the dresser. I told my neighbor about the missing hairbrush. She began telling me that this has happened to her since she has lived here with not only her hairbrush missing but her comb and pieces of jewelry. She says everything is returned when asked.

Monday, 9 July 2012, I have had to put my little faithful companion, Buster, to sleep. We had slept on the floor the night before with him struggling for every breath. All I could do was lay beside him so that he was not alone, stroking him, telling him how much he was loved when he became restless. I was heartbroken and will miss him. I rearranged the flower garden and buried him by the small patio under the bird feeder by the back porch door. I sprinkled lavender, sage and flat leaf cedar over his body. That night when I closed my eyes, the first thing I saw was his sweet little face outlined with golden light. And if cats can smile, which he could and did when receiving his nightly head scratch, he was smiling at me. I have since seen and heard him in the house along with Jezebel.

Chapter 48

Monday, 16 July 2012, the beings continue to focus on trying to solve the problem of getting past my hair barrier. Last night after I had covered my left eye with hair to block the rectangle that was aiming light at my left eye, a wad of white lit fibers appeared between my face and the hair barrier. Apparently they have decided to use light fibers the same size as my hair fibers to worm through the tiny spaces between the hairs. The result was as if someone had removed the hair from my brush which then formed a wadded cluster of hair, and that is what their lit fibers looked like, a wadded cluster of thin lit fibers.

Tuesday, 31 July 2012, I lay in bed reading when the lights flickered followed by a power failure. Apparently there was a ball lying on the pillow next to my head. When the light stayed off the ball began to shine, dulled then became brilliant. I had the impression that it was creating light so that I could continue reading but it went out and the power came back on. There seems to be only one white ball here now and it is the one who leads me into the bathroom and sits on my hand.

Tuesday, 14 August 2012, 11:30 PM, I was awakened by the intense odor of a being and see a design on the wall I am facing. It is an odor not likely to be forgotten once smelled. It lingered in the bedroom all night forcing me to get up and down several times.

Thursday, 16 August 2012, early this morning I dreamed of cooking and looking at recipes. This morning I went food shopping. There is no doubt the shopping was needed, my cupboards were bare. What had concerned me was just prior to dreaming I thought I heard the closet door open and after the dream ended, I heard it shut. I have no animals to cause noises.

I find myself becoming depressed without my cats.

Friday, 17, August, 2012, I was taken last night.

I got up to go to the bathroom and when I returned to bed I felt the familiar being-taken feeling, yelling "No, no, no!" and fought thinking I had won. I grabbed the corn next to me and started throwing it emptying the container. They went away but the feeling came back and not having any corn left, I ran into the dark living room, and grabbed the basket of corn off of the table. When I removed the lid from the basket, within was what I perceived to be corn silk strands with pieces of corn attached almost like corn meal as well as corn kernels. It didn't matter, corn is corn. I began to throw what was in the basket at them all the while thinking I had bested them and thwarted their attempts to take me.

I looked at the clock, it was 5 AM. The container of corn in the bed remained full of corn. The basket on the table was also full of corn kernels. There was no corn lying around the rooms. It was all in my head. I got up, went to the bathroom, they took me for an undetermined length of time and brought me back but within my mind I created the episode of throwing corn. Why would I have perceived the corn in the basket as if eaten by meal worms creating a nest? Did I grab something on their ship and throw it thinking it was corn? Were they telling me the corn is

ineffective against them? Did I have an OOBE?
Perhaps they simply did not want me to throw more corn.

Tuesday 4 September 2012 I slept heavily last night and woke up tired. It's been cloudy for days, and I seem to be one of those people who needs a little sun every day. I went for a doctor appointment and on my return, I fell asleep. I became aware that letters were being shown then suddenly my right eyelid popped open. Lying on the bed in front and facing me was the curled cover of the paperback book I had been reading with a lit rectangle about three by five inches sitting on it. On the rectangle were multicolored figures all too small to distinguish what they were. The whole panel of figures was zipping upwards at a rapid pace like a slot machine. Was I being fed information? I laid there for awhile watching it thinking I am so sick of this shit. Slowly I maneuvered my left arm under the blanket to the back of the book cover and slammed it closed. A lot of good that did because it was probably a hologram, but it made me feel good to have surprised them with a good one!

it is after 3 AM. I can see the little rectangle in my closed left eye with patterns swirling and moving fast, but because the light is on, the patterns are faint, and I think they are having no effect on me until they swirl to the right and I feel dizzy. I go into the bathroom satisfied that I have beaten them at their own game.

Wednesday, 11 September 2012, they were here last night. As I readied for bed I knew they were coming. I sat the corn in the bed within easy reach and read, became restless, got up, had a snack, and went outside for another cigarette. It is impossible to explain what I saw outside or felt, it was nothing specific other then I knew they were coming. I reset the security alarm before going back to bed and this time I left the light on falling into a deep sleep. Suddenly I am awake with only my right eye open and glance at the clock, The rest of the night I am restless. I am awakened after 5 by the two warning beeps of the security alarm and the heavy smell of the little one by my bed. I think that he has come to take me since the first attempt was a failure, the smell fades away. I roll over and try to go back to sleep, but the silent alarm again beeps the two warning sounds a few minutes later again the warning beep sound. I get up and reset it leaving the light on when I return to bed. After six o'clock, I turn off the light and think about what has happened.

Light or no light, holograms or no holograms, I was taken and the beeps were my notification that I am back in my bed. The light did not stop them, they simply went about it in a different manner, and this morning I have the heaviness of a hangover. What is it they want from me?

It has been seven years since I first saw the space suit in the bedroom doorway.

Saturday, 22 September 2012, I am a happy woman today. My son has sent me money and I have gone to the county animal shelter and adopted two male kittens, an all black four month old who I will name Ace, and a two month old fluffy tiger stripe who I will name Tom. It is already settled between the two, Ace is the dominant cat. Next we will have to work on who is dominant of this house. Ace is strong willed, an alley cat survivor I suspect

Saturday, 20 October 2012, I've stopped writing about the beings hoping they would get the message to leave and stay away, and although I see the small white orb on the walls in the evening watching me, I ignore it as though it isn't there. Other times I try to destroy it with thought but it disappears and reappears in another spot. It doesn't allow enough time to beam in and "gotcha" it. They have been here twice this month. I have no memory of the first visit. On the second visit when the little one came, I told him that I did not want to go, and he replied that I had no choice that I had too. My only memory is when I popped out of my body seeing me lying on a table with my eyes closed and mouth open. There is a being or a figure standing at the head of the table looking into my mouth, and I hear a thought or words say, "She needs to get her teeth cleaned." That is a true statement. Two days later we part-timers receive notice that we are eligible for dental benefits. The notice comes a few days before the sign-up period ends. I sign up.

I awoke feeling well and proceeded with my normal morning routine and found that I needed to visit the bathroom repeatedly. Following the many trips I began to feel really bad then the chills set in. I have some sort of bug. I called out of work and sat around as I was unable to relax enough to lie down. Both little kitties took turns sitting on my lap; they are my source of daily joy. My mind becomes fixated drifting from one negative thing to another, and I feel as if I am becoming insane and terrified of this thought, I talk with God. It is as if I become cloaked with a mantle of protection and calm; the negativity leaves as quickly as snapping your fingers. It is gone. I know that I have experienced something malicious trying to mess with my mind.

I eat, feed the babes and finish a mystery book then pick up the Tanakh and continue reading marking the passages that God appears in what has to be human form or the "gods" are spoken of. I think that the translation may well be correct. I fall asleep.

I am dreaming.

I enter through a door directly into the dining room thinking that I am visiting friends that I am very happy to see. To my left is an open door leading directly into a bedroom. I can see a bed and am aware of activity in the room. My friend comes out, but he doesn't seem right rather nervous which is very unlike him. I can see a woman standing in the bedroom who I think is his wife, but her hair is too long. She nods to me and hurries off into an area of the bedroom where I cannot see her. Two children, around the age of nine, noisily chase each other through the dining room laughing. My friend is still standing in front of me nervously shifting his weight from one foot to the other.

I explain that I am there to add something under their bathroom sink in the cabinet area, and raise my left hand that is holding a small brown cardboard box, than raise my right hand that is holding a screw driver. He nods and runs into the bedroom and stands by the bed holding his wife. I enter into the bedroom and find the sink immediately on my left thinking this is an unusual setup not at all like our homes. I kneel down, open the cabinet doors and know that my friends are not my friends, but a tall grey and a female grey, and they are terrified of me. I close the cabinet doors and slide the box between the wall and the side of the cabinet, rise and say to my friend who is still holding the woman that the item is still in the box, and he can attach it whenever he wishes.

I rise and walk into the dining room, set down in a chair, place my elbow on the table and prop my head on my hand. I feel down, the beings are afraid of me. The children, two small greys, run behind me into the bedroom with the other two greys. I wake up.

They truly mess in my life. I can understand why people have committed suicide or possibly done any number of things of which I don't know but I do know that when your head is messed with, unless you are strong or have protection, you might do something that you normally would never think of doing. If the beings are role-playing to tell me that I frighten them, and that now seems to be the case, I'm aware of the message but I am unmoved. Logically this idea is pure nonsense. I simply want them to leave;

they have nothing to offer me nor I to them.

Tuesday, 30 October 2012, I turned off the bedroom light and saw a lit ball on the wall at the foot of the bed. The room then became lit with the large white rectangle on the wall by the window. It remained lit then the light went out and appeared again slightly to the left of where it had been before. I reached beside me placing my fingers in the small container of Indian corn, selected a few kernels and threw them at the large lit rectangle. The light went out, waited a few seconds and lit up again in the same spot. I waited for the compartments to appear, and as they began to become clear, I threw another handful of corn at it. The light went out, and I went to sleep.

Thursday, 1 November 2012 I awoke from a sound sleep with the room brightly lit by an unformed mass of what I assumed was energy on the window side of the bed. It seemed to be collecting, forming what I know not nor did I want to see. It was fascinating to watch, forming unrecognized multiple star-like designs, and becoming brighter as if gaining strength. I threw corn at it hitting it directly in the middle and watched it lose a bit of its shape then reform but weaker than before. The entire room seemed to jump and undulate with flashes and floating clear balls, and then the unshaped form began collecting its energy and formed again. I threw more corn at it and watched it struggle then become fragmented and disappear. I fell asleep.

Early Saturday morning, 3 November 2012, I looked at the clock; it was 5:10 am. I had been dreaming.

My mother and others familiar are there but who I do not remember. My mother, at first thought to be my earth mother, is a tall pale woman with long black hair, and I suspect we had been either role playing or having a meeting of sorts, because there is a lot of activity in the room. She suddenly turns facing me, looks at me with anger in her eyes, points a finger at me and with that motion I know I am being taken. I am aware I am in bed because I can feel it under me but the awful feeling of being taken is unmistakable. Fight! My mind demands, and I began yelling "No, no, no". Struggling against the force, I break free and grab what is closest, the neck of the small grey on my right and the neck of the small grey on my left before they can react. My elbows are resting on the bed and I begin to pull my hands with their necks enclosed in my fists across the front of my body back and forth, back and forth, as if I am exercising using hand weights, and feel them becoming limp like rag dolls. Something snaps in the neck of the one on my right. I am awake, hot, covered in sweat and breathless. I fall asleep. Why don't they leave me alone?

Friday, 23 November 2012, they were back last night and very aggressive at least the one ball of light was that kept shining light in my face sending pictures of scary monsters, lots of them, worse than a nightmare. I pulled my hair over my eyes, put corn kernels over the left eye and believe this made it even angrier because a short time later it flew in front of my right eye and exploded with a tremendous flash of light that left me dizzy. I fought it off with my will and won. I watched it fly to and out through the window. I got up, read more of a book, had a snack, went back to bed and slept well.

Thursday 29 November 2012, after work I sat on the front porch sipping a cup of coffee and smoking a cigarette. The full moon was beautiful. I am unable to see the stars well as there are too many street lights in front, however if I go into the back they are clearly visible. In front I watched one "star" which began to meander around little by little seemingly getting closer to my area. I finished my cigarette inside not waiting until the beams hunted me out. It felt like a repeat of the experience in Mississippi. Inside I hung Indian corn in the window so the moon and sun would shine upon it.

I am dreaming.

I am with others. I have no idea where I am or who I am with but it seems like a regular dream, a nonthreatening one. Suddenly I am aware that I must go to a group of houses near where I live to retrieve something, I think, or do I have to give them something or perhaps, information, but I must go. I find myself standing in a desolate area at the bottom of a manmade hill with a chain link fence running around the top. I am surrounded by trees and can see a dirt road passing through the trees. I think that I am near where I use to live in the country.

There are tall grasses and weeds growing on the hill and surrounding area, bent as if they had been covered by fast flowing water and had yet to recover. I stand at the bottom surveying the hill not wanting to enter into it, the hidden area, but know that I must. I climb the hill at an angle looking for the hidden path that will lead me into the area when I see that a car has driven up and stopped not far from where I had been standing at the bottom of the hill. The car is dark, old and dusty. I do not like this as there should be no one else here, and hesitate watching the vehicle. I pop out of my body and see myself on the hill then I start to move on upward when a sudden feeling of foreboding surrounds me. I stop to look back at the car. I wake up.

Something sinister is here with me, and I open my eyes to see a lit square a few feet above my head. There seems to be a design, a figure or face within it that reminds me of a spider. Could it be a spider? It isn't clear enough to determine what is in the square. It could even be a grid of some sort but I'm not sure. I reach for some corn in its container in my bed and quickly throw it at the square. The square moves onto the wall above my head on my left, and I quickly get on my hands and knees and throw more corn. It moves directly in front of me as it glides across the surface of the wall towards the bathroom. I'm still not sure what is in the square but think it is some sort of spider, and throw more corn as it moves further along the wall. I throw corn again and again knowing that I am hitting it direct on without influence. The light in the square extinguishes and the room is dark once more. I glance at the clock, it is 5 AM. I am alone and waiting to see what it will do next but it does nothing more. I wonder if this was a hologram then why was there no interruption when it passed in front of me?

Where was the source if it was a hologram?

Chapter 49

Friday, 30 November 2012, after I turned off the light last night and got comfortable on my left side, the light began to worm its way between the pillows and my face shining on my left eye. I maneuvered around until I realized it is settling in for the evening, rolled onto my back, and opened my eyes. Hanging above my head was the square with the spider. I only got a glimpse, and I can forthrightly say I don't know what the hell it is. There are four rectangular bars extending from each corner towards the center. In the center is what I assume to be a head with large slanted yellow eyes.

Surrounding the head I'm left with the impression that there are hair-like projections the coloring similar to a honey bee. Is this what I am seeing, the head of a honey bee? I don't know. The light went out and appeared on the wall at the head of my bed then again went out and made a short leap to its right, my left. By this time I am on my knees with a handful of corn. It stops on the wall in the center of the head board and is now a white lit slit the height of the square. I threw the corn at it and it went out. I slept.

Saturday, 1 December 2012, when I turned out the bedroom light there were dozens of white lit balls hanging about the room. I see the square flash above me then become a slit. I have corn in my hand ready to throw. The lit slit flashes on the wall above the head of my bed and disappears. I know who it is, it is the bug. I fall asleep.

I am dreaming.

I am in the New Jersey Pine Barrens, blueberry and cranberry country, and can see rows upon rows of blueberry bushes. I am visiting a young couple who have youngsters. The house and furniture are rugged but pleasant and comfortable. They leave as they have somewhere else they have to be. It is dark and late at night, so I go to bed. Suddenly I am being held down while something sinister is trying to get at the back of my neck. It wants to kill me. I fight pulling on my physical and inner strength. It is a test of wills. I pop out of my body and see that the bed linen has been wrapped around me used as a restraint. I am almost in a sitting position within the wrap, on my right hip with my legs bent propped up by my right arm. My will is stronger than it. I wake up. It is 3:30 AM.

I am dreaming again. I am in an isolated place and battling something that I cannot see but I can feel its energy. It is trying to get at the back of my neck and telling me that it will place a black diamond shape there that will kill me and laughs. I once again wake up. It is 5 AM and I am awake for the day.

I know there is one of the beings that does not like me. Perhaps it has to do with the being that burned in front of me but I do not know for sure. It could be the one who surrounded me in a vacuum several times because I "gotcha" and placed many balls in vacuum containers. I have also suspected the one who grabbed my foot and was thrown through the bedroom door. So chances are there are several beings who do not like me but I suspect it is just the one, the same one for all three reasons. One of the ghost hunters had picked up on that I was hated by something. How extraordinary to be hated by extraterrestrials! How many earthlings can claim that? How many earthlings can claim a "hit-bug" has been sent after them?

However, these beings take what is already in your mind and distort it seeking the answer to whatever their question of the day is. Several days ago I finished reading a popular mystery novel that had a kill method similar to the diamond shape on the back of my neck. I do not know for sure but suspect they have used this to frighten me. It didn't work.

Today is Tuesday, December 18, 2012. They do not like corn thrown at them and avoid presenting themselves in a situation where I can. There were no balls on the wall at night, no hanging orbs, red blobs, etc above me. Their entire presentation of blinking lights and flashes has become muted and nano-quick. If I had not been trained by them on what to look for I would not see it.

Last Saturday night I was awake all night with them pestering me with the light by my eyes. I got up and did all of the chores I would have done on Sunday. While washing clothes I saw that the guest bathroom door was pulled shut. I did not close the door and if the cats while playing in the room, which they do, and had somehow closed the door, they would have been trapped in the bathroom, but they weren't. No one was in the bathroom when I opened it, and I wondered if there had been when I got up. I finally fell asleep around 5AM, their active time.

I am dreaming.

I am in a room with a table in front of me and someone that I cannot see is standing on my left. I am being instructed about the items on the bright lime colored tray on the table. On the tray are many instruments not like our instruments but long rectangular in shape somewhat like a travel toothbrush holder. I am struck with the thought that the tray and its contents look like a tray of vegetables because they are the color of fruits and vegetables, bell pepper green and red, lime green, carrot orange and lemon yellow. I wake up and watch two balls fly out through the bedroom window while several others remain in the room blinking.

I understand that when I remember dreams it is within that period between deep sleep and awareness.
 Sunday, I took a sleeper and was unaware of anything. Monday night they were annoying again but backed off when I mentally asked them why they are still here. I feel some sadness to miss an opportunity to learn about beings from another world.

Sunday, 27 January 2013, it was obvious that the balls of black and white were more numerous and active than usual but thought little of it. It was a full moon and for once I could see it without massive cloud cover. I had read all of the library books and finding myself very tired, I turned out the light looking forward to sleep. It was not to happen.

The rectangular light was persistently brilliant at left eye level, and the smell of the little one permeated the bedroom. I asked, "What are you doing here?" and he replied, "I've come to take you." "No, I'm not going," I stated. I began to feel my body becoming numb and my mind as if drugged. Fighting off this feeling, struggling to gain control, I staggered off to the bathroom and when I returned, I turned on the bedroom light. I lay on my left side willing the little one to leave when suddenly I am out of bed and in the living room.

I am walking towards the kitchen counter to get my billfold then I turn to go to the computer desk to retrieve my library card to put in the billfold which had been one of my last thoughts before falling asleep. Having done this, I turn to walk back to the kitchen to place the billfold in my purse. I am only a few steps from the desk when I feel the ominous feeling of being taken. "No!" I yell. Suddenly there is the presence of a being next to me and we struggle. I turn to gain a better position when he suddenly grabs me from the back tightly wrapping his arms around my waist pressing his head against the small of my back. I can't reach him at my back! What can I use to get him off of me? I find that I am holding my purse with a long shoulder strap! The purse is of heavy leather and with the weight of the contents, if I could hit him in the head with it, he would let go of me or it would knock him out. I swing the purse aiming for his head instead hitting the back of the high back chair. He has somehow gotten me into an enclosed area where there is little room to maneuver. Suddenly I am back in bed and alert.

Leaving the light on I slept little. I got up around 5AM to go to the bathroom and turned off the light when I returned to the bed. Lined up against the top of the curtain were five blinking balls, and to their right was a deep red blotch. I turned the light back on and continued a restless sleep. When I got up for the day I felt drugged and out of sorts. My conclusion is I had an OOBE experience since I was aware that I was in bed until I found myself in the living room. At that point I was only aware of what was happening out of the bed. I think that I was being taken when the OOBE occurred and that is the reason for the struggle. I can think of nothing else that makes sense, but nothing concerning them makes sense.

Wednesday morning, 30 January 2013, 7:55 AM, I have finished my book and am a bit out of sorts as what to do with myself. I worked on genealogy yesterday then puttered around feeling bored. After my usual routine I turned off the light around 11 PM. Only one ball blinked, and I became concerned because it is often on "quiet" nights like this that they come. I felt like I knew the ball and found it was the one that leads me into the bathroom. I told him that I wished they would all leave and it was a shame that their visits hadn't worked out as I had looked forward to learning about them and how they lived. He told me that his family was well and that they do not live in a family unit like we do. I was unable to sleep, got up and played computer games until a little after 2 AM.

I had not turned on the bedroom light when I had gotten out of bed nor had I turned on the light by the computer, so the house was dark except for the computer monitor. To anyone outside it would appear that the house was dark. I turned the computer off and entered the dark bedroom. I could see flashing lights penetrating through the black-out curtain on the bedroom window thinking this strange as the motion detector is stationary with one light. This light was rapidly moving blinking lights. My first thought was this was caused by an emergency vehicle but why would one be at my bedroom window, and the lights were white not red and blue?

Standing at the side of the window, I peeked behind the drop-down shade. The motion detector light was on illuminating a craft sitting in my backyard mere yards from the house!

The craft itself was shadowed. The rounded top central portion was small but large enough for one person as I had seen on 1 April 2007 and again on 9 September 2008. The bottom also appeared to be rounded. Around the middle there was a slightly angled ledge extending outward perhaps, two or more feet from the center of the rounded portions. Spaced evenly around the rim of the ledge were six lights producing bright cold white light. The lights lit one at a time running clockwise around the ledge producing a blinking effect. No doubt about it, I can now say I have seen a UFO, a UFO setting in my backyard mere feet from my bedroom window.

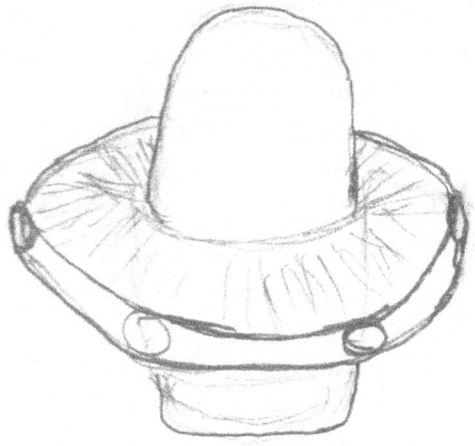

I slowly stepped back from the window so as not to attract attention. The motion light turned off and I peeked around the drop-down curtain again. There was nothing there, no ship, no lights. Had they come for me? Was I supposed to run out the back door and jump in? Well, that's not going to happen.

I crawled into bed and watched a thick mist began to form across the windowed wall extending out into the bedroom. It was so thick the window was nearly hidden behind it. I grabbed the container of corn in the bed and began throwing handfuls at it watching the mist thin out. My container was nearly empty, so I dashed into the living room for more. Grabbing the corn basket and my cell phone, I ran back into the bedroom. I turned on the bedside light as I crawl back into bed knowing this was going to be another long sleepless night but that is not what happened, I slept, a twilight sleep but I slept. What the hell are they doing? I so want them to leave!

Friday, 1 February 2012, I think the beings are trying to get rid of me, not remove me from their rolls but rid me from this earth. I have not been cooperating with them and attempting to evade everything they throw in my path, at least that is what I think I have been doing, at least that is what I remember trying to do. Are the beings evil? I don't think any more evil than we humans. They carry the same emotions as we do such as hate, vengeance and the desire to wipe out those who do not cooperate with them. I won't venture to say they are all that way just as humans are not all that way, but there are some who are vengeful, and if they are leaders they can force their will upon others.

I am not sleeping at night, and becoming confused with dreams and reality. Which is which? They are all mixed together. I feel like an entity floating with neither foot on the ground nor hand holding onto a grounded object. I need to be grounded.

Tuesday, 5 February 2013, I worked yesterday 11 AM to 4 PM. I had been straightening up the shelves when I became so dizzy that my vision faded out, my brain was swirling and I thought I was going to drop to the floor. There were small children and parents in the shop, and I didn't want to frighten them and cause a commotion. I have been having these episodes lately but none as severe as this one. I stood there until it subsided enough that I could walk to the chair at the end of the aisle and sit down. I sat there a few minutes until the feeling passed, got up and finished straightening the shelves. I have also been having strange headaches lately.

Last night I stayed up late to finish a book by P. C. Doherty, I enjoy his series with Hugh Corbett, and turned off the light somewhere around 3 AM. A blue round sphere with an eye in the center was upon me as soon as the light went out. I pulled the hair over my left eye, the blue light with the eye zoomed in then went out followed by a bright light shining above the hair over my left eye, then that too went out, and I fell asleep.

I am dreaming.

I am standing at a door holding Tom, my new kitty; a woman is standing on the other side of the door. I tell her, "Just a minute, I have to go to the bathroom," and put Tom down on the floor.

I am now awake looking towards the bathroom door and see a short grey standing by the bureau. I ask, "What are you doing here?", as I get up to go into the bathroom. When I return to the bed there is a large amount of stick designs forming nothing specific except there seemed to be a larger amount gathered at the bathroom door, I threw corn. Heaviness in my head began as if something was pressing on both temples at the same time, I fell asleep. Did they take me? It's possible, I remember nothing.

Saturday, 6 April 2013, I am dreaming.

I am in a large room with others who are working on projects, giving them encouragement to complete their chosen task when my college age son enters the room and draws me aside. He tells me he is leaving for fifteen days and has come to tell me goodbye. I ask him if I am to come with him, and he replies that I can if I wish but we are to leave right away, that the plane will be here any minute. He will be with his college friends and not wanting to interfere, I decide not to go, and he seems relieved. I have made the right choice. We exit the side of the building and walk around to the front where I can see the front end of the vehicle waiting for him. The front looks like a bus with a slanted windshield. He is excited. I hug him telling him that I love him, and he nods hugging me back then enters the bus. I return to the building and find that everyone is finished with the projects they had been working on and are readying to leave.

My sister is with me, but I don't think this is my sister. It is nighttime when we leave the building. I am in a wheelchair being pushed by my sister heading to the street corner by the building we have just left. There is a streetlight on our corner at this crossroad. Staying on the same street, we cross at the corner when I hear someone clearly calling my name several times and look around to see who it is. I see the person across the street sitting in a chair on the small front porch waving to me. We cross the street. She is a cheerful friendly plump elderly woman who talks to us and although I understood everything she said at the time, I remember nothing she said now.

When she is finished talking, my sister and I continue on our way down the dark street entering onto a dark path of yellowish-red hard packed soil surrounded by flat leaf cedar pines pressed closely together. They have nearly covered the narrow path causing us to brush against them as we continue towards the opening at the end. My sister says, "I am afraid. I do not like this," and I respond, "Do not be afraid, there is nothing to be frightened of," but I hear her continued mumbling behind me. I am surprised the wheelchair can pass through the path with the trees so closely grown together but they are soft causing no harm. The path ends by opening into a dark area but we do not enter into the open space because I am suddenly torn from this dream, harshly yanked twice to exit it, feeling each yank until I am awake staring at the ceiling looking at white wisps that begin to form a face. The face is truly ugly, and although I do not feel evil from it I know that it is not of the Light. It was 5:13 AM, their time for dreams.

Sunday, 7 April 2013, the balls and flashes continue although greatly diminished. I am able to see their lit balls on the wall and ceiling especially when I am watching TV. I continue to see the blue rectangle, a tiny one. The less intense balls appear before my closed eyes when I go to bed far less often, and not at all when I am praying. However, during the night when I get up to go to the bathroom they do appear but by that time all I want to do is go back to bed and sleep giving them little thought except to be aware of their presence. Essentially they seem to have become more respectful and less aggressive in their actions or that is what they want me to think. I still dream vivid dreams working with others seldom remembering even a small part. The dreams that I am aware having have changed as well in that they are calmer and less dramatic.

As I leave this story, if I could impart one word to you regarding the beings that one word would be

.... BEWARE..............

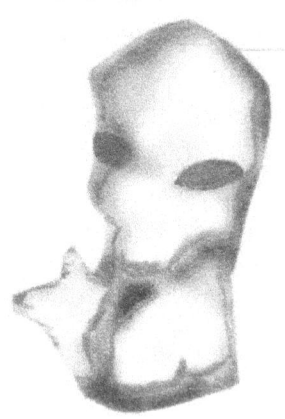

In July, 2010, my buddy sent an email about another type of ship spotted by accident. Apparently it is a type of drone which follows people around and is only seen when something interferes with their wave lengths.

I began thinking about what I have learned about the beings and started this list:

- The little ones have pointed teeth
- They cannot smile but grimace instead
- There are many different types of beings
- The skin of the little ones is rough like sandpaper which isn't abrasive
- The cellular level of skin is white, 8 sided with a darkened area in the middle which causes them to look grey
- There is always a guide at your side during learning
- They have vocal cords and can speak
- They can see clearly in the dark with some sort of apparatus which only lights up the target
- There are groups of beings who do specific things
- There are strict schedules
- They can bond only to be moved to a different location when the relationship is discovered
- They have artistic ability
- They like to entertain us and watch our reaction
- They use symbols for written communication
- Several different types of symbols can be used simultaneously depending on where you look

- They like vivid colors
- They can control an individual when they want
- They are here to study humans
- They can and will intimidate to get results
- They can be injured
- They react to inflicted pain
- Individuals have a specific odor
- The strength of the stench of the greys odor depends on when they have fed
- They have a sense of humor
- Their presence occurs around the full moon
- They perform procedures on your body
- They are unsure of my abilities
- They use eye movements during sleep
- They use either the iris or pupil in some way
- They use holograms sent to/implanted in the eye
- They use some sort of paralyzing current which can be overcome
- Their vehicle can lay flat on the wall yet have depth and have multiple compartments

www.ingramcontent.com/pod-product-compliance
Lightning Source LLC
Chambersburg PA
CBHW060448090426
42735CB00011B/1946